19 95

D0771864

CLAIMING AMERICA

IN THE SERIES

ASIAN AMERICAN HISTORY AND CULTURE

EDITED BY SUCHENG CHAN, DAVID PALUMBO-LIU,
AND MICHAEL OMI

A list of books in the series appears at the back of this volume

CLAIMING AMERICA

CONSTRUCTING CHINESE

AMERICAN IDENTITIES

DURING THE EXCLUSION ERA

EDITED BY

K. SCOTT WONG AND

SUCHENG CHAN

305.895
c.1

 TEMPLE UNIVERSITY PRESS

PHILADELPHIA

Temple University Press, Philadelphia 19122
Copyright © 1998 by Temple University.
All rights reserved
Published 1998
Printed in the United States of America

Interior design by Richard E. Rosenbaum

∞ The paper in this publication meets the requirements
of the American National Standard for Information Sciences—
Permanence of Paper for Printed Library Materials, ANSI Z39.48–1984.

Library of Congress Cataloging-in-Publication Data

Claiming America : constructing Chinese American identities during the
  exclusion era / edited by K. Scott Wong and Sucheng Chan.
      p.   cm. — (Asian American history and culture)
      ISBN 1-56639-575-5 (cl: alk. paper)/ISBN 1-56639-576-3 (pb: alk. paper)
      Includes bibliographical references.
    1. Chinese Americans—History. 2. Chinese—United States—Social
  conditions. I. Wong, Kevin Scott. II. Chan, Sucheng. III. Title:
  Chinese American identities during the exclusion era. IV. Series.
  E184.C5C57   1998
  973'.04951—DC21   97-2539

Contents

Preface

More than thirty years have passed since Roger Daniels wrote, "Other immigrant groups were celebrated for what they had accomplished; Orientals were important for what was done to them."[1] In the meantime, great strides have been made in recovering and reconstructing the Asian American past, but more remains to be done. Still noticeably lacking in the literature are studies that rely primarily on the voices of Asian immigrants and their American-born offspring. For example, in *Entry Denied: Exclusion and the Chinese Community in America, 1882–1943*, edited by Sucheng Chan, with the exception of the chapter by Sau-ling C. Wong, the other chapters do not examine how the Chinese immigrants and their American-born progeny perceived themselves and how those perceptions might have been affected by the harsh conditions under which they lived during the sixty-one years of Chinese exclusion from 1882 to 1943. As indicated in the preface to *Entry Denied*, "The most glaring omission . . . is the absence of any essays on the second, American-born generation: what it was like for them to grow up in a ghettoized setting, the schooling they received, the employment opportunities denied them, and the myriad, cultural, social, intergenerational, and interracial conflicts they experienced."

Designed to be a companion volume to *Entry Denied*, and to meet the implied challenge of Daniels to write Asian American history from Asian American perspectives, *Claiming America* contributes to the ongoing effort to fill important historiographical gaps. Within the seven chapters in this volume. Chinese immigrants and Chinese

Americans express themselves not only about their lives in the United States, but also about how the politics and rhetoric of exclusion shaped their attempts to claim a place in the American polity.

In *Claiming America*'s subtitle, the concept of identity is used in the plural because scholars have argued persuasively that people's sense of who they are is not unitary and unchanging. Rather, individuals continually engage in a process of constructing and negotiating their identities—identities that vary with time and space, depending on the particular subject positions that they occupy during different points in their lives. Identity in the singular implies an essentialism that is limiting in scope and blind to the process of historical change. At the same time, it is difficult for historians to think in terms of fragmented subjects and elusive, floating signs without any moorings, as some scholars in other disciplines have proposed we should do. Most historians are not yet ready to jettison the idea of an object world made up of parts that bear some discernible relationship to one another. In particular, scholars who study groups who have been left out of the master narratives of historical scholarship have barely begun the challenging task of resurrecting the existence of people who have been neglected and hence silenced or even totally erased from historical memory. If we do not want our forebearers to be consigned to permanent oblivion or, at best, to what the British social historian Edward P. Thompson has called the "enormous condescension of posterity,"[2] we must recover their voices and assert, on their behalf, their agency.

Mere inclusion, however, is not enough. Rather, we must write corrective histories—accounts that simultaneously, in Joan Scott's words, supplement and replace the established histories.[3] A supplement, as Scott explains, is "both an addition and a substitute." When we write the histories of Asians in America, we add something to U.S. history; by inserting such supplements, we replace a story that, to this point, has been full of gaps and omissions.

The methodology that seems most comparable with the present Asian American project of historical reconstruction is one that anthropologists John and Jean Comaroff have characterized as neomodern (in contrast to postmodern). It is an approach that "seeks to construct . . . accounts at once social and cultural, both imaginative in their grasp of the interior worlds of others and yet . . . respectful of the real."[4] In the kind of historical ethnography that the Comaroffs champion, documentary evidence is considered "as much the subject as the means of inquiry." In other words, scholars should not take the historical texts that they unearth at face value but should inquire into how these texts were produced in order to understand "the role of inscriptions of various kinds in the making of ideology and argument."[5] Although the authors of the chapters in this book do not use the term "neomodern," the manner in which they investigate their topics certainly resonates with the interrogative spirit that the Comaroffs call for.

Compared with European immigrants, Chinese immigrants and their American-born children have left relatively few historical records. However, documents including some in English, *do* exist. Each contributor to this volume used a set of these English-langauge writings—many hitherto unexamined by historians—to reconstruct the thoughts and sentiments of their authors and to offer insights into the social milieu in which these writings were produced. Many of the quotations in this book are long because we want to introduce the voices of Chinese Americans—persons with names and individualized life stories—into the historical record. Chinese, and other Asian Americans, have been depicted far too often only as nameless and faceless masses, a practice that has made stereotyping them easy. Lengthy quotations are also justified because the number of available sources is so small. The available evidence cannot help but carry a greater burden than that used to study topics with a richer documentary record. Thus, scholars who rely on such sources must exercise greater caution when generalizing from them.

Thin as the documentary record may be, three fairly reliable conclusions emerge from the chapters in this book. First, the individuals who have left us writings, including those who were not native speakers of English, had mastered the language so well that they penned eloquent essays in English. To be sure, these individuals were not representative of the general Chinese population in the United States. However, because they had been educated in English, were articulate, and had managed to have their writings published, or, as in the case of Wong Chin Foo, had captured the attention of reporters from some of the most important newspapers in the nation, they were, and can in retrospect be treated as, spokespersons of their communities. Although none of them was an "average" Chinese immigrant or Chinese American, the *sensibilities* that they expressed reflected their peers' concerns.

Second, the writers whom we examined had a deep understanding of American society and had apparently embraced its professed values. Whether they invoked democracy, freedom, and equality because they truly believed in them or merely for strategic reasons is less important than the fact that they insisted that such ideals were applicable to the

Chinese who were living in the United States. In multiple ways, they called attention to the discrepancy between the American creed and the reality that Chinese settlers faced. In short, they did not hesitate to "claim" America. Such active efforts to demand for themselves the same rights that all Americans are supposed to enjoy stand in sharp contrast to the timeworn portrait of a population whose members allegedly refused to assimilate. Just as important, the evidence indicates that the desire to be accepted as Americans began developing much earlier in Chinese American history than was previously assumed.[6]

Third, in addition to cultural differences (or ethnicity), other factors—in particular, race, gender, and class—played significant roles in shaping the identities of Chinese Americans. Although most of the writers investigated in this book thought in dichotomous, or binary terms—seeing clear-cut differences between "Chinese" and "American" cultures—in retrospect their identities were fluid and multidimensional. For some individuals, their sense of who they were changed from one phase of their life cycle to the next. Their understanding of their "place" in the world shifted, as well, in response to broad historical transformations in China and in the United States and to structural changes within the Chinese American communities themselves. Our findings therefore accord more with the insights of the social scientists who argue that ethnic identities are constructed, emergent, or situational than with those who believe that ethnic loyalties are primordial.

Investigating both the immigrant and American-born generations illuminates the continuities as well as the ruptures in the experiences of successive generations. Diverse attitudes within the same generation are also revealed. In the opening chapter, K. Scott Wong shows that members of the immigrant generation did not speak with a single voice and used different arguments to make their cases, and that the process of Americanization had begun among Chinese immigrants in the nineteenth century. The next three chapters discuss organizations formed to promote the rights of persons of Chinese ancestry. Qingsong Zhang and Renqiu Yu focus on the Chinese Equal Rights League and the Chinese Hand Laundry Alliance—organizations formed by immigrants—respectively, whereas Sue Fawn Chung presents the history of the Chinese American Citizens Alliance, which was established by U.S.-born Chinese Americans. Although the founders of these associations belonged to different generations, their goals and the ideology that they espoused were similar. In the last three chapters, Sucheng Chan, Gloria Chun, and Henry Yu look at the thoughts and feelings of various individuals and analyze the social contexts in which their consciousness as Chinese Americans emerged. Chan and Yu are especially sensitive to how gender complicates the process of identity construction.

Finally, because each chapter in this book was written to stand alone, inevitably some redundancy can be found in the book as a whole. We retained a little of the repetitious information and perhaps conflicting interpretations of certain events or historical processes to preserve the authorial integrity of each study.

Santa Barbara, California and   —Sucheng Chan and
Williamstown, Massachusetts   K. Scott Wong

Notes

1. Roger Daniels, "Westerners from the East: Oriental Immigrants Reappraised," *Pacific Historical Review* 35 (November 1966): 375.
2. Edward P. Thompson, *The Making of the English Working Class* (London: Victor Gallencz, 1963, reprint, 1980; New York: Vintage, 1963), 12–13.
3. Joan Scott, "Women's History," in *New Perspectives on Historical Writing,* ed. Peter Burke (University Park: Pennsylvania State University Press, 1991), 49–50.
4. John and Jean Comaroff, *Ethnography and the Historical Imagination* (Boulder, Colo.: Westview Press, 1992), ix.
5. Ibid., 34.
6. Roger Daniels, for example, stated that this "turn" toward America occurred only in the 1940s. Roger Daniels, *Asian America: Chinese and Japanese in the United States since 1850* (Seattle: University of Washington Press, 1988), 98–99.

PART I

THE IMMIGRANT
GENERATION

CHAPTER I

Cultural Defenders and Brokers: Chinese Responses to the Anti-Chinese Movement

K. SCOTT WONG

THE ANTI-CHINESE MOVEMENT AGAINST WHICH IMMIGRANTS and American-born Chinese fought during the mid-nineteenth and mid-twentieth centuries existed simultaneously on several levels. In addition to the numerous mechanisms used to bar Chinese from mainstream American institutions and the physical intimidation and violence that they encountered regularly, the Chinese in America were confronted with an organized campaign to defame them in prose and in illustrations. Thus, the anti-Chinese movement was an early example of what is now often called a "culture war." Much of this "war" was a battle of words, waged in print as well as through other forms of public discourse. The exclusionists published an enormous number of pamphlets, essays, articles, novels, political cartoons, and other literary products advocating the exclusion of Chinese immigrants from the United States. This body of literature expressed the fears of what was known as the "Yellow Peril" in America.

In contrast, the Chinese had little recourse against their accusers. There is not much evidence to indicate that the Chinese physically retaliated against their attackers, although recent scholarship has revealed that the Chinese sought to challenge the discrimination that they faced by going on strike and by filing lawsuits in the American legal system.[1] Another avenue of resistance open to the Chinese was print journalism. By adopting the same rhetorical tactics as their critics—writing in English and publishing in some of the same periodicals, such as the *North American Review* and the *Overland Monthly*—the

Chinese elite in America attempted to gain some control over the images of the Chinese that were being presented to the American public. By offering alternative representations of themselves and by answering some of the charges levied against them, these writers hoped that attacks against the Chinese would lessen, that immigration legislation would be liberalized, and that the Chinese would eventually find acceptance in the American polity.

These writings by Chinese spokespersons in America also revealed how they viewed themselves. Writing in self-defense, they used four distinct, yet overlapping strategies: They denied the anti-Chinese charges and paraded the virtues of Chinese history and culture; they sought equal treatment with other groups in America on the basis of class similarities; they defended the presence of the Chinese in America by comparing themselves favorably with others or by denigrating other immigrant and minority groups, often in Sinocentric terms; and they turned American democratic ideals back on their accusers, demanding that they live up to their own professed standards. The Chinese joined their critics in a "culture war of words" in an attempt to defend their presence in the United States.

To investigate these debates, I focus mainly on competing Chinese positions. I start with a variety of anti-Chinese passages to set the rhetorical context for the Chinese response. Next, I discuss several Chinese-authored pieces that refute the critics; these writings demonstrate that Chinese diplomats, intellectuals, and community leaders, acting as cultural defenders, actively challenged the prevailing negative images of the Chinese created by the exclusionists, while defining their own lives and culture in terms of China's glorious past. Finally, by examining Yung Wing's life and career as a cultural broker, a role that contrasts with that of the Chinese elite spokespersons, I argue, on the basis of his love of American social values and the democratic ideals of inclusion, rather than his being a member of a formerly resplendent civilization, that his life in the United States can be viewed as the earliest recorded attempt by someone to find a niche in American society as a *Chinese American*. Although often at odds with one another, these divergent approaches by the Chinese in America to combat the exclusionists articulate an early Chinese American consciousness or identity—a blend of Sinocentric attitudes and an understanding of and appreciation for American civic ideals. Given the magnitude of anti-Chinese sentiments during this period, these writings reveal that much more effort was expended in attempts to negate unfavorable images than in the expression of a clearly defined Chinese

American sensibility that could develop independently of the anti-Chinese movement. Therefore, these examples of an incipient Chinese American consciousness were usually a form of self-defense rather than a celebration of the value and vitality of the Chinese American community.

The Anti-Chinese Movement: The Rhetoric of Exclusion

American opposition to the Chinese presence in the United States centered on two main issues, economics and race, both of which were usually framed as a critique of Chinese culture. Euro-American politicians, missionaries, labor leaders, and journalists argued that the Chinese degraded American labor by working for wages well below the standards needed to sustain an American family. And, because of the nature of their economic arrangements with their employers or mutual aid societies, the Chinese were accused of fostering a new system of slavery, or coolieism, in the United States. These economic issues were entwined with American racial antipathy toward the Chinese, who were considered immoral and unclean, biologically inferior, and perhaps most important, unassimilable. These two broad categories of opposition to the Chinese contributed to the belief that the Chinese immigrant presence in America was a threat to American institutions and "civilization."

Two of the richest sources of American images of Chinese immigrants are the 1876 California State Senate hearings and the U.S. congressional hearings on Chinese immigration.[2] A written memorial from the California Senate to the U.S. Congress argued that the Chinese were unfair competition in the labor market:

> The male element of this population, where not criminal, comes into a painful competition with the most needy and most deserving of our people—those who are engaged, or entitled to be engaged, in industrial pursuits in our midst. The common laborer, the farm hand, the shoemaker, the cigar maker, the domestic male and female, and workmen of all descriptions, find their various occupations monopolized by Chinese labor, employed at a compensation upon which white labor cannot possibly exist.[3]

Besides the belief that the Chinese undercut wages, a strong conviction was held that the Chinese labored for bosses under a system akin to slavery. This misunderstanding arose when many Euro-Americans failed to distinguish between two streams of Chinese emigrants: the Chinese taken to Cuba and Peru in the coolie trade and those who came to the United States as free or "semifree" emigrants with the aid of the so-called credit-ticket system.[4] Equating these two groups of emigrants and misunderstanding the credit-ticket system, many commentators called Chinese immigration a new form of slavery—one that enslaved both male laborers and female prostitutes.[5]

Racially and culturally, the Chinese were frequently compared with black Americans and white Americans—comparisons that stressed racial hierarchies, the perceived immorality of the Chinese, their supposed cultural inferiority, and their ultimate unassimilability into American society. On the one hand, Chinese were considered as inferior as black Americans, "incapable of attaining the state of civilization [as] the Caucasian."[6] On the other hand, Chinese were regarded as less assimilable than black Americans because, it was believed, the Chinese had once had an advanced civilization to which they clung. One witness at the congressional hearings declared:

> I think the Chinese are a far superior race to the negro race physiologically and mentally. That may probably not be the case with some neat mulattoes who have white blood; that is different. I think that the Chinese have a great deal more brain power than the original negro. The negro, however, has never had any discipline; he has never had in Africa a regular religion as the Chinese have had. His mind is undisciplined, and it is not as systematic as the Chinese mind. For that reason the negro is very easily taught; he assimilates more readily. The Chinese are non-assimilative because their form of civilization has crystallized, as it were.[7]

These state and federal hearings helped contribute to the national mood that led to the passage of the first Chinese Exclusion Act in 1882. However, the anti-Chinese movement continued unabated long after the exclusionists had carried the day. The original exclusion legislation of 1882 was repeatedly extended and strengthened through federal legislation in 1888, 1892, 1894, 1898, 1902, and 1904.[8] Much of the rhetoric that surfaced in official documents also found expression in popular periodicals and in pamphlets published by labor organizations in their campaigns to extend Chinese exclusion legislation as each act came up for renewal.

In response to an earlier article by Ho Yow, the Chinese consul general in San Francisco, James D. Phelan, then mayor of San Francisco, published an article in the *North American Review* in 1901 entitled "Why the Chinese Should Be Excluded."[9] Advocating the renewal of the Chinese Exclusion Act for the second time, Phelan wrote, "Has there been any change in the nature of the evil, or in the sentiments of the people? Certainly not on the Pacific Coast, where the lapse of time has made still more evident the non-assimilative character of the Chinese and their undesirability as citizens."[10] Phelan then proceeded to explain why Chinese exclusion legislation should be continued, basing his argument on American concepts of free labor, civilization, citizenship, and racial hierarchies. Regardless of how much or how little Chinese workers were paid, Phelan declared, "For all purposes of citizenship their usefulness ends with their day's work; and whatever they are paid, they are paid too much, because they make no contribution by service or citizenship or family life to the permanent interest of the country."[11] Although ideals of citizenship and family life are frequently linked in American civic discourse, Phelan disregarded the impact of exclusion legislation on the Chinese immigrant community. Such legislation had barred the Chinese from citizenship and greatly curtailed female immigration. The growth of Chinese American families and communities had thus been severely stunted, which rendered Phelan's complaint almost meaningless.

Near the end of his article, Phelan alluded to the Chinese as a disease, another prevalent theme in the anti-Chinese literature of this period. Chinese were often accused of carrying diseases, the men leprosy and the women various venereal diseases.[12] At the same time, the Chinese were deemed a social disease infecting the American body politic. As Phelan stated, "The Chinese may be good laborers, but they are not good citizens. They may in small numbers benefit individual employers, but they breed the germs of a national disease, which spreads as they spread, and grows as they grow."[13]

The idea that the Chinese were diseased or biologically inferior was widely articulated. One of the most subtle but significant examples can be found in the 1880 California Constitution. Its Article II outlined the rights of suffrage and stated: "No native of China, no idiot, insane person, or person convicted of any infamous crime, and no person hereafter convicted of the embezzlement or misappropriation of public money, shall ever exercise the privileges of an elector in this State."[14] In short, Chinese were equated with idiots, insane persons, and convicted criminals, an association that would later find expression in other realms of popular consciousness. For example, "Mongolian" and "Mongoloid," originally anthropological labels used to classify Chinese and other Asians, became code words to denote various forms of mental retardation.[15]

The theme of the Chinese as a disease was reiterated in the brochure published in 1902 by the American Federation of Labor (AFL), *Some Reasons for Chinese Exclusion: Meat vs. Rice; American Manhood against Asiatic Coolieism. Which Shall Survive?* Early in the document, the following assertion is found: "An advancement with an incubus like the Chinese is like the growth of a child with a malignant tumor upon his back. At the time of manhood death comes of the malignity."[16] Published as part of organized labor's attempt to influence public opinion in favor of renewing the Chinese Exclusion Act, this text contains many of the fundamental themes of the anti-Chinese movement. Following the title page, an illustration is captioned "The American Gulliver and Chinese Lilliputians." The "American Gulliver," resembling Abraham Lincoln, is being shackled to the floor by hordes of tiny Chinese, complete with queues and buckteeth. They are securing "Gulliver" to the floor with bands and spikes; the words "cheap labor," "heathen competition," and "starvation labor" are written on the bands. In the distance, countless Chinese await entry. The bottom caption asks, "Shall the last spike be driven?" Was the American Gulliver/Great Emancipator/American Workingman to have the last blow dealt him by the relaxation of exclusion legislation? Just as a disease spreads throughout the body, invading cells without discrimination, so the masses of China, undifferentiated in appearance, were poised at the gate to overwhelm the American labor force, already on its back from years of "heathen competition."

Even more important than labor competition was the quality of American life. The main body of the AFL pamphlet concludes with the exclusionary rhetoric of Senator James G. Blaine (1830–1893) from Maine. Blaine, moving the stakes to a level far higher than mere wage differences, declared:

> You cannot work a man who must have beef and bread, and would prefer beef, alongside of a man who can live on rice. In all such conflicts, and in all such struggles, the result is not to bring up the man who lives on rice to the beef-and-bread standard, but it is to bring down the beef-and-bread man to the rice standard.
>
> We have this day to choose whether we will have for the Pacific Coast the civilization of Christ or the civilization of Confucius.[17]

Blaine's "choices" point to fundamental issues in American immigration history in general, and conflicts over Chinese immigration in particular. The tension between pluralism and the desire for homogeneity stands here in bold relief. Believing that Americans had to choose between the "civilization" of Christ or Confucius, those advocating exclusion cast the Chinese as perpetual foreigners, who because of their race and culture could never appreciate the fruits of American civilization. Such an attitude set the terms for the interaction between Euro-Americans and Chinese immigrants and placed the burden of proof on the Chinese to demonstrate their desirability as fellow citizens. When the first exclusion legislation was passed in 1882, American immigration policy crossed a line, as did the American self-image: No longer a nation freely open to all immigrants, the United States had chosen homogeneity and racial superiority over pluralism, while the American self-image was recast in response to the presence of an Other.

The Chinese Elite Response: In Defense of Culture

Given the rabidity of the anti-Chinese movement and its accompanying rhetoric, the Chinese had a tremendous task before them in their attempts to maintain a lasting presence in the United States. Appointed Chinese officials in the United States and local Chinese elites sought to lessen the sting of anti-Chinese activities by trying to control and protect the immigrant community through institutional means and moral exhortation. Among other things, they published articles and gave public speeches to defend the immigrant community (in the process developing a self-definition that reflected not only shifts in the worldview of the Chinese elite in America, but also the limits of their racial and cultural discourse), which often placed them in the position of having to define who the Chinese were *not*, rather than who they were.

Of the Chinese foreign ministers assigned to the United States, Wu Tingfang (1842–1922) was the most active in writing and giving public lectures on behalf of the Chinese immigrant community in the United States. Rather than simply attack American exclusion policy as immoral or unjust, Wu tried to convince the American public that the policy was detrimental to U.S. interests. He first stressed the trade potential between the two countries. In the *North American Review*, a periodical that frequently printed anti-Chinese articles, Wu stated: "Let the products of American farms, mills, and workshops once catch the Chinese fancy, and America need look no further for a market. . . . I would suggest that American farmers and manufacturers might find it to their advantage to study the wants and habits of the Chinese and the conditions of trade in China."[18]

Wu also encouraged using American capital to invest in China's future by providing aid for the construction of railroads and various public works. Wu argued that, seen in the light of reciprocal business relations between the two countries, such trade and investment not only would be a great benefit to both parties, but also would facilitate better relations.

However, full reciprocity could not exist if the United States maintained its exclusionary immigration policies toward China. This recognition framed Wu's second theme: equal treatment for the Chinese. He wanted American immigration policy to reflect parity between the two nations, and he demanded that Chinese immigrants be treated the same as others:

> Justice would seem to demand equal consideration for the Chinese on the part of the United States. China does not ask for special favors. All she wants is enjoyment of the same privileges accorded other nationalities. Instead, she is singled out for discrimination and made the subject of hostile legislation. Her door is wide open to the people of the United States, but their door is slammed in the face of her people. I am not so biased as to advocate any policy that might be detrimental to the best interests of the people of the United States. If they think it desirable to keep out the objectionable class of Chinese, by all means let them do so. Let them make their immigration laws as strict as possible, but let them be applicable to all foreigners.[19]

Wu was careful not to challenge the right of the United States to determine the nature of its immigration laws, but he made a strong appeal to ideals of equal treatment. Thus, he placed the onus for the immigration crisis on the American government rather than on the supposed cultural flaws of the Chinese.

In his defense of the Chinese, however, Wu's class and racial biases became evident. His distance from the working classes and his belief in Chinese cultural superiority are obvious in many passages of his writings. While decrying the treatment of Chinese students and merchants in the United States, he drew a clear distinction between desirable and unwanted immigrants:

> It [the Chinese Exclusion Act] aimed to provide for the exclusion of Chinese laborers only, while freely admitting all others. As a matter of

fact, the respectable merchant, who would be an irreproachable addition to the population of any country, has been frequently turned back, whereas the Chinese high-binders, the riff-raff and scum of the nation, fugitives from justice and adventurers of all types have too often effected an entrance without much difficulty. This is because the American officials at the entrance ports are ignorant of Chinese character and dialects and cannot always discriminate between the worthy and unworthy.[20]

Not only did Wu sound like an anti-Chinese exclusionist at times, he also echoed sentiments held by nineteenth-century anti-immigrant nativists. In his published memoir, written in English, *America Through the Spectacles of an Oriental Diplomat,* he wrote:

In a large country like America where a considerable portion of the land remains practically uncultivated or undeveloped, hardy, industrious, and patient workmen are a necessity. But the almost unchecked influx of immigrants who are not desirable citizens cannot but harm the country. In these days of international trade it is right that ingress and egress from one country to another should be unhampered, but persons who have committed crimes at home, or who are ignorant and illiterate, cannot become desirable citizens anywhere. They should be barred out of the United States of America.[21]

Whether or not Wu included Chinese laborers in this group is uncertain, but clearly he embraced class attitudes similar to those of Americans who favored immigration restriction.

On the other hand, Wu often spoke of the Chinese in terms that placed them above other races. Speaking against exclusion, he stated, "So long as honest and steady workmen are excluded for no reason other than they are Asiatics, while white men are indiscriminately admitted, I fear the prosperity of the country cannot be considered permanent."[22] More directly, he glorified the past achievements of Chinese civilization vis-à-vis Western achievements, claiming,

It is too often forgotten that civilization, like religion, originally came from the East. Long before Europe and America were civilized, yea while they were still in a state of barbarism, there were nations in the East, including China, superior to them in manners, in education, and in government; possessed of a literature equal to any, and of arts and sciences totally unknown in the West. Self-preservation and self-interest make all men restless, and so Eastern peoples gradually moved to the West taking their knowledge with them; Western people who came into close contact with them learned their civilization. This fusion of East and West was the beginning of Western civilization.[23]

Having "established" the origins of Western civilization, Wu took the moral high ground, using language rooted in Sinocentrism to condemn white supremacy:

Those who support such a policy hold that they, the white people, are superior to the yellow people in intellect, in education, in taste, and in habits, and that the yellow people are unworthy to associate with them. Yet in China we have manners, we have arts, we have morals, and we have managed a fairly large society for thousands of years without the bitter class hatreds, class divisions, and class struggles that have marred the fair progress of the West. We have not enslaved our lives to wealth. We like luxury but we like other things better. We love life more than chasing imitations of life.[24]

Finally, Wu warned the exclusionists, "I only wish to give a hint to those white people who advocate an exclusive policy that in their next life they may be born in Asia or in Africa, and that the injury they are now inflicting on the yellow people they may themselves have to suffer in another life."[25]

Educated primarily in Western institutions, Wu had adopted many Western attitudes, most notably his respect for the concepts of equal treatment under the law and reciprocity in international relations. In his defense of the Chinese and Chinese culture, however, his Sinocentrism surfaced. By claiming that the Chinese had developed a high civilization long before the West had done so and by castigating the exclusionists as morally deficient, Wu implied that Americans were inferior to the Chinese. Working constantly for the repeal of the exclusionary statutes, Wu was among the most articulate Chinese of his era in his efforts to defend the Chinese, but his writings also reveal the limits of his worldview. Unable to effect changes in U.S. immigration policy, Wu could only protest through his writings, often using Sinocentric rhetoric, unable to bridge fully the cultural gulf between the two nations.

During Wu's first term as minister (1896–1902), his brother-in-law, Ho Yow, served as China's consul general in San Francisco. A graduate of Oxford University, Ho also used the press to defend the Chinese in America.[26] He first published an article in 1901 in the *North American*

Review, "Chinese Exclusion, a Benefit or a Harm?" which elicited James Phelan's response two months later. Ho began by denouncing isolationism, equating the Great Wall of China with American exclusion policy. Both, he believed, were obstructions to greater understanding. He wrote,

> In the fourteenth century the Ming emperors constructed of brick and mortar in China on the north and west a memorable obstacle to intercourse with the people beyond the border; that barrier is crumbling to ashes, and we have been prone to look upon it as a relic of old China. But this most enlightened nation of the illuminated West, in the height of its glory and splendor, revives what is dead and past with us, and enthrones it into a living, active principle. Bricks and mortar do not comprise [sic] the Great Wall which the United States has built against China. It is the old idea, the folly of which we of China have long seen, rehabilitated and swathed in modern attire; its bricks are printed words, and the base upon which it rests is a solemn code; but its parapets are none the less patrolled, and from its battlements gleam the steel of the mediaeval soldier.[27]

However, recognition of the failings of mutual ethnocentrism soon gave way to a defense of the Chinese: "In point of fact the immigration which has come to the United States from Asia has been in all respects as good as that which has come from Europe. In some respects it has been a great deal better; for we have never aided thither paupers, criminals nor insane persons, and this slough comprised so considerable a percentage of the European immigration that it became necessary for Congress to enact a law extending to them the treatment which it visits upon the Chinese."[28] Ho Yow thus used a tactic similar to Wu Tingfang's: When cast as the undesirable Other, reverse the gaze and subject your accuser to the same process of alterity.

Ho continued his defense of the Chinese the following month with an article, "The Chinese Question," in the *Overland Monthly.* Illustrated with photographs of San Francisco's Chinatown by Arnold Genthe, this article answered a number of charges against the Chinese.[29] Again, Ho compared the Chinese with European immigrants, this time drawing a distinction between "American" labor and immigrant labor. He claimed,

> We contend that the Chinese do a different class of work than the true white laborers. The Chinese work at manual, unskilled occupations,

doing a lower class of work than the great majority of the whites. The Americans are more skilled, requiring and possessing technical education and high manipulative and administrative ability, fitting them particularly for foremen, engineers, draftsmen, high-grade mechanics, and the like, while the Chinese do more of fruit picking, truck gardening, and work of a lower type, and are not what would be considered skilled laborers. The Chinese, in a measure, do conflict with the imported pauper labor of Europe, which in no sense can be termed typical white labor.[30]

In this case, Ho subordinated the Chinese to "American" labor but implicitly placed the Chinese above newly arrived immigrants from Europe. Following a line of thought similar to Wu Tingfang's, Ho appealed to American commercial interests with the hope of lessening the hostility against the Chinese: "By admitting the Chinese, this country would gain many more advantages than it does from the admission of the same classes from other countries. You would get commercial and other beneficial returns from China in a large and profitable measure, while you would not get half as much from the others."[31] In passages such as these, the Chinese spokespersons, like their detractors, clearly viewed exclusion not merely in terms of race, but also in terms of class.

Answering the charges against the Chinese for being unclean and diseased, Ho further raised issues of class:

As to the question of cleanliness, the Chinese laboring class is just as clean as the corresponding class of any other nationality. If a comparison could be instituted right here in San Francisco of the same classes of all nationalities, my statement would be verified. The Chinese in this country must be regarded, generally, as of the laboring class and adjudged as such. It is unfair to compare the Chinese laboring classes with the white middle or higher classes. There is no reason why the Chinese are likely to introduce more diseases into this country than any similar classes from other countries. Were the Chinese responsible for the great historical plague of London? There were no Chinese in London then. The Chinese are laboring under many disadvantages, but there is no reason why they should be made into bacilli to suit the pleasure of the selfish and spiteful.[32]

By depicting Europeans as equally disease prone as the Chinese, Ho was seeking a degree of parity. Although he was committed to the defense of the Chinese, Ho's Sinocentric worldview, based to a large degree on social hierarchies, prevented him from offering any fresh argument as to why exclusion should be repealed. He could see only the differences and the convenient similarities between the two cultures and ranked the Chinese higher than European immigrants to advance the status of the Chinese. In this way, Ho and Wu Tingfang both used European immigrants as a foil to deflect the tensions between the Chinese and the Americans.

In addition to the appointed officials, the resident Chinese elite also published works in response to the exclusionists' rhetoric. Based primarily in San Francisco, but in cities such as New York as well, some of the individuals (often merchants) who served as spokespersons for the community had been educated in American schools or missionary institutions. This training not only provided them with the writing skills needed to challenge their accusers, but no doubt also informed their perception of their situation and shaped their response to it.

One of the earliest statements made by Chinese in San Francisco appeared in response to Governor John Bigler's letter of April 23, 1852, to the Senate and Assembly of the State of California calling for the exclusion of Chinese laborers.[33] Bigler referred to the Chinese as "Coolies," claiming that they were unfit to testify in American courts and, because of their culture and pecuniary interest in mining gold, did not want to become American citizens.[34] In a letter dated April 29, 1852, and reprinted in the July issue of *Living Age,* two Chinese met Bigler's accusations and requests for immigration restriction head on. Hab Wa and Long Achick of Sam Wo Company and Ton Wo Company, respectively, claimed to have been educated in American schools and could therefore read the Governor's message and explain it to other Chinese in California.[35] These authors first explained that the Chinese laborers in California were not "Coolies" in the pejorative sense of the word. Instead, they pointed out that the word "Cooly" [sic] was not a Chinese word, but one of foreign (Indian) origin.[36] To the Chinese, the term had come to mean a common laborer, not one "bound to labor under contracts which they can be forcibly compelled to comply with."[37] Keeping to this simple definition, the authors maintained, "The Irishmen who are engaged in digging down your hills, the men who unload ships, who clean streets, or even drive your drays, would, if they were in China be considered 'Coolies.'"[38] Like the Chinese officials who came after them, these early writers sought to deflect criticism of the Chinese by pointing out that the Chinese were similar to the other working people in America.

After making lengthy comparisons that favored Chinese laborers over other immigrants in America and after praising the economic possibilities of Sino-American trade relations, Hab Wa and Long Achick addressed Bigler's charge that the Chinese were neither fit for nor desirous of American citizenship. After forcefully defending the integrity and honesty of the Chinese, qualities that would make them good citizens, the authors concluded:

> There is a Chinaman now in San Francisco who is said to be a naturalized citizen, and to have a free white American wife. He wears the American dress, and is considered a man of respectability. And there are, or were lately, we are informed, Chinamen residing in Boston, New York, and New Orleans. If the privileges of your laws are open to us, some of us will, doubtless, acquire your habits, your language, your ideas, your feelings, your morals, your forms, and become citizens of your country—many have already adopted your religion as their own—and we will be good citizens. There are very good Chinamen now in the country, and a better class, will, if allowed, come hereafter—men of learning and of wealth, bringing their families with them.[39]

This document, and this passage in particular, is an important testimony to the depth of conviction that some Chinese held with regard to living in the United States. It demonstrates a willingness on the part of the Chinese, as early as 1852, to adapt to American social mores and embrace American civic values in order to live a life of equal status in America. Also apparent are the beginnings of a rhetorical strategy that would be used for years to challenge the exclusionists and to attempt to claim a place for the Chinese in American society: refuting anti-Chinese charges, offering alternative readings of the Chinese presence in the United States, equating Chinese immigrants with other immigrant groups, and stating a desire to sink roots among the people of America.

Three years after the letter in *Living Age,* Norman Asing also responded to Governor Bigler's call for exclusion by writing a letter to the *Daily Alta California.* Asing argued that China's ancient civilization was an indication of China's cultural superiority. He remarked, "But we would beg to remind you that when your nation was a wilderness, and the nation from which you sprung barbarous, we exercised most of the arts and virtues of civilized life."[40] This all-too-common Sinocentric attitude was then followed by a rather eloquent dismissal of racial hierarchies based on skin color:

As far as regards the color and complexion of our race, we are perfectly aware that our population have been a little more tan than yours. Your Excellency will discover, however, that we are as much allied to the African race and the red man as you are yourself, and that as far as the aristocracy of skin is concerned, ours might compare with many of the European races; nor do we consider that your Excellency, as a Democrat, will make us believe that the framers of your declaration of rights ever suggested the propriety of establishing an aristocracy of skin.[41]

Asing's response to those who advocated restriction or exclusion was consistent with the tone and approach of many of the publications of that era, as well as those that appeared later.

Also speaking to Bigler's call for exclusion, Lai Chun-chuen, representing the Chinese merchants of San Francisco, wrote: "But of late days your honorable people have established a new practice. They have come to the conclusion that we Chinese are the same as Indians and Negroes, and your courts will not allow us to bear witness. And yet these Indians know nothing about the relations of society; they know no mutual respect; they wear neither clothes nor shoes; they live in wild places and in caves."[42] Lai thus shared Asing's tactic of privileging Chinese culture to downplay the achievements of the West and to degrade other peoples.

Nonwhite peoples were not the only groups that the Chinese cited as inferior in their attempts to deflect criticism. Yan Phou Lee, a former student brought to the United States by the Chinese Educational Mission in Hartford, Connecticut, a graduate of Yale University, and a naturalized citizen, remarked in the *North American Review:* "Why is it that the American laborer was soon raised to a higher social and industrial plane, and ceased to fear Irish competition, while the Irish still dread the competition of the Chinese? It is simply because the Irish are industrially inferior to their competitors. They have not the ability to get above competition, like the Americans, and so, perforce, they must dispute with the Chinese for the chance to be hewers of wood and drawers of water."[43] Thus, Lee denigrated the Irish in order to find acceptance for the Chinese. Employing a discourse that was influenced not only by Confucian concepts of social hierarchy, but also by Western notions of racial hierarchy and the progressive development of culture, these Chinese spokespersons were often unable to provide any alternative to the prevailing popular discourse in which American race relations were framed.

Yan Phou Lee also engaged in a brief dispute with publisher and Chinese-rights activist Wong Chin Foo over the supposed benefits of Christianity.[44] In the August 1887 issue of the *North American Review,* Wong had published an article, "Why Am I a Heathen?" in which he pointedly attacked what he saw as the hypocrisy of American Christians who preached the doctrines of equality and good will and yet supported the exclusion of Chinese. Remarking on the practice of the New Dispensation (the forgiveness of sins), Wong pondered, "Applying this dogma, I began to think of my own prospects on the other side of Jordan. Suppose Dennis [sic] Kearney, the California sand-lotter, should slip in and meet me there, would he not be likely to forget his heavenly songs, and howl once more: 'The Chinese must go!' and organize a heavenly crusade to have me and others immediately cast out into the other place?"[45]

Wong continued in a similar vein, casting Christianity as a doctrine of deception. And, like others before and after him, Wong claimed that Western civilization was "borrowed, adapted, and shaped from our [Chinese] older form."[46]

Yan Phou Lee, a devout Christian, took exception to Wong's views. Writing in the next issue of the *North American Review,* Lee argued that the Americans who supported exclusion policies were not true Christians. His Christian faith was so deep that he answered Wong Chin Foo by stating, "Such, indeed, is its [Christianity's] power to change the heart of man, that even if Dennis [sic] Kearney should slip into the Heavenly Jerusalem, he would be lamb-like and would be heard to say: *The Chinese must stay!* Heaven is incomplete without them.'"[47] In the remainder of the article, Lee extolled the virtues of Christianity, maintaining, "It is the Christian who looks on me as his equal and who thinks that the Chinese are as well endowed, mentally, as he."[48]

The content of the exchange between Wong and Lee is perhaps less significant, however, than the fact that their conflicting views appeared in English in a popular periodical of the time. The publication of these articles is important because it publicized the views of two Chinese writing in English in competing discourses, but both grappling with the problems of exclusion and the attempt by the Chinese to establish themselves in America. Therefore, the Chinese response to the anti-Chinese movement was not monolithic but, rather, multifaceted, disclosing both Chinese and Western influences on an emerging Chinese American consciousness.

Most of the time, the local elite used the same approach as the appointed officials: They refuted the charges made against the Chinese and stressed the ideals of equality and fair treatment. Writing President Ulysses S. Grant in 1876, the Chinese Consolidated Benevolent Association (CCBA, also known as the Chinese Six Companies) declared that not all Chinese women in the United States were prostitutes and that white men were a part of this sordid business as well; that the Chinese diet, although different from that of many Americans, was hardly a cause for immigration restriction; that the Chinese Six Companies was not a secret tribunal; and that the Chinese in America were wage earners, not slaves. As the CCBA stated, "If these men are slaves, then all men laboring for wages are slaves."[49] These authors also pointed out that the United States had a policy to "welcome immigration," that the Burlingame Treaty of 1868 provided for Chinese immigration to America, and that the Chinese had "neither attempted nor desired to interfere with the established order of things in this country, either of politics or religion."[50] In other words, no cause existed for the Chinese to be singled out for exclusion.

These views on race and justice were apparently shared by some Chinese working people. One of the few writings left by a Chinese launderer from this period stated:

> Irish fill the almshouses and prisons and orphan asylums, Italians are among the most dangerous of men, Jews are unclean and ignorant. Yet they are all let in, while Chinese, who are sober, or duly law abiding, clean, educated and industrious, are shut out. There are few Chinamen in jails and none in the poor houses. There are no Chinese tramps or drunkards. Many Chinese here have become sincere Christians, in spite of the persecution which they have to endure from their heathen countrymen. More than half the Chinese in this country would become citizens if allowed to do so, and would be patriotic Americans. But how can they make this country their home as matters are now? They are not allowed to bring wives here from China, and if they marry American women there is a great outcry.
>
> All Congressmen acknowledge the injustice of the treatment of my people, yet they continue it. They have no backbone.
>
> Under the circumstances, how can I call this my home, and how can any one blame me if I take my money and go back to my village in China?[51]

For the most part, however, the diplomats, intellectuals, and local elite who spoke out against exclusion and American attitudes toward the Chinese maintained a Sinocentric worldview, playing the role of cultural defenders. Coming from a country that had traditionally considered itself the center of the civilized world, these members of the Chinese elite protested American immigration policy because it offended their Chinese sensibilities. They demanded fair treatment for themselves and their lower-class compatriots on the basis of China's great civilization and past achievements. When seeking treatment equal to that of other immigrant groups, these individuals often resorted to denigrating the other groups to elevate the status of the Chinese. Even their appeals to American standards of justice and fairness were a tactic designed to make Americans live up to the rhetoric of democracy, but there is little indication that these Chinese spokespersons personally believed in democratic practices. One man, Yung Wing, however, stood in contrast to most of his peers. Acting as a cultural broker between Chinese and American worldviews, he rejected Sinocentrism, embraced American political and civic values, and made the United States his adopted home.

Yung Wing: Challenging Sinocentrism and American Ideals of Inclusion

Yung Wing and a number of the young Chinese who were educated in the United States underwent a cultural metamorphosis during their time in America. Those who returned to China with a Western education to serve their country aided China's entry into the modern family of nations, which underscores the fact that China's modern transformation was shaped in part by the Chinese experience in America. This process produced a new model of Chinese intellectuals and immigrants through hybridization.[52] No longer exclusively Chinese subjects in America, Yung Wing and the others who remained in or later returned to the United States were among the first transplanted Chinese in America who clearly demonstrated that psychocultural development could occur despite legal constraints.

Yung Wing was born on November 17, 1828, in the village of Nam Ping on Pedro Island, about four miles southwest of the Portuguese colony of Macao. When Yung was seven years old, his father, for unknown reasons, enrolled him in a missionary school in Macao run by the Reverend Charles Gutzlaff's wife. Yung would henceforth receive mainly an American education, primarily in English. This alone set him apart from most of the Chinese of his time, and his life foreshadowed the cultural evolution that many Chinese would undergo in the late nineteenth and early twentieth centuries.

After Yung Wing had attended this school for about four years, Mrs. Gutzlaff returned to the United States and the school was disbanded. Yung then returned to his village and resumed studying Chinese. During this period, his father died and the children had to support the family. Yung sold candy on the street and gleaned rice in the fields. Soon, he found employment in the office of a Catholic priest who needed someone who could read Arabic numerals to assist in various clerical duties. After four months in this position, Yung was able to resume his education. He received word from one of Mrs. Gutzlaff's friends that he could attend the Morrison Education Society School in Macao, then under the direction of the Reverend Samuel R. Brown (Yale, 1832) and his wife.

The Morrison School had opened in 1839; when Yung entered it in 1841, five other Chinese boys were already enrolled, Wong Shing, Li Kan, Chow Wan, Tang Chik, and Wong Foon.[53] The students studied arithmetic, geography, and reading, and attended classes in English-language training in the morning and Chinese in the afternoon. At the end of the first Opium War in 1842, the school was moved to Hong Kong, where it remained until it closed in 1850. In 1846, the Reverend Brown announced that he was returning to the United States because of ill health but hoped that a number of his students would accompany him to complete their education in America. Yung Wing, Wong Foon, and Wong Shing volunteered and received permission from their families to go abroad. Several patrons were found in Hong Kong who pledged to support the students' families during their expected two-year sojourn in the United States. These patrons also helped defray the students' expenses. Yung and his classmates arrived in America in April 1847 and were enrolled in the Monson Academy in Monson, Massachusetts, under the direction of the Reverend Charles Hammond (Yale, 1839).

Wong Shing had to return to China in the spring of 1849 because of his failing health, but he subsequently played important supporting roles in Sino-American diplomacy.[54] Wong Foon and Yung Wing, however, did not want to return to their native country at the completion of their studies at the Monson Academy. To prolong their stay abroad, Yung and Wong had to gain permission and further aid from their benefactors in Hong Kong, who agreed to continue to support their education if they would attend the University of Edinburgh. Wong Foon accepted this offer, but Yung Wing chose to remain in the United States, hoping to attend Yale University. Wong Foon graduated from the University of Edinburgh and returned to China in 1857 as China's first Western-trained physician.[55]

That Yung decided to remain in the United States, rather than to return to China or continue his education in Scotland, reveals his strong attraction to American life. His serious reevaluation—and rejection—of Chinese culture led to his decision. In a letter to Samuel Wells Williams, the American chargé d'affaires in China and a Morrison Education Society trustee, a lifelong friend whom Yung had first met when he was a student in Hong Kong, Yung explained his desire to remain in the United States:

> Of course you are aware that my feelings would not allow me to leave my mother and the brothers and sisters, since I promised them all when I left China to return in two or three years and you know ful [sic] well the prejudice of the Chinese, how they misrepresent things, and that they are not able to see as you or any enlightened mind do, the object, the advantage, and value of being [Western] educated. Ignorance and superstition have sealed the noble faculties of their minds, how can they appreciate things of such worth?[56]

This passage reveals that Yung had already distanced himself from a strictly Chinese worldview and was privileging Western learning. He contrasted what he saw as Chinese "prejudice" and "ignorance and superstition" with the "enlightened mind" produced by an American education. He believed that fundamental differences existed in the manner in which Chinese and Americans viewed the world and that the American approach was better.

Yung Wing entered Yale soon after Wong Foon departed for Edinburgh. There, his appreciation of American culture became even more pronounced. He became a naturalized American citizen on October 30, 1852, in New Haven,[57] a fact that spoke strongly of his changing self-perception: He was no longer simply a Chinese student in America; he was formally staking his claim as a Chinese American.

Another indication of Yung's embrace of Western culture was his active Christian affiliation. According to his friend, the Reverend Joseph Twichell, Yung's conversion to Christianity occured while he was attending the Monson Academy, when he became a member of the Monson Congregational Church.[58] Yung's faith appears to have been sincere; his personal writings are replete with references to God and the importance of good works. His conversion was more than a break with fundamental Chinese cultural traditions; it marked a conscious separation from his family and a significant break with Confucian tenets of filial piety. Yung did not even return to China in 1850 to mourn the death of his oldest brother. He wrote to Samuel Wells Williams that he was concerned for his mother's condition but "the only thing that I can do for them now is to pray for them."[59]

Yung Wing's lengthy exposure to Western educational practices and values, and his own transformation thereby, led him to believe that China's salvation depended on training China's youth in Western learning. Yung believed that by fully adopting the educational practices and models of the West, China might be able to reclaim its place among the powerful nations of the modern world. He wrote,

> Before the close of my last year in college I had already sketched out what I should do. I was determined that the rising generation of China should enjoy the same educational advantages that I had enjoyed; that through Western education China might be regenerated, become enlightened and powerful. To accomplish that object became the guiding star of my ambition. Towards such a goal, I directed all my mental resources and energy. Through thick and thin, and the vicissitudes of a checkered life from 1854 to 1872, I labored and waited for its consummation.[60]

Driven by this patriotic devotion to regenerate China through the adoption of American educational ideals, Yung strove to strip away Sinocentrism to allow new and fresh ideas to emerge, and thereby to transform China into a new nation just as he had been changed by his exposure to the West. He devoted much of his career to remaking China into a modern nation through the adoption of Western-style education.

Yung Wing and the Chinese Educational Mission

Soon after Yung graduated from Yale, he returned to China in the company of the Reverend William A. Macy (Yale, 1844), who had formerly taught at the Morrison School in Hong Kong and was now returning to China as a missionary for the American Board of Commissioners for Foreign Missions (ABCFM). For the next several years, Yung worked at various jobs. He first became the private secretary to Dr. Peter Parker, a former medical missionary with the ABCFM who had been appointed as the temporary U.S. commissioner to China. Later, Yung became a translator for the Imperial Customs House in Shanghai, worked a short stint as a clerk for English tea and silk merchants, and made ends meet by translating works for both Chinese and Western business firms.[61] Yung also accepted an offer to travel to the tea districts in Zhejiang, Hubei, and Hunan to learn the business of packing tea for transport and export. He made a name for himself by going into territory occupied by the Taiping rebels and bringing out tea held by them. Such ventures earned Yung a favorable reputation and he was able to conduct his own commission business for the next three years.[62]

Yung Wing had returned to China during a period of great civil unrest marked by a series of rebel movements. The longest and best known was the Taiping Rebellion (1850–1864), a tremendous anti-dynastic uprising that pit huge armies of disenchanted peasants, influenced by an ideological blend of millenarian Christianity and anti-Manchu sentiments, against imperial troops. The rebel forces proved to be formidable opponents to the state, and nearly fourteen years passed before the central government suppressed the movement.[63] An important consequence of the Taiping Rebellion was the elevation of regional figures to national prominence. One such man was Zeng Guofan (1811–1872), who after defeating the Taiping rebels in 1864 was promoted to viceroy of Liangjiang (Jiangsu and Jiangxi provinces). In this position, Zeng sought to strengthen China through the modernization of its military. Hearing of Yung's education and experience in America, Zeng summoned him for an audience. The two spoke of Zeng's aspirations for a modern China. Zeng soon commissioned Yung to travel to the United States to purchase machinery to equip what would become the famous Jiangnan Arsenal in Shanghai.

Yung arrived in the United States in 1864. Because of the Civil War, most American machine shops were working at full capacity to fill orders for the armies. Nevertheless, Yung managed to engage Putnam and Company of Fitchburg, Massachusetts, to fill his order. While waiting for the machinery to be manufactured, Yung visited Yale and even traveled to Washington, D.C., to volunteer for the Union Army, clearly demonstrating his self-identification as an American citizen and his dedication to duties that he saw as obligatory. His enlistment was not accepted, however; the officials of the Volunteer Department declined to interfere with his obligations to the Chinese government.[64]

Upon his return to China with the machinery in 1865, Yung was rewarded for his service. Zeng recommended to the Qing court that he be granted a regular official rank. He was appointed as an official of the fourth grade and made an Expectant Taotai, which made him eligible for appointment to an administrative post on a subprefectual level when one became available.[65] It was not a powerful or significant position in the grand scheme of the Chinese bureaucracy, but it conferred on the foreign-educated Yung permanent official status normally earned only by Confucian-educated literati in China. While awaiting an administrative appointment, he became an interpreter and translator for the government in Shanghai.

Although Yung had wanted to promote his idea of sending Chinese students to America since he first returned to China, no opportunity arose until 1870. That year, a number of European missionaries (predominantly French) and other foreign citizens were killed by an antiforeign Chinese mob in Tianjin. Zeng Guofan and his protégé, Li Hongzhang (1822–1901), were among the imperial commissioners assigned to settle the affair with the French authorities. Yung Wing was appointed secretary to the commission. In the aftermath of the settlement, he was invited to submit recommendations for China's modernization.

Yung presented four recommendations: forming a fully Chinese-owned steamship company charged with transporting tribute rice to the capital from the southern provinces, sending youths abroad to be educated in Western schools for the service of the country, exploiting China's mineral resources, and prohibiting missionaries from exercising any kind of jurisdiction over their converts. The educational proposal proved attractive to Ding Zhichang (1823–1882), the governor of Jiangsu, who sent it to the throne in a series of memorials under Zeng Guofan's and Li Hongzhang's names.[66] Chen Lanbin, a secretary with the Board of Punishments, and Yung Wing were chosen as commissioner and associate commissioner, respectively, to head the Chinese Educational Mission to the United States.

The Mission was to send 30 students between the ages of twelve and sixteen to the United States each year for four years. These 120 students would study in America for fifteen years and would be allowed to travel for another two years before returning to China. They would then report to the Zongli Yamen for assignment to useful occupations in service to the country.[67] Chen was to be in charge of their Chinese education, and Yung was responsible for their Western curriculum. The commissioners were to ensure that the students read the *Sacred Book of Imperial Edicts* at specified times and that Chinese almanacs would be distributed to enable the students to observe the proper rituals, so that they could preserve and maintain their sense of Chinese propriety and reverence for Chinese tradition.[68] The Mission would be funded by the income collected from the Shanghai Customs, with an estimated 1.2 million taels (U.S. $1,680,000) needed to fund the whole project.[69]

In 1871, a training school was established in Shanghai from which students for the Mission would be selected. The students in this school were recruited on the basis of ability, age, health, and family background. They were instructed in both Chinese and English and were required to pass an examination to qualify for consideration.[70] In an 1872 letter to the president of Yale, Yung Wing noted that the Mission students would be interested in "military and naval science, medicine, the law, engineering, chemistry, Natural philosophy, geology, and astronomy."[71]

Despite official support for the Mission, the Chinese government, from the earliest stages of the project, had reservations about the possible cultural impact that the United States might have on the young Chinese students. To recognize the benefits of Western learning was indeed a step away from the traditional Sinocentric worldview that placed Chinese learning above all others, but the manner in which the Chinese hoped to operate the Educational Mission reveals that the supporters of the Mission cleaved to the *ti-yong* idea that Western learning was best for application, whereas Chinese learning was best for cultural rectification.[72] As the Mission took root in the United States, the tensions inherent in this dichotomous approach to modernization became increasingly clear.

After the first group of thirty students was selected from the preparatory school in Shanghai, they traveled to the United States under the care of Chen Lanbin and other members of the Mission staff.[73] Yung had departed for America a month earlier to finalize housing arrangements for the students. He first established the headquarters of the Mission in Springfield, Massachusetts, because he considered it the most central point from which to locate the students in area homes. The students were housed by twos and threes in private homes throughout the Connecticut valley.[74] In these homes, the boys were taught English and activities such as singing, dancing, piano playing, drawing, and oil painting.[75] The Mission later moved to Hartford, Connecticut, where it remained for its duration.

Soon after the Mission was established in Hartford, Yung Wing, Chen Lanbin, and eventually Wu Jiashan clashed over the direction, operation, and goals of the Mission, as well as over the students' behavior. At the core of the official concern over the students' attitudes and behavior was the fear that their experiences in America would undermine the original purpose of the Mission. The officials who did not share Yung's attraction to American culture worried that the students would become deracinated by adopting Western ideas and practices that contradicted fundamental aspects of Chinese culture. The officials also worried that the students would reject their own culture and, in turn, lose their nationalistic desire to serve China. This would not only be a failure, but also signify the officials' loss of control over their wards. Therefore, those in charge of the Mission wanted the students to be extremely aware of the situation in China and their expected role in its eventual development into a modern nation.

The differences between Chinese and American approaches to education and the question of how the Mission students should behave were best captured in Yung's discussion of the reasons for Chen Lanbin's dissatisfaction with the Mission:

> He had never been out of China in his life until he came to this country. The only standard by which he measured things and men (especially students) was purely Chinese. The gradual but marked transformation of the students in their behavior and conduct as they grew in knowledge and stature under New England influence, culture and environment produced a contrast to their behavior and conduct when they first set foot in New England that might well be strange and repugnant to the ideas and senses of a man like Chin Lan Pin [*sic*], who all his life had been accustomed to see the springs of life, energy and independence, candor, ingenuity and open-heartedness all covered up and concealed, and in a great measure smothered and never allowed their full play. Now in New England the heavy weight of repression and suppression was lifted from the minds of these young students; they exulted in their freedom and leaped for joy. . . . He must have felt that his own immaculate Chinese training had been contaminated by coming in contact with Occidental schooling, which he looked upon with evident repugnance.[76]

The depth of Yung's attachment to what he perceived as the superior qualities of Western society is strikingly clear in this passage. Contrasting American "energy and independence, candor, ingenuity and open-heartedness" with a Chinese tendency to "cover up, conceal, and smother," Yung rejected what he viewed as the restrictive character of Chinese cultural traditions and chose instead the "springs of life" that he found in New England.

The closing of the Educational Mission in 1881 has often been attributed to personal conflicts among Yung Wing, Chen Lanbin, and Wu Jiashan, or to the Zongli Yamen's disappointment that the students had not received enough technical or miltary training and were not admitted to American military academies, or that too few had graduated from college. The conflict that caused the closure was, in fact, much more fundamental.[77] It was part of the crisis in which Chinese intellectuals found themselves as they attempted to carve out a new place for China in the modern family of nations while still retaining a Sinocentric worldview. This combined goal proved unattainable in the case of the young students sent to live and study in the United States. These students, like Yung Wing, were harbingers of a new era in Chinese history, as well as in Chinese American history. While they were being educated to help transform China into a modern nation, they also unwittingly adopted a lifestyle and ethos that a Sinocentric worldview could not encompass.

Yung Wing's Place in Chinese American History

Because Yung Wing's career was primarily in the service of the Chinese government, he is often neglected in the study of Chinese Americans. In fact, he was an important figure in the development of late-nineteenth- and early-twentieth-century Chinese American history, representing the transition from a primarily China-oriented life to an America-oriented life. His faith in American educational practices and goals was a strong challenge to the Sinocentric notion of cultural superiority. His affinity for American culture certainly contradicted the belief that Chinese could never live in the United States alongside Euro-Americans as moral and social equals. His devotion to American ideals of democracy and inclusion also shaped his response to the anti-Chinese movement. Although he did not publish articles in the same manner as those discussed in the first part of this chapter, his surviving writings and remarks on the exclusion of the Chinese clearly show that he opposed such policies and those who formulated them. He was well aware of the poor treatment afforded most Chinese in the Americas. In addition to his work to curtail the coolie trade to Cuba and Peru, he voiced his opposition to the anti-Chinese forces in the United States. Assailing the many statements made by Senator A. A. Sargent and Frank Pixley at the 1876 congressional hearings on Chinese immigration, Yung wrote to Samuel Wells Williams, "Sargent and Pixley are what people call 'politicians.' What they think and say either on American or Chinese matters do not carry any great weight with the thinking public, though it cannot be denied that they do exercise an influence with the 'herd.' I have great confidence in such men as [President Rutherford B.] Hayes and [Secretary of State William Maxwell] Evarts. They mean well and will act as they mean. I think they will do justice to China and the Chinese."[78] Yung's forecast was too optimistic. In 1880, he complained to Secretary of State Evarts about the continuing poor treatment of Chinese in America:

> You will pardon me for stating my views on the subject with entire frankness. I will not venture to measure the powers of the general government of the U.S. in the enforcement of Treaties, or suggest that it could have acted more vigorously against the trespassers upon Treaty rights. I am not unmindful of the Executive veto of the "Chinese bill," or of the decision of a U.S. Court that the "queue ordinance" was unconstitutional. But at the present time the Treaty of 1868 is practically a dead letter in one of the States of the Union where tens of thousands of my countrymen are by law deprived of shelter and prohibited from earning a livelihood and are in hourly expectation of being driven from their homes to starve in the streets. Under such circumstances I could not acquit myself of my duty if I did not protest earnestly, but most respectfully, against the wrong to which they have been subjected.[79]

Yung's gentlemanly protestation did little good. Years later, Yung would state his case in much more emphatic terms, placing the blame for the exclusion of Chinese fully on the American government's failure to live up to its own ideals of inclusion and democracy. He wrote: "In view of what the United States government has done, for the past twenty years, in the way of enacting obnoxious laws against the Chinese, and without any provocation flinging insult after insult in the very teeth of the Chinese government, I cannot for the life of me see how republicanism is to become universal, or how the torch of American liberty is to enlighten the eastern races when they are shut out from its light."[80]

This theme was reiterated by former student of the Chinese Educational Mission and Yale graduate Yan Phou Lee. His 1889 article, cited previously, contained a plea for equal treatment similar to the position taken by Yung:

> No nation can afford to let go its high ideals. The founders of the American Republic asserted the principle that all men are created equal, and made this fair land a refuge for the whole world. Its manifest destiny, therefore, is to be the teacher and leader of nations in liberty. Its supremacy should be maintained by good faith and righteous dealing, and not by the display of selfishness and greed. But now, looking at the ac-

tions of this generation of Americans in their treatment of other races, who can get rid of the idea that that Nation, which Abraham Lincoln said was conceived in liberty, waxed great through oppression, and was really dedicated to the proposition that all men are created to prey on one another?

How far this Republic has departed from its high ideal and reversed its traditionary *[sic]* policy may be seen in the laws passed against the Chinese.[81]

Thus, Yung, and in this passage Yan Phou Lee, did not rely on China's past greatness to demand fair treatment in America, nor did they attempt to denigrate others to elevate the status of the Chinese. Instead, Yung Wing embraced fully the values and ideals of his adopted country and pointedly asked that America live up to those ideals, especially in the case of the cruel treatment of the Chinese in America.

Despite his fervent attachment to American ideals, Yung, while visiting China in 1898, lost his American citizenship as a result of the enforcement of the 1878 *In re Ah Yup* decision, which declared Chinese immigrants ineligible for American citizenship.[82] Education, religion, family concerns, and cultural affinities notwithstanding, in the eyes of the law Yung was still an excludable alien in the United States. Nevertheless, Yung managed to return to the United States, where he lived in semiretirement, writing his autobiography, visiting friends, corresponding with his sons, keeping current with events in China, and even receiving visits from Liang Qichao in 1903 and Kang Youwei in 1905.[83]

Contrary to the racist thinking that deemed Chinese unassimilable during the anti-Chinese movement, Yung Wing's life in America was the quintessential example of assimilation. He was more than able to adapt and contribute to American society. His American education, religious conversion, family, friends, and career were all part of and products of a worldview that was fundamentally American. In rejecting much of the traditional Chinese approach to education and social conventions, Yung sought to become American. Yung Wing may have lost his American citizenship because of American anti-Chinese legislation, but he had lost much of his purely Chinese identity long before that, and America was where he chose to live until his death in 1912.

Yung straddled two worlds, that of a Chinese reformer dedicated to bringing China into the modern family of nations and that of a Chinese American husband and father, concerned with the affairs of his family in Hartford, Connecticut. These roles do not appear to have been contradictory for Yung. A career devoted to serving China did not preclude a desire to be an American. Acting as a cultural broker, he sought to bridge the distance between the Chinese and American perspectives by shedding the Sinocentric approach to international relations while fully maintaining concern for China's future and compassion for his Chinese compatriots.[84] At the same time, he was profoundly disappointed in the failure of American policy makers and the people of the United States to fulfill their commitment to democracy and the ideals of pluralism.

Conclusion

Chinese immigration to the United States created a situation in which three parties found themselves in crisis: Euro-Americans who were opposed to the Chinese immigrant presence, the Chinese government, and Chinese immigrants in America. Euro-Americans, in acknowledging that they did not want Chinese immigration, were forced to reevaluate American ideals of equality and free immigration. Racial and cultural differences, wage competition, and questions of assimilability were fundamental concerns for the Americans involved in the debate over Chinese immigration, but these questions were only specific manifestations of a larger issue: Should America remain a country of free immigration, or should it restrict immigration on the basis of racial, class, and cultural grounds? In this debate, specific charges were made and refuted or supported, and important issues of race, culture, and power were presented, but the underlying concern was the fate of American society.

The Chinese government, too, had to reevaluate its policies regarding its subjects abroad. Faced with the recognition that Chinese immigrants were often the victims of restrictive legislation and brutal discrimination, the Chinese government, largely Sinocentric in its approach to international relations, decided to break with tradition in 1875 and establish a formal foreign legation in the United States. The Chinese government was forced to acknowledge that the Chinese immigrant presence in America called for new approaches to understanding China's position in the modern world. No longer merely Chinese subjects bound to the culture of China and its long history, the Chinese in America, and the Chinese officials who dealt with the immigrants, found themselves in a "new world," confronted with conflicting values and changing social relations. Many Chinese, therefore, first came into contact with the "modern family of nations" as unwelcome immigrants in the United States. Their response to this process, in turn, was a vital part of China's overall response to the West.

Meanwhile, Chinese immigrants, unable to defeat the anti-Chinese movement, nonetheless attempted to contest legislation in the courts and to publish articles in support of their mode of life in America. These articles, filled with indignation and frustration, reveal that the Chinese in America, regardless of class, while bound by their own notions of race and hierarchy, were simultaneously aware and appreciative of American political and civic ideals and sought acceptance in the American polity. Although pecuniary interests were often assumed to be Chinese immigrants' sole concern, this was not the case. A number of them did attempt to find a home in the "Land of the Flowery Flag." They sought to escape the stigma of being aliens ineligible for citizenship by emphasizing the glories of Chinese civilization, by comparing themselves favorably with members of other groups, and by appealing to American values of inclusion, thereby seeking to wrest control of their image out of the hands of the exclusionists.

On the other hand, Yung Wing, took a divergent path in his response to the crisis engendered by the Chinese presence in America. Educated primarily in American-run schools, and the first Chinese to graduate from an American university, Yung fully embraced American civic and political values. He rejected the Sinocentric worldview that placed Chinese culture above all other cultures and devoted his career to modernizing China by using the United States as his model. This dedication to China, however, did not dampen his resolve to live in the United States as an American citizen. He saw no contradiction in serving the land of his birth while fully embracing the values of his adopted country.

The Chinese in America during the late nineteenth and early twentieth centuries were acutely aware that theirs was a community under siege. Thus, more often than not, the consciousness of the early Chinese Americans was shaped by the need to respond to their accusers; it was a consciousness that reflected a blend of and a conflict between Chinese and American cultural ideals. Acting as both cultural defenders and cultural brokers, they sought to find acceptance in American society. However, although they were engaged in a process of resistance and self-definition, they were forced to focus more of their attention on defending their presence than on developing an identity with an accompanying body of literature to define and celebrate their existence in America.

Notes

1. The earliest recorded strike carried out by Chinese laborers in America occurred in 1867, when thousands of Chinese who were employed in building the first transcontinental railroad went on strike for better wages and working conditions. However, the strike lasted only a week because the railroad company cut off the laborers' food supply. No in-depth study of this strike exists, but brief accounts can be found in Thomas W. Chinn, H. Mark Lai, and Philip P. Choy, *A History of the Chinese in California: A Syllabus* (San Francisco: Chinese Historical Society of America, 1969), 45–46; and Sucheng Chan, *Asian Americans: An Interpretive History* (Boston: Twayne Publishers, 1991), 81–82. This strike is also the subject of David Henry Hwang, "The Dance and the Railroad," in David Henry Hwang, *FOB and Other Plays* (New York: New American Library, 1990), 53–86. The most extensive study of how the Chinese used the courts to challenge the anti-Chinese movement is Hudson N. Janisch, "The Chinese, the Courts, and the Constitution: A Study of the Legal Issues Raised by Chinese Immigrants to the United States, 1850–1902" (J.D. dissertation, University of Chicago, School of Law, 1971). More recent studies include Charles J. McClain and Laurene Wu McClain, "The Chinese Contribution to the Development of American Law," and Christian G. Fritz, "Due Process, Treaty Rights, and Chinese Exclusion, 1882–1891," both in *Entry Denied: Exclusion and the Chinese Community in America, 1882–1943*, ed. Sucheng Chan (Philadelphia: Temple University Press, 1991), 3–24; 25–56; Charles J. McClain, *In Search of Equality: The Chinese Struggle against Discrimination in Nineteenth-Century America* (Berkeley and Los Angeles: University of California Press, 1994); and Lucy E. Salyer, *Laws Harsh as Tigers: Chinese Immigrants and the Shaping of Modern Immigration Law* (Chapel Hill: University of North Carolina Press, 1995).

2. California State Senate, *Chinese Immigration, Its Social, Moral, and Political Effect* (Sacramento: State Printing Office, 1878), hereafter cited as Califormia State Senate, *Chinese Immigration*; and U.S. Congressional Joint Special Committee to Investigate Chinese Immigration, *Report*, 44th Cong., 2d sess., Senate Report 689 (Washington, D.C.: Government Printing Office, 1877), hereafter cited as U.S. Joint Special Committee, *Senate Report* 689.

3. Calfornia State Senate, *Chinese Immigration*, 61. In this case, a "memorial" refers to a statement of facts presented to a legislative body as the grounds for a petition. These arguments would continue to frame the discussion of the drive for the exclusion of Chinese immigrants.

4. In this system of debt bondage, various individuals—returned emigrants, Chinese merchants, Western labor recruiters, ship captains—and Chinese fraternal associations provided emigrants with tickets on credit for the voyage abroad. These indebted emigrants were then obligated to repay their fares out of their future earnings upon arrival at their destination, often at a high interest rate. This description is based largely on Sucheng Chan, *This Bittersweet Soil: The Chinese in California Agriculture, 1860–1910* (Berkeley and Los Angeles: University of California Press, 1986), 26, which, in turn, relies on Persia C. Campbell, *Chinese Coolie Emigration to Countries within the British Empire* (1923; reprint, New York: Negro University Press, 1969). According to

Chan, Campbell may have been the first author to use the term "credit-ticket." I also adopt the term "semifree" from Chan to describe those who used this financial arrangement to emigrate. To trace the English-language historiography of the coolie trade and the use of the credit-ticket system, see Mary R. Coolidge, *Chinese Immigration* (New York: Henry Holt, 1909); Ch'en Ta, *Chinese Migrations, with Special Reference to Labor Conditions* (Washington, D.C.: Government Printing Office, 1923); Harley Farnsworth McNair, *The Chinese Abroad: Their Position and Protection, a Study in International Law and Relations* (Shanghai: Commercial Press, 1951); Watt Stewart, *Chinese Bondage in Peru: A History of the Chinese Coolie in Peru, 1848–1874* (Durham: Duke University Press, 1951); Gunther Barth, *Bitter Strength: A History of the Chinese in the United States, 1850–1870* (Cambridge, Mass.: Harvard University Press, 1964); Arnold Joseph Meagher, "The Introduction of Chinese Laborers to Latin America: The 'Coolie Trade,' 1847–1874" (Ph.D. dissertation, University of California, Davis, 1975); Kil Young Zo, *Chinese Emigration into the United States, 1850–1880* (1971; New York: Arno Press, 1978); Robert L. Irick, *Ch'ing Policy towards the Coolie Trade, 1847–1878* (Taipei: Chinese Materials Center, 1982); Rebecca J. Scott, *Slave Emancipation in Cuba: The Transition to Free Labor, 1860–1899* (Princeton: Princeton University Press, 1985); Patricia Cloud and David W. Galenson, "Chinese Immigration and Contract Labor in the Late Nineteenth Century," *Explorations in Economic History* 24 (1987): 22–42; Charles J. McClain, "Chinese Immigration: A Comment on Cloud and Galenson," *Explorations in Economic History* 27 (1990): 363–378; Evelyn Hu-DeHart, "Coolies, Shopkeepers, Pioneers: The Chinese of Mexico and Peru (1849–1930)," *Amerasia Journal* 15, no. 2 (1989): 91–116; and Wally Look Lai, *Indentured Labor, Caribbean Sugar: Chinese and Indian Migrants to the British West Indies, 1838–1918* (Baltimore: Johns Hopkins University Press, 1993). The English-language text of the Chinese report on the coolie trade in Cuba was recently reprinted as *The Cuba Commission Report: A Hidden History of the Chinese in Cuba,* with an introduction by Denise Helly (Baltimore: Johns Hopkins University Press, 1993).

5. Studies that address the issue of Chinese prostitution in America include Lucie Cheng, "Free, Indentured, Enslaved: Chinese Prostitutes in Nineteenth-Century America," in *Labor Immigration under Capitalism: Asian Workers in the United States before World War II,* ed. Lucie Cheng and Edna Bonacich (Berkeley and Los Angeles: University of California Press, 1984), 402–434; George Anthony Peffer, "Forbidden Families: Emigration Experiences of Chinese Women under the Page Law, 1875–1882," *Journal of American Ethnic History* 6 (1986): 28–46; Sucheng Chan, "The Exclusion of Chinese Women, 1870–1943," in *Entry Denied,* ed. Chan, 94–146; and Benson Tong, *Unsubmissive Women: Chinese Prostitutes in San Francisco, 1849–1882* (Norman: University of Oklahoma Press, 1994). See also Peggy Pascoe, *Relations of Rescue: The Search for Female Moral Authority in the American West, 1874–1939* (New York: Oxford University Press, 1990), and Judy Yung, *Unbound Feet: A Social History of Chinese Women in San Francisco* (Berkeley and Los Angeles: University of California Press, 1995), 26–37, 73–77.

6. U.S. Joint Special Committee, *Senate Report* 689, 289.

7. Ibid., 942.

8. The evolution of these laws can be traced in 22 *U.S. Statutes at Large* 58–61; 25 *U.S. Statutes at Large* 476–479; 27 *U.S. Statutes at Large* 25–26; 28 *U.S.*

Statutes at Large 1210–1212; 32 *U.S. Statutes at Large* 176–177; 33 *U.S. Statutes at Large* 428; and 43 *U.S. Statutes at Large* 153–169.

9. James D. Phelan, "Why the Chinese Should Be Excluded," *North American Review* 173 (November 1901), 663. The initial article by Ho Yow is discussed later in this chapter.

10. Ibid., 663.

11. Ibid., 668.

12. Testimony concerning leprosy among the Chinese can be found in California State Senate, *Chinese Immigration*, 74, 152, 154, 183, 197; U.S. Joint Special Committee, *Senate Report* 689, 13, 131–132, 180, 182, 199–205, 646, 1100. Similar testimony concerning the diseases allegedly carried by Chinese prostitutes can be found in California State Senate, *Chinese Immigration*, 153, 168, 172, 178, 196; and U.S. Joint Special Committee, *Senate Report* 689, 14, 97. Studies on the racial politics of diseases in San Francisco's Chinatown include Philip A. Kalisch, "The Black Death in Chinatown: Plague and Politics in San Francisco, 1900–1904," *Arizona and the West* 14 (Summer 1972): 113–136; John B. Trauner, "The Chinese as Medical Scapegoats in San Francisco, 1870–1905," 57 *California History* (1978):70–87; and Charles J. McClain, *In Search of Equality*, 234–276.

13. Phelan, "Why the Chinese Should Be Excluded," 674–675.

14. *Statutes of California* (1880): xxiv.

15. One definition of "Mongolian" listed in the *Compact Oxford English Dictionary* is "a type of idiot characterized by a physiognomy resembling that of the Mongolians," page 1837. The earliest entry under this definition reads, "1892, J. L. Down in Tuke, *Dict. Psychol. Med* II.644 'Ten per cent. of all cases of idiocy arrange themselves around a highly characteristic type which the writer has proposed to call the Mongolian variety.'" As recently as 1980, the *American Oxford Dictionary*, page 430, defined "Mongolism" as "an abnormal congenital condition in which a person suffers from mental deficiency and has a Mongoloid appearance." The "Mongoloid appearance" was apparently in reference to the shape of the affected person's eyes. This condition is now usually referred to as "Down syndrome."

16. American Federation of Labor, *Some Reasons for Chinese Exclusion: Meat vs. Rice, American Manhood against Asiatic Coolieism. Which Shall Survive?* (Washington, D.C.: American Federation of Labor, 1902), 5. In response to this publication, a "pro-Chinese" pamphlet was published entitled *Truth without Fiction. Justice versus Prejudice. Meat for All, Not for Few*. The author, publisher, and date of publication of this tract are uncertain. It may have been produced by American missionaries sympathetic to the Chinese immigrant presence.

17. American Federation of Labor, *Some Reasons for Chinese Exclusion*, 31. Blaine's statements here are taken from his remarks as a member of the U.S. Senate during debates on Chinese immigration in 1879. He later became secretary of state under Presidents James Garfield and Chester Arthur (these positions were held only briefly because of Garfield's assassination and Arthur's change of administration), and President Benjamin Harrison. Blaine remained a staunch opponent of Chinese immigration for many years.

18. Wu Tingfang, "Mutual Helpfulness between China and the United States," *North American Review* 171 (July 1900): 4–5. The *North American Review* frequently published articles about China and the Chinese in America. In print from 1815 to sometime in the 1930s, this was one of the leading period-

icals in the country. The early editors, mostly intellectuals from New England, promoted a policy of scholarly and political debate, which gave anti- and pro-Chinese writers the opportunity to state their views. For brief commentaries on the character of the *North American Review*, see Stuart Creighton Miller, *The Unwelcome Immigrant: The American Image of the Chinese, 1785–1882* (Berkeley and Los Angeles: University of California Press, 1969), and John Tebbel and Mary Ellen Zuckerman, *The Magazine in America, 1741–1990* (New York: Oxford University Press, 1991).

19. Wu, "Mutal Helpfulness," 9.

20. Ibid., 10.

21. Wu Tingfang, *America through the Spectacles of an Oriental Diplomat* (New York: Frederick Stokes, 1914), 16–17.

22. Ibid., 117.

23. Ibid., 146.

24. Ibid., 180.

25. Ibid., 186.

26. Ho Yow was unpopular among many of the Chinese immigrants in America because of his efforts to control their behavior, especially that of Chinese immigrants in secret societies, by threatening their relatives in China. He was later accused of corruption, fraud, incompetence, and consorting with prostitutes. Wu Tingfang relieved Ho of his post in 1902. See Shih-shan Henry Tsai, *China and the Overseas Chinese in the United States, 1868–1911* (Fayetteville: University of Arkansas Press, 1983), 129.

27. Ho Yow, "Chinese Exclusion, a Benefit or a Harm?" *North American Review* 173 (September 1901): 315.

28. Ibid., 327. The exact congressional act to which Ho refers in this passage is unclear.

29. Ho Yow, "The Chinese Question," *Overland Monthly* 34, no. 1 (October 1901): 249–257. For studies of Arnold Genthe's representations of the Chinese of San Francisco, see Maxine Hong Kingston, "San Francisco's Chinatown," *American Heritage* 30, no. 1 (December 1978): 37–47; John Kuo Wei Tchen, *Genthe's Photographs of San Francisco's Old Chinatown* (New York: Dover Publications, 1984); and Toby Gersten Quitslund, "Arnold Genthe: A Pictorial Photographer in San Francisco, 1895–1911" (Ph.D. dissertation, George Washington University, 1988).

30. Ho, "The Chinese Question," 253.

31. Ibid., 254.

32. Ibid., 250–253.

33. John Bigler, *Governor's Special Message* (April 23, 1852). All citations of this document refer to the reprint in *Asian Americans in the United States*, vol. I, ed. Alexander Yamata, Soo-Young Chin, Wendy L. Ng, and Joel Franks (Dubuque, Iowa: Kendall/Hunt Publishing, 1993), 173–179.

34. Ibid., 173–174.

35. Hab Wa and Long Achick, "The Chinese in California: Letter of the Chinamen to His Excellency Gov. Bigler," *Living Age* 34 (July 1852): 32. I thank Sucheng Chan for supplying me with a transcribed copy of this document.

36. Ibid. For a convincing argument on the origins of the word, see Irick, *Ch'ing Policy toward the Coolie Trade*, 2–6.

37. Hab and Long, "The Chinese in California," 32.

38. Ibid.

39. Ibid., 33.

40. Norman Asing, "To His Excellency Governor Bigler," *Daily Alta California*, San Francisco (May 5, 1855), included in *To Serve the Devil*, Vol. 2, *Colonials and Sojourners*, ed. Paul Jacobs and Saul Landau with Eve Pell (New York: Vintage Books, 1971), 127. Asing was among a few Chinese immigrants who had managed to become naturalized citizens at this early date.

41. Ibid., 128.

42. Lai Chun-chuen, *Remarks of the Chinese Merchants of San Francisco, upon Governor John Bigler's Message and Some Common Objections; with Some Explanations of the Character of the Chinese Companies, and the Laboring Class in California* (San Francisco: Office of the Oriental; Whitton, Towne and Company, 1855), 5. These remarks were originally written in Chinese and translated into English by local supporters of the Chinese.

43. Yan Phou Lee, "The Chinese Must Stay," *North American Review* 148 (April 1889): 477.

44. Wong's life and career are covered in much more detail in Chapter 2 of this book.

45. Wong Chin Foo, "Why Am I a Heathen?" *North American Review* 145 (August 1887): 171.

46. Ibid., 174.

47. Yan Phou Lee, "Why I Am Not a Heathen: A Rejoinder to Wong Chin Foo," *North American Review* 145 (September, 1887): 308.

48. Ibid., 311.

49. Chinese Consolidated Benevolent Association, *A Memorial to His Excellency U.S. Grant, President of the United States from Representative Chinamen in America* (n.p., 1876), 6–9.

50. Ibid., 3-4.

51. Lee Chew, "The Biography of a Chinaman: Lee Chew," *Independent* 55 (February 19, 1903), included in *The Life Stories of Undistinguished Americans as Told by Themselves*, ed. Hamilton Holt (New York: James Pott and Company, 1906), 298–299.

52. Paul Cohen spoke briefly of a hybridization process that occurred in China with American missionaries. He pointed out that they were transformed by their experience in China, becoming a "Westerner-in-China" rather than remaining a "Westerner pure and simple." Paul A. Cohen, *Discovering History in China: American Historical Writing on the Recent Chinese Past* (New York: Columbia University Press, 1984), 13–14.

53. Yung Wing, *My Life in China and America* (New York: Henry Holt, 1909), 13. Yung wrote this autobiography when he was in his late seventies and his memory of certain events is at odds with the accounts of others.

54. Wong Shing regained his health in China and soon went to work for James Legge, assisting him in his pioneering translation of the Chinese classics into English. Later, Wong returned to the United States as a teacher with the Chinese Educational Mission. When the Chinese foreign legation was established in Washington, D.C., Wong became the head translator and interpreter. See Thomas E. LaFargue, *China's First Hundred: Educational Mission Students in the United States, 1872–1881* (Pullman: State College of Washington Press, 1942), 21; and Yung Wing to Samuel Wells Williams, August 23, 1878, *Yung Wing Papers* (New Haven: Manuscripts and Archives, Yale University Library), microfilm.

55. Yung, *My Life in China and America*, 31–33, and LaFargue, *China's First Hundred*, 19–21.

56. Yung Wing to Samuel Wells Williams, April 15, 1849, *Yung Wing Papers*.

57. Edmund H. Worthy, "Yung Wing in America," *Pacific Historical Review* 34 (August 1965): 270. Yung was one of a few Chinese who had managed to attain American citizenship before the 1882 Chinese Exclusion Act. For an important study of early Chinese American communities on the East Coast in which some of the Chinese attained citizenship, see John Kuo Wei Tchen, "New York Chinese: The Nineteenth-Century Pre-Chinatown Settlement," in *Chinese America: History and Perspectives, 1990* (San Francisco: Chinese Historical Society of America, 1990), 157–192.

58. Reverend Joseph H. Twichell, "Address before the Kent Club of the Yale Law School, April 10, 1878," included in Yung, *My Life in China and America,* 254. Yung's membership in the Monson Congregational Church is mentioned in the introduction to the *Yung Wing Papers*. Also contained in this collection is a letter dated December 2, 1887, requesting that his membership in the Yale Congregational Church be transferred to the Asylum Hill Congregational Church in Hartford.

59. Yung Wing to Samuel Wells Williams, December 25, 1850, *Yung Wing Papers*.

60. Yung, *My Life in China and America,* 41.

61. For Yung's account of these occupational endeavors, see Ibid., 58–70.

62. For details of Yung's experience in the tea business, see Ibid., 79–112.

63. For major studies of the Taiping Rebellion, see Franz Michael and Chang Chung-li, *The Taiping Rebellion: History and Documents,* 3 vols. (Seattle: University of Washington Press, 1966–1971); Vincent Shih, *The Taiping Ideology: Its Sources, Interpretation, and Influence* (Seattle: University of Washington Press, 1967); John K. Fairbank, eds. *The Cambridge History of China,* vol. 10 (Cambridge: Cambridge University Press, 1978), 264–317; and Jonathan D. Spence, *God's Chinese Son: The Heavenly Taiping Kingdom of Hong Xiuquan* (New York: W. W. Norton, 1996).

64. LaFargue, *China's First Hundred,* 27.

65. For details on this title, see Charles O. Hucker, *A Dictionary of Official Titles in Imperial China* (Stanford: Stanford University Press, 1985), 489.

66. Kim Man Chan, "Mandarins in America: The Early Chinese Ministers to the United States, 1878–1907" (Ph.D. dissertation, University of Hawaii, 1981), 26. A partial translation of Zeng's and Li's memorial can be found in *China's Response to the West: A Documentary Survey, 1839–1923,* ed. Ssu-yu Teng and John K. Fairbank (New York: Atheneum, 1965), 91–94.

67. The Zongli Yamen was established in 1861 as a governmental agency to deal specifically with foreign relations. It was involved with treaty negotiations, the establishment of foreign-language schools, the research of Western forms of government, and the study of international law. For a study of its creation, see Masataka Banno, *China and the West, 1858–1861: The Origins of the Tsungli Yamen* (Cambridge, Mass.: Harvard University Press, 1964).

68. Y. C. Wang, *Chinese Intellectuals and the West, 1872–1949* (Chapel Hill: University of North Carolina Press, 1966), 43.

69. K. M. Chan, "Mandarins in America," 26.

70. Of the 120 students who eventually traveled to America, more than 70 percent were from areas around Canton, with 37 students from Yung Wing's home district. Thomas LaFargue points out that no Manchu youths volunteered for the Mission. LaFargue, *China's First Hundred,* 33–34. Brief biographical and later occupational sketches of the students can be found in Ibid., 173–176; Yung Shang-him, "The Chinese Educational Mission and Its

Influence," *T'ien Hsia Monthly* 9, no. 3 (October 1939): 241–256; Liu Boji, *Meiguo Huaqiao shi* [A history of the Chinese in the United States of America], vol. I (Taipei: Liming wenhua, 1976), 379–385; and Ruthanne Lum McCunn, *Chinese American Portraits: Personal Histories, 1828–1988* (San Francisco: Chronicle Books, 1988), 17–25.

71. Yung Wing to Noah Porter, February 17, 1872, *Yung Wing Papers.*

72. The concept of *ti-yong* was popular among those who supported gradual reform. They thought that China would be best served by following the tenets of "Chinese learning as the essence with Western learning for practical development." This approach would ensure that Chinese culture would always be viewed as superior to Western culture.

73. One contemporary source lists a Chan Laisun as a secretary to the Mission. He is claimed to have been educated at Hamilton College and to have been a member of the First Congregational Church in Springfield. See James L. Bowen, "Yung Wing and His Work," *Scribner's Monthly Magazine* 10 (May 1875): 107. However, I cannot find another reference to this individual. A Tsang Laisun is mentioned in other sources as being on the Mission staff, but neither an American education nor a religious affiliation is mentioned.

74. Yung, *My Life in China and America,* 189.

75. Wang, *Chinese Intellectuals and the West,* 44.

76. Yung, *My Life in China and America,* 202–203.

77. Huang Zunxian focused on the personal conflicts between the principal figures as the reason for the Mission's closure, writing, "So we have let a magnificent, far-sighted policy, be ruined by some private quarrels." William Hung, trans.,"Huang Tsun-hsien's Poem: 'The Closure of the Educational Mission in America,'" *Harvard Journal of Asiatic Studies* 18 (1955): 50–73. Hung also translated a letter from Li Hongzhang to the Zongli Yamen, stressing his hope for cooperation among the three, "I shall of course write now and then to Messrs. Ch'en, Yung, and Wu, urging them to reconcile their differences in the interest of public good and for the purpose of joint success," Hung; 69. Charles A. Desnoyers points out that Li Hongzhang expressed his concern that the students had not become proficient in modern mining technology and was angry that Chinese students would not be allowed to attend U.S. military academies. See Charles A. Desnoyers, "Chinese Foreign Policy in Transition: Ch'en Lan-pin in the New World, 1872–1882" (Ph.D. dissertation, Temple University, 1988), 355–357. At the time of the Mission's recall, only two students had graduated from college, whereas six were in college and the rest were still in high school. Wang, *Chinese Intellectuals and the West,* 45.

78. Yung Wing to Samuel Wells Williams, June 7, 1877, *Yung Wing Papers.* During the hearings, when informed of Yung's objection to the treatment of Chinese in the United States, Pixley threatened to cut off Yung's queue. U.S. Joint Special Committee, *Senate Report 689,* 461.

79. Yung Wing to Secretary of State William Maxwell Evarts, March 9, 1880. Notes from the Chinese Legation to the Department of State. Quoted in Worthy, "Yung Wing in America," 280.

80. Quoted in W.A.P. Martin, "As the Chinese See Us," *The Forum* 10 (September 1890): 688.

81. Lee, "The Chinese Must Stay," 476.

82. *In re Ah Yup,* C.C.D. Cal (1878). The federal circuit court denied Chinese immigrants the right of naturalization because they were neither "a free white person nor a person of African nativity or descent." See Janisch, "The Chi-

nese, the Courts, and the Constitution," 201. This ruling was reiterated in the 1882 Chinese Exclusion Act. 22 *U.S. Statutes at Large* 61. For details about Yung losing his citizenship and his reentry into the United States, see Worthy, "Yung Wing in America," 283–285.

83. Liang Qichao, *"Xin dalu youji jielu"* [Selected memoir of travels in the New World], in *Yinbingshi heji zhuan* [Collected writings from an ice-drinker's studio], vol. 22 (Shanghai: Zhonghua shuju, 1936), 47; and Robert L. Worden, "A Chinese Reformer in Exile: The North American Phase of the Travels of K'ang Yu-wei, 1899–1909" (Ph.D. dissertation, Georgetown University, 1970), 178.

84. Because of Yung's opposition to the Qing conservatives and his novel approach to China's modernization, he gained a favorable reputation among contemporary Chinese scholars as a patriot. For example, see Dai Xueji, "Aiguo Huaqiao xuezhe zhi qiaochu—Jung Hung" [A standout among patriotic overseas Chinese scholars—Yung Wing], in *Huaqiao shi lunwen ji* [Essays on the history of overseas Chinese], vol. 1 (1981), 125–160. In Dai's essay, Yung is portrayed as undermining the agenda of using "Chinese learning as the base" for reform, thus contributing to the fall of "feudal" China.

CHAPTER 2

The Origins of the Chinese Americanization Movement: Wong Chin Foo and the Chinese Equal Rights League

QINGSONG ZHANG

ON JULY 30, 1884, TWO YEARS AFTER THE U.S. CONGRESS PASSED the first Chinese Exclusion Act, which not only prohibited the immigration of Chinese laborers to America, but also banned the naturalization of Chinese in the United States,[1] a group of Chinese who had been naturalized before the Act was passed gathered at 32 Pell Street, New York City. Their goal was to organize themselves into a political association to "obtain representation and recognition in American politics."[2] This meeting, which produced perhaps the first Chinese voter association in the United States, was organized by Wong Chin Foo.

Wong, who had returned to China after receiving an American education, was forced to flee to the United States in 1873 to escape the Qing government's persecution of his heretical beliefs. Thereafter, he devoted himself to improving the conditions of his countrypeople in the United States. There is good reason to regard Wong as an unsung hero in Chinese American history—he was one of the most active and devoted community leaders of Chinese immigrants in the nineteenth century—yet his name has rarely been mentioned in studies of the Chinese experience in the United States.[3]

By piecing together excerpts from scattered historical documents, this chapter offers a sketch of Wong's beliefs and activities. Besides being a devoted community leader, he was an unheralded civil rights activist and a pioneer of the Chinese Americanization movement. Historians have generally regarded the Native Sons of the Golden State (NSGS) as the pioneers of this movement.[4] Established in 1895, the

NSGS aimed to promote the political awareness of American-born Chinese. Its major influence was on the West Coast (see Chapter 4 of this book). However, Wong had begun similar activities in the mid-1880s on the East Coast, his goal to obtain civil and political rights for all the Chinese in the United States.

Portraying Wong as a courageous civil rights activist helps counter the image of Chinese Americans as "sitting ducks." Standard textbooks on the Chinese American experience, as historian Roger Daniels noted, have often been written "from the excluders' perspectives" while overlooking the reactions and responses of the excluded.[5] The six decades of Chinese exclusion were the "dark ages"[6] in Chinese American history, during which the Chinese were always the underdogs, endlessly persecuted and seemingly never retaliating.[7] In recent decades, historians have begun to reevaluate, revise, or repudiate the traditional biased and distorted stereotypes imposed upon the Chinese during the exclusion years.[8] This chapter shows that some Chinese dreamed of an America that would live up to its proclaimed principles of justice and equality for all, and they had a leader in Wong Chin Foo.

Wong's story also challenges the conventional interpretation of the reasons for the exclusion of the Chinese. Anti-Chinese groups claimed that the Chinese were clannish, were unassimilable, and showed no interest in Americanization; therefore, they must be excluded.[9] Some historians, who have based their research entirely on English-language sources, have also attributed exclusion to the unwillingness of Chinese immigrants to join mainstream society.[10] Such a blame-the-victim approach, however, neglects the fact that various laws prevented the Chinese from integrating into the larger society. The Chinese were simply not given a chance to share in the American dream. In other words, Chinese alienation in America was not the cause of but rather a product of Chinese exclusion. Wong's unsuccessful endeavor to obtain equal rights for the Chinese supports this conclusion.

Wong Chin Foo: The Early Years

In 1868, at age seventeen, Wong Chin Foo first arrived in the United States to receive an education sponsored by an American woman missionary in China. After a preliminary course of instruction in Washington, D.C., he entered a Pennsylvanian college (name unknown). Having studied with a zeal that pleased and astonished his professors, he graduated with honors and became one of the few Chinese other than

Yung Wing to possess an American college degree before the advent of the Chinese Educational Mission in the 1870s.[11]

Wong was as devoted to China's modernization as Yung Wing was. Yung took an elitist approach by soliciting support from top Chinese government officials for a Chinese Educational Mission, the construction of modern factories, and the modernization of the military.[12] In contrast, Wong took a grassroots approach, focusing on the enlightenment of the common people. After graduation, Wong spent time trying to understand the organization and management of social and political clubs, benevolent societies, and trade unions. He "grasped at the information which was conveyed to him so easily and discoursed upon it with so much elegance as to attract the favorable attention of those with whom he came in contact."[13] In a few years, he declared that he had accomplished all that he desired. He went to San Francisco and boarded a ship to China.

Entering government service as an interpreter and traveling from place to place in China to give speeches on China's need for a social and cultural reformation, he called for the abolition of opium smoking, the adoption of certain American social customs, and the elevation of the masses. He also organized societies aimed at the improvement of the mental, moral, and physical state of the people. However, Wong's aggressive activities soon caused concern to the Qing government, which traditionally dealt with independent social organizations with an iron fist. The government issued an order to suppress Wong's activities and forced him to go underground. A second order mandated the dismantling of the societies that he had set up and the imprisonment and execution of Wong's followers.[14] With a $1,500 reward on his head, Wong was hunted for months and lost all his belongings. A Japanese sailor came to his aid, however, and Wong managed to escape to Japan, where he obtained help from C. O. Saeppard of Buffalo (then the U.S. consul at Yokohama) and boarded a ship bound for San Francisco.[15]

Twenty-five years later, in 1898, Yung Wing followed Wong's steps and fled China after the defeat of the One-Hundred-Day Reform in which he was involved. Perhaps not coincidentally, two of the earliest American-educated Chinese had to flee their homeland after the failure of their reform efforts. Wong Chin Foo left the country early, whereas Yung maintained closer ties to China and is known mainly for his role in the Chinese Educational Mission. Consequently, Yung is regarded as a modern Chinese hero, but Wong is not well known in China.

When Wong stepped on American soil for the second time, in 1873, he found that his compatriots' situation in the United States had dramatically deteriorated. In the 1850s and 1860s, anti-Chinese actions were generally confined to discriminatory laws, ordinances, and taxes in California and its neighboring states. In the 1870s, however, anti-Chinese sentiments intensified and spread like an epidemic. The Workingmen's Party of California spearheaded the movement. Both major political parties adopted anti-Chinese platforms. Negative stereotypes saturated the media. Violence was frequently committed upon Chinese persons and properties, and federal restrictions on Chinese immigration gained widespread support.[16] Without knowing when he could return to his homeland, Wong decided to devote his talent and knowledge to improving the conditions of the Chinese in the United States.

Wong believed that cultural misunderstanding was the origin of anti-Chinese sentiments. His approach was to educate Americans about the essence of Chinese culture, traditions, and customs. After spending one year studying in a college in Washington, D.C. (name unknown), Wong began to tour eastern cities such as Boston, New York, and Philadelphia, as well as midwestern cities such as Chicago. In 1876, he gave more than eighty lectures to "explain away certain misapprehensions concerning his country and people which prevail among Americans."[17]

Harper's Weekly described him as an "intelligent, cultured gentleman, who speaks English with ease and vivacity, and has the power of interesting his audiences."[18] The *New York Times* described Wong's appearance at one of his lectures in the following manner:

> Wong was dressed in a dark suit, in shape not unlike that of the ordinary Chinaman, though of richer material and more elaborate make. His only jewelry consisted of a gold watch and rich neck-chain of the same metal. He appeared to the audience as a young, courteous, and well-bred Mongolian of about 26, with a thoughtful cast of features and an expressive countenance. He was graceful in his movements, perfectly self-possessed, and comported himself throughout with as much tact and propriety as though he had been a "society man" of years' standing. His English was generally fluent and well chosen, but he experienced some difficulty in conveying certain ideas in clear and unambiguous language.[19]

Religious Differences

Wong realized that religious differences were a major argument against Chinese immigration. He was indignant at Americans' prejudice against non-Christians and annoyed that his compatriots were called "heathens," "pagans," "celestials," and "idolaters." While attempting to refute Americans' negative stereotypes (such as the notion that all Chinese ate rats and puppies), Wong focused his lectures on dispelling the misapprehensions about Chinese religions. His emphasis on the subject, however, led many people to mistake him as a Chinese missionary who wanted to convert Americans to Buddhism.[20] Denying that he was a Buddhist missionary, he insisted that his knowledge of Buddhist theology was no more than that of an ordinary educated young Chinese and that he had merely entered upon his present course of action for the purpose of "disabusing the American mind of the gross errors and absurdities respecting the religion of China."[21]

Wong attributed the prejudice against Chinese religions to the Christian missionaries in China who painted false pictures of Chinese degradation, immorality, and idolatry in order to wring more money from American donors. He tried to stress the similarities and downplayed the differences between Christianity and Chinese religions. He pointed out that the Chinese also believed in an all-seeing and all-powerful God and that they worshiped idols in the same way that Westerners worshipped the Virgin Mary and the Cross. He claimed that God had given to every race of people a religion peculiar to their nature, noting that the Buddha lived four hundred years before Christ and had taught essentially the same moral truths. Wong also refuted the view of the "damnation of the heathen." He found the idea preposterous that the Chinese who had upheld and shared so many moral and ethical values with Christians would be unmercifully consigned to hell's everlasting fire no matter how virtuously they had lived, while in the land of the Christians some lifelong criminals, murderers, cutthroats, and thieves would become pure as newborn babies after a few short hours of conversion.[22]

Wong's lectures were met with unfriendly commentaries from the media, which persistently portrayed him as a Buddhist missionary, even though he continued to assert that he was attempting only to promote mutual respect and understanding between the Chinese and the Americans. That would be "uphill work," a Philadelphia newspaper reporter commented, because "Christianity has developed astonishing civilization among those races that adopted it. Buddhism meanwhile has kept all of its professing peoples in a condition of semi-barbarism."[23] Wong's criticism of missionaries in China also caused resentment. A newspaper reported Wong's lectures with this headline: "The Heathen among Us. His Horrible Heterodox Views of Christian Missions in China."[24]

Responding to these charges, Wong demanded fair play and a chance to be heard. The following is the text of a letter he sent to the *New York Herald:*

> Since I have been in this country teaching the religion and describing the social life and political affairs of my native land, China, I have never slandered, abused and swindled in many [*sic*] places. I have tried to show the Christians how an honorable Chinamen [*sic*] looks and talks. You send your missionaries to us and we listen to them. Is it unfair for me to ask them to hear what we have to say? They say that, we, hea-thens, are to be eternally damned, no matter how honest, moral and sincere we may be. We think Christians will be damned if they behave like very wicked Buddhists.[25]

The editors of the *Herald* titled Wong's letter "A Heathen's Chal-lenge."[26]

Throughout his life, Wong's refusal to convert to Christianity dis-tinguished him from many other Americanized Chinese. His article "Why Am I a Heathen?" published in the *North American Review* gave his reasons for not accepting Christianity. He acknowledged that during his childhood he had been under considerable Christian influ-ence (as mentioned previously, his U.S. education had been sponsored by a missionary family), and for a while he had planned to become a missionary. But besides his rejection of the "damnation of the hea-then" philosophy, he was bewildered by the multiplicity of Christian sects, "each one claiming a monopoly of the only and narrow road to heaven."[27] He examined the major denominations of Christianity and was attracted to none, not "merciless" Presbyterianism, "divided" Baptism, "noisy" Methodism, "elitist" Congregationalism, "skepti-cal" Unitarianism, or "eccentric" Quakerism.[28] Wong's approach to re-ligion was functional—he evaluated religions by the moral and ethical principles that their ministers preached, and by their values for the well-being of society. As alluded to previously, he believed that the ba-sic Christian moral and ethical values had already been taught by an-cient Chinese philosophers such as Confucius thousands of years before and had been practiced by the Chinese people ever since.

The treatment of the Chinese in the United States was also a factor in his decision. In this land of Christians, he contended, brotherly love and fairness were often talked about and preached about, but in reality, the Chinese were murdered, robbed, discriminated against, and perse-cuted. Therefore, while promoting greater Chinese participation in

American society, Wong felt no embarrassment to remain an uncovered "heathen." "I earnestly invite the Christians of America to come to Confucius," he declared.[29]

The Chinese in the American Political Arena

Wong Chin Foo's lecturing in the eastern states was not an isolated event. In the West, the leading Chinese organization known as the Chinese Six Companies published its own pamphlets, sent petitions to the federal government, and sponsored the publication of books written by Americans who were friendly to the Chinese.[30] All these activities reflected a conscious effort by the Chinese in the 1870s to answer the charges against their immigration and to correct the misconceptions about their culture, traditions, and immigrant life. These efforts, however, failed to reverse the trend toward exclusion and in 1882 the first Chinese Exclusion Act was passed.[31]

The passage of this act prompted the Chinese to reexamine their experience in the United States and to find the reasons for their ineffectiveness in fighting against the anti-Chinese movement. Wong was one of the first Chinese to recognize that a lack of political influence was one of the deciding factors in the failure of the Chinese to defeat the exclusion legislation. The solution was, therefore, greater Chinese participation in American politics.

The Chinese and their friends considered the explicit prohibition on Chinese naturalization as the "most obnoxious" feature in the 1882 Chinese Exclusion Act because it barred the entire Chinese race from naturalization "regardless of qualifications or earnest desire on their part to become citizens."[32] On the other hand, the Act also made the Chinese who were naturalized before 1882 appreciate the value of their citizenship.

On July 30, 1884, fifty naturalized Chinese, along with a dozen American sightseers, convened at 32 Pell Street, New York City, to organize themselves into a political association. Wong was appointed the secretary and Li Quong (president of the Chinese Cigarmakers' Union), the temporary chairman of the meeting. Wong gave an eloquent speech that summarized the reasons why the group wanted to form a voters' organization.[33]

He observed that the meeting was the first effort by the Chinese in America to take an active part in American politics and to unite in all matters concerning their dignity as U.S. citizens. Their purpose was to "obtain representation and recognition in American politics." Such an effort might be a small drop in the mighty ocean of American politics, Wong noted, but he believed that had such organized attempts been made earlier, the anti-Chinese bill would not have been passed. Wong's remarks showed his keen understanding of the essence of American politics:

> Remember the politicians who lord it over you today is [sic] an arrant coward and times his [sic] sails to every breeze that blows. When you don't vote and don't wish to vote, they denounce you as a reptile; the moment you appear at the ballot box you are a man and a brother and are treated to cigars, whiskeys and beers. Why can't we make our marks in politics as well as any of our brother races? Why can't we become good and substantial citizens like those from England, Ireland, Germany and other European, Asiatic and even African countries?[34]

The year 1884 was a presidential election year. When asked which platform the Chinese would support, Wong replied that they were not committed. The Chinese were disappointed with the Republicans because under the Republican administration "we have been prohibited from becoming citizens of the United States, a privilege that is granted to all other races of men, and our fellow countrymen were for ten years forbidden upon a free and Republican shore."[35] The Democrats could not be trusted either. "Democrats are robbers and thieves who will plunder and rob the U.S. Treasury. When they got into power . . . every citizen have [sic] to go about them [sic] armed to teeth for self-protection."[36] The third party, the Greenbackers, meanwhile, "was too young with no character to amount to anything," Wong said.[37] Clearly, he and the other naturalized Chinese were hoping that their political involvement would help sway the major parties away from anti-Chinese platforms.

Wong's Newspaper

Another significant event parallel to the political initiative was the appearance of the first Chinese newspaper on the East Coast, edited and published by Wong Chin Foo. The title and format of the paper clearly indicate that part of Wong's efforts was to promote a mutual understanding between the Chinese in America and the larger society. The paper, a weekly first published on February 3, 1883, was entitled the *Chinese American (Hua Mei Xin Bao).*[38] Although the term "Chinese American" has been used extensively in recent decades, its appearance in 1883, only one year after the enactment of the first Chinese exclusion law, has significant implications. It was perhaps the first attempt by the Chinese to identify themselves as "Americans of Chinese origin" rather than as "sojourners" or "subjects of the Yellow Emperor." It was refreshing and earthshaking for the Chinese to identify themselves as Americans in an era when they were usually referred to by such insulting terms as "heathens," "celestials," "John Chinaman," and "Chink." It was also a challenge to the popular stereotype that the Chinese were not interested in becoming American citizens, and it reflected the desire of Wong and other naturalized Chinese for respect, recognition, and equal rights from their adopted country. To help Americans better understand the life and interests of the Chinese community, the paper was published in both Chinese and English.[39]

However, Wong had difficulties in finding financial support for the *Chinese American.* The paper could not sustain itself through subscriptions because it had a limited circulation and readership. Consequently, it ran for only less than a year. In a report dated January 21, 1884, a New York journalist referred to Wong, as "the ex-editor of the late *Chinese American.*"[40] Therefore, by January 1884, the *Chinese American* had apparently ceased publication.

In the meantime, Wong continued to work to improve the image of Chinese immigrants in the United States. Within the Chinese community, he tried to unite all the factions into a consolidated group and to eliminate such bad habits as opium smoking, prostitution, and gambling among the Chinese.[41] Outside the community, he continued efforts to reduce the prejudice and hostility against the Chinese people and their culture. He published an article entitled "The Chinese in the United States" in *The Chautauquan* and another entitled "The Chinese in New York" in *Cosmopolitan,* in which he explained in detail the personal and community lives of Chinese immigrants, hoping to offset the negative stereotypes prevalent among Euro-Americans.[42] His articles "The Story of San Tszon" in the *Atlantic Monthly* and "Political Honors in China" in *Harper's Weekly* aimed to acquaint Americans with the cream of Chinese civilization.[43]

Insurmountable Obstacles

Wong's push for greater Chinese participation in American society soon after the passage of the first Chinese exclusion law showed his courage and optimism. However, he had many kinds of difficulties to overcome both within and outside the Chinese immigrant community.

To organize his countrypeople around one cause was difficult because the Chinese community was often divided along clan or geographic origins and lacked intergroup communication and cooperation. His approach was to maintain a distance from the clan organizations. When disputes occurred, he took a neutral position and urged restraint and peaceful negotiations.[44] His effort to unite the Chinese community sometimes caused resentment, however, because he was thought to be stepping over traditional lines dividing groups.[45]

Wong also had to deal with pressure from the secret societies that were behind most of the extralegal businesses such as gambling, opium trafficking, and prostitution. These societies were angry at Wong's strong editorials (in the *Chinese American*) against such vices. Once, the gambling-den bosses hired an assassin to kill Wong and silence his criticism. The *New York Times* reported in 1883,

> Wong Chin Foo, the editor of the *Chinese American*, who is better known in literary circles as Ah Wong, appeared in the Tombs Police Court yesterday afternoon as a complainant against another Celestial gentleman named Ching Pong Tip of No. 15 Mott Street. Mr. Wong charges that Tip assaulted him at No. 10 Pell Street at about 3:30 o'clock yesterday afternoon. Mr. Wong was conversing with a number of Chinese gentlemen of his acquaintance [and] casually remarked upon the extreme heat of the weather when Tip without any provocation rushed at him and called for someone to give him a revolver, with a view to disposing of the amicable Mr. Wong without further delay. Tip was prevented from carrying out his design and Mr. Wong had him arrested and taken to the Tombs. The court had adjourned and the Justice was no longer upon the bench, so Tip was taken to the 6th Precinct Police Station, and the case will be brought up today. Mr. Wong says that the attack upon him was the outcome of a strong feeling aroused against him among the Chinese residents of Mott Street and the vicinity by the vigorous articles directed against the opium and gambling dens. He also said that Tip tried to kill him once before in Chicago, but fortunately did not find him at home.[46]

Furthermore, Wong had to amend his relationship with the Chinese who had converted to Christianity. Wong's "heathenishness" alienated him from the Christianized Chinese, although they, like him, had strong desires for recognition and respect from the larger society. When he was in Chicago, Wong's relationship with the Chinese Sunday School was not harmonious.[47] His article "Why Am I a Heathen?" drew a sharp rejoinder from Yan Phou Lee, a Yale graduate who was naturalized, Christianized, and married to an American woman.[48] Lee's article "Why I Am Not a Heathen" appeared in the same year (1887) and in the same magazine—the *North American Review.*[49]

Although problems within the Chinese community might have been resolvable, the legal and political barriers separating the Chinese from the rest of society were virtually insurmountable. The 1882 Chinese Exclusion Act marked the beginning of a miserable era in which anti-Chinese sentiment became a national phenomenon. Hoodlums and government officials worked hand in glove to persecute the Chinese. As the legislative objective changed from temporary suspension to absolute exclusion, the exclusionists demanded the complete elimination of the Chinese from American territory, and the laws became increasingly punitive and more rigidly enforced. Chinese communities were under constant harassment and Chinese visitors were subjected to cruel and humiliating treatment at the ports. Such a hostile and volatile environment had an intimidating effect upon the Chinese and offset Wong's endeavor to unite the two societies.

The largest and strongest obstacle to Wong's Americanization initiative was Section 14 of the 1882 Chinese Exclusion Act, which explicitly prohibited U.S. courts from naturalizing the Chinese.[50] This policy fixed the status of the Chinese as "permanent sojourners," which institutionally suppressed the growth of any desire among the Chinese to "belong to America." Section 14 maintained the Chinese as excludable aliens; thus it restrained them from engaging in activities that might be judged offensive to the government or threatening to public security.[51] It excluded the Chinese from the political sphere, neutralizing appeals such as Wong's for political participation. This status was applied to all Chinese, so the aspirations of those who wanted to become American citizens were thwarted. Hence, because most Chinese were barred from the voting booth, Wong's drive for political participation could appeal to only a tiny group of Chinese who had been naturalized before 1882.

However, even these naturalized Chinese did not receive acceptance and respect from the larger society. The U.S. government refused to recognize their rights. They were ineligible for U.S. passports, diplomatic protection from U.S. consulates in foreign countries, and employment in professions requiring citizenship (such as attorneys and legal counselors), and they were not exempt from the Chinese exclusion laws. Therefore, the Chinese—"sojourners" and naturalized citizens alike—were denied the opportunity to join the American social and political mainstream.

Not only did Wong have difficulty reaching his goal of greater Chinese participation in the political and social arenas, but he could not even maintain his own status as a naturalized American citizen. In 1898, he went to Hong Kong to organize a cultural delegation to participate in an international exhibition in Omaha. He applied for and received a passport from the U.S. consulate general in Hong Kong on the basis of a naturalization certificate issued to him by the Circuit Court of Michigan in 1874. However, the passport was later recalled and canceled by R. Wildman, U.S. consul, by order of the U.S. State Department. The consul was told that he should not "issue passports to Chinese holding naturalization papers that were issued before March 6, 1882 or at any other date."[52]

The Chinese Equal Rights League

Despite the many adversities facing him, Wong continued to work to improve the status of the Chinese in the United States, but with a new emphasis—the attainment of equal rights. In the wake of a nationwide movement among the Chinese to protest the passage of the Geary Act of 1892, Wong helped organize the first Chinese civil rights organization in America—the Chinese Equal Rights League.

On September 1, 1892, Chinese community leaders of the eastern states held a convention in New York City to discuss ways to counter the vicious exclusion laws. The Chinese Equal Rights League was formed, with a membership of 150 English-speaking merchants and professional men. Lee Sam Ping, a Philadelphia merchant, was installed as president, and Wong was elected secretary. On September 22, the League held a mass meeting at Cooper Union in New York City in which more than 1,000 Americans and 200 Chinese merchants attended. "All the Mongolians wore American clothes, and most of them had on patent-leather shoes and white neckties," the *New York Times* reported.[53] After Wong and several prominent Americans gave their speeches, the meeting members adopted a resolution denouncing the 1892 Geary Act.

The notorious Geary Act not only extended Chinese exclusion for another ten years, but also, to the indignation of the Chinese, required

Chinese laborers in the United States to register for certificates of residence and imposed heavy penalties on violators of this provision.[54] The Geary Act faced organized resistance from Chinese communities across the nation, of which the meeting at Cooper Union was a vital part. The resulting resolution denounced the Geary Act as "monstrous, inhuman and unconstitutional."[55]

The Chinese Equal Rights League was not formed just to protest the Geary Act, however. As its name suggested, its founders had a higher goal in mind, which was laid out in a pamphlet published by the League in 1892.[56] The pamphlet contained an "Appeal of the League to the People of the United States," which began by denouncing the Geary Act. It contended that the Act "was made to humiliate every Chinaman, regardless of his moral, intellectual and material standing in the community; neither was his long residence in the country considered. By this mean and unjust Act discriminating between foreign residents from different countries, [it] has traversed and contraversed the fundamental principles of common law."[57]

The appeal then exposed the deeper interests of the League—equal franchise for the Chinese. The author of the pamphlet declared that the Chinese were industrious, law-abiding, and honest people; they had paid taxes and had thus supported the nation and the government; they loved and admired the U.S. government and were appreciative of its "unwavering love of human rights." "Our interests are here, because our homes, our families and all our interests are here. America is our home through long residence,"[58] declared the author, who then raised the specific demand: "We, therefore, appeal for an equal chance in the race of life in this our adopted home—a large number of us have spent almost all our lives in this country and claimed no other but this as ours. Our motto is: Character and fitness should be the requirements of all who are desirous of becoming citizens of the American Republic."[59]

Previously, in 1877, in the wake of rising anti-Chinese sentiment, the Chinese community had produced an important document, *Memorial of the Chinese Six Companies to the Congress of the United States.* A comparison of that document with the appeal of the Chinese Equal Rights League of 1892 reveals the differences between the two. In the 1877 memorial, the Chinese Six Companies took a defensive tone, depicting themselves as guests, asserting treaty rights, and demanding hospitality and international justice.[60] The Equal Rights League of 1892 was more aggressive and assertive; its members wished to be treated as part of the nation and demanded a common humanity and equal rights, including the franchise.

Unfortunately, the change from a defensive approach to an aggressive strategy could not alter the established national policy of Chinese exclusion from both immigration and naturalization. A *New York Times* editorial illustrates how the League's appeal was construed:

> The Chinese Equal Rights League has not chosen a very favorable time for agitating for the repeal of the Chinese Exclusion Act, just when the public mind is occupied with the question of drawing closer the lines for excluding undesirable alien elements from our population. The Geary Act was unnecessarily harsh and created an invidious distinction, and it would be well if all except the section continuing the present restrictions could be repealed, but the matter is hardly likely to receive favorable consideration at present. The statement of the league put the case rather too strongly and ask [sic] rather too much. . . . It is asking too much to demand that Chinese residents here be "forthwith admitted to citizenship and given the franchise of the nation." The Chinese Equal Rights League should be more moderate in its presentations and more modest in its demands.[61]

The Chinese community leadership experienced a major setback in 1893, when the U.S. Supreme Court declared in the case of *Fong Yue Ting* v. *United States* that the Geary Act was constitutional and forced the Chinese to abandon their boycott against registration.[62] The Chinese Equal Rights League's plea for the franchise was also rejected by the Supreme Court, which announced in the same decision, "Chinese persons not born in this country have never been recognized as citizens of the United States, nor authorized to become such under the naturalization laws."[63]

In 1893, under the shadow of the defeat of the anti–Geary Act campaign, Wong left New York City and returned to Chicago. In the early 1890s, Chicago's Chinatown experienced a rapid expansion, partly because of Chicago's emergence as a major metropolis and partly because more and more Chinese were crossing the U.S.-Canadian border and entering Illinois through northwestern and northeastern border states.

In Chicago, Wong continued his drive for equal rights for the Chinese community. He resumed publishing the *Chinese American*[64] and established a Chicago branch of the Chinese Equal Rights League. A Chinese named Chinn Wing contributed two dollars and became a member of the League in 1897. A certificate of contribution issued to Chinn Wing can be found in Thomas W. Chinn's *Bridging the Pacific*, revealing important information about the league.[65] The certificate indicates that in 1897 the League's full name was "Chinese Equal Rights League of America," with Wong Chin Foo as president, Tom Yueh as secretary, Yee Ming as Chinese secretary, and Wong Kee as treasurer. The League's mission was "demanding equality of rights for Americanized Chinese of the United States." A statement was also printed on the certificate that read, "We ask and demand for an equal franchise for the Americanized Chinese of the United States."[66]

In addition to the handful of naturalized Chinese, American-born Chinese, whose rights and privileges as citizens were often ignored and violated by the government, could become members of the League. Although the Fourteenth Amendment had established universal birthright citizenship, and even though the federal courts had repeatedly confirmed the citizenship of American-born Chinese, the administrative branches of the U.S. government continued to treat American-born Chinese as aliens and tried to apply the Chinese exclusion laws to them. Protecting the political rights of the American-born Chinese was thus an important part of the League's agenda.[67]

In 1897, Wong and the League initiated a franchise movement to persuade Congress to repeal the Chinese exclusion laws passed after 1882 and to extend the right of suffrage to the Chinese. In a newspaper interview, Wong explained: "We want Illinois, the place that Lincoln, Grant, and [John Alexander] Logan called their home, to do for the Chinese what the North did for the Negroes. Why should we not have a voice in the municipal and national affairs like other foreigners? There are 50,000 Chinese in this country who are desirous of becoming citizens."[68] He told reporters that a mass meeting had been planned in Chicago and that similar meetings would be held in other parts of the country.

On November 27, 1897, more than two hundred Chinese gathered at Chicago's Central Music Hall. Presided over by Wong, the meeting resulted in the adoption of a declaration of principles that reads as follows:

> Whereas, there is now organized and formed under and by virtue of the laws of the State of Illinois an organization known as the Chinese Equal Rights League of America, under the management and control of that widely known, highly educated, and patriotic Chinaman, also an American citizen, Wong Chin Foo, its President, the object of which league is to secure for the American resident Chinese the rights and privileges of American citizenship.
>
> We therefore pledge to the said league, and to said Wong Chin Foo our free, full and hearty cooperation in bringing about the successful ac-

complishment of the purposes of said league, and the restoration of the rights of said resident Chinese citizens to naturalization under the constitution of the United States.[69]

After the resolution was adopted, a white man rose in the middle of the hall and declared that the action was arbitrary and that both sides should have a hearing. He took the platform and stated that he would "stand by the law that was passed a hundred years ago which said no Chinaman can be a citizen of the republic." He left the stage after the audience expressed indignation.[70]

Responses from the larger society were not encouraging. An editorial forecast the doom of the Chinese suffrage movement. "There is little likelihood that the meeting will have any tangible results," the *Chicago Tribune* predicted. It contended, "Chinese in this country are not numerous enough to make their political adherence and support desirable to the politicians, and consequently the laws discriminating against them will probably not be repealed. We welcome all other foreigners to citizenship, but the Chinese must continue to be aliens in the land of their residence."[71]

Such negative commentaries, however, did not dampen the spirits of the League's members. They continued their plan and soon made some progress. On December 16, 1897, George W. Smith, a member of the U.S. House of Representatives from Illinois, introduced a bill (H.R. 5182) entitled "To Permit the Naturalization of Americanized Chinese," which was perhaps the first bill introduced after 1882 that advocated the naturalization of the Chinese. However, the introduction of the bill was all that the League achieved. The bill was referred to the House Committee on Immigration and Naturalization and was soon forgotten.[72]

In early 1898, the United States was preparing to go to war with Spain. Collaborating with the Chicago initiative, the New York branch of the Chinese Equal Rights League, headed by Lee Sam Ping, disclosed a proposal to form a Chinese militia company as evidence of American patriotism. Lee told reporters that the New York Chinese community was planning to organize volunteer troops to render their service for the protection of the United States. Between thirty and forty Chinese had already enrolled, Lee said, and they could provide their own uniforms and equip themselves if they received permission to do so. The movement was intended to "illustrate to Congress the patriotism and Americanism of Chinamen who wish to be citizens."[73]

Permission was never granted, though, because the Spanish-American War of 1898 did not last long and the service of the Chinese militia was not needed. However, many Chinese did join the U.S. armed services. More than eighty Chinese served in the U.S. Navy's Asiatic Squadron, which in the Battle of Manila Bay in 1898 sustained only minor injuries while destroying the Spanish fleet. The Chinese were praised by all the officers and soldiers for their display of courage and heroism. After the war, however, these patriotic Chinese heroes were not allowed to come to the United States to participate in the victory celebration. Their requests for citizenship were denied.[74]

Wong Chin Foo's Legacy

Although this chapter provides a summary of Wong Chin Foo's struggles for equal rights for Chinese immigrants from 1874 to 1898, little can be said about Wong's life and activities after 1898 because of a lack of documentary sources. A book published in 1904 indicates that the New York branch of the Chinese Equal Rights League was still functioning in that year, "The building at No. 5 Mott Street also contains the Oriental Club, which is a dozen years old and devotes itself to Americanizing its members and aiding the illumination of China." This description matches perfectly with the League established by Wong in 1892.[75] However, little more is known of Wong or the League.

Wong's three-decade struggle did not lead to any changes in the law and the exclusion system. Wong did, however, play a pioneering role in the Chinese civil rights movement. His cause—demanding citizenship and voting rights for the Chinese—was carried on by his compatriots long after he disappeared from the scene.

In 1895, the American-born Chinese established their own organization, the Native Sons of the Golden State (later known as the Chinese American Citizens Alliance), to promote Americanization and protect the rights and interests of Chinese American citizens.[76] (See chapter 4 of this book.) The Hawaiian Chinese, in the wake of the U.S. annexation of Hawaii in 1898, sent petitions to Congress demanding U.S. citizenship. In 1900, Congress did pass an act extending citizenship to Chinese who were citizens of the Republic of Hawaii at the time of annexation.[77] By 1901, even the Qing government began to advocate and lobby for American citizenship for the Chinese in the United States.[78] And by 1906, Ng Poon Chew, the famous Chinese American journalist, had emerged as the leader of the cause spearheaded by Wong—fighting against prejudice, and advocating Chinese Americanization, equality in society, and citizenship for the Chinese.[79]

Although the ban on Chinese naturalization was not abolished until 1943, the Chinese successfully defended their birthright citizenship. In 1898, the U.S. Supreme Court confirmed the citizenship of native-born Chinese in the famous decision, *Wong Kim Ark* v. *United States.*[80] Furthermore, despite the rigors of exclusion, the population of American-born Chinese steadily increased. In the 1880 census, only 1,183 Chinese were reported as American citizens. By 1940, however, 40,262 Chinese had American citizenship, an increase of 3,400 percent during the six decades of exclusion. In fact, by 1940, Chinese American citizens had outnumbered Chinese aliens (37,242). Therefore, three years before the repeal of the Chinese exclusion laws and the granting of the right of naturalization to the Chinese in 1943, Chinese communities in the United States had already transformed themselves from a sojourner society to a citizen-dominated society.[81]

Conclusion

Wong Chin Foo, an American-educated Chinese, political exile, journalist, social worker, and civil rights leader, was one of the pioneers of the Chinese Americanization movement. He was perhaps the first to use the term "Chinese American," the first to attempt to form a Chinese American political association and civil rights organization, and the first to initiate a drive to demand citizenship for the Chinese. He committed his life to the struggle against racial prejudice; to the protection of the rights and interests of his countrypeople; to the promotion of fairness, justice, equality, and racial harmony; and to the fulfillment of the American dream. He was not as renowned as black civil rights leaders such as Martin Luther King, Jr., and Malcolm X, but he shared the same dream and was devoted to the same cause—social justice and racial equality. His life and activities are a forgotten chapter in the history of the American civil rights movement. Nevertheless, he was a true Chinese American hero.

Notes

1. The text of the Chinese Exclusion Act of 1882 is found in 22 *U.S. Statutes at Large* 58–61.
2. "The Chinaman Organizing," *New York Times,* July 30, 1884.
3. Him Mark Lai, "Shijiu shiji Meiguo Huaren baoye fazhan xiaoshi" [A brief history of the development of Chinese American newspapers in the nine-

teenth century], in *Huaqiao shi yanjiu lunji* [Research papers on the history of Chinese in other countries], vol. 1, ed. Wu Zhe (Shanghai: Huadong Shida Chubanshe, 1984), 349.

4. Loren W. Fessler regarded the Native Sons of the Golden State, which later became the Chinese American Citizens Alliance (CACA), as the pioneers in Chinese Americanization. He stated in *Chinese in America: Stereotyped Past, Changing Present* (New York: Vantage Press, 1983), 192–193, "The formation of the Alliance signified the first organized attempt by Chinese Americans to protect and further their rights and interests as American citizens and for that reason could be regarded as the first conscious Chinese effort to activate the process of assimilation. . . . There seems no denying the CACA's pioneering role in trying to get for Chinese in America those rights which the Constitution says belong to everyone in America." For a similar view, see Roger Daniels, *Asian America: Chinese and Japanese in the United States since 1850* (Seattle: University of Washington Press, 1988), 98–99. Also see Sue Fawn Chung in Chapter 4 of this book.

5. Daniels, *Asian America*, 5. See also Peter Kwong, "The Challenge of Understanding the Asian-American Experience," *Ethnic and Racial Studies* 13 (October 1990): 584–585.

6. Sucheng Chan, ed., *Entry Denied: Exclusion and the Chinese Community in America, 1882–1943* (Philadelphia: Temple University Press, 1991), x.

7. A discussion on a computer network illustrates such an approach. One student observed: "Throughout history, minorities in the U.S. have suffered from racial discrimination. But they have different reactions. We all know Martin Luther King, Malcolm X, etc.; they were all heroes of blacks. They were famous and fought against the injustice of the society." Then he asked, "Chinese are [sic] also victims in the old days. . . . Why there is [sic] no one like them that are Chinese? Why there is [sic] no Chinese Martin Luther King? Where is our hero?" Another student commented: "The blacks fight [sic] back when they were treated unfairly. . . . When Chinese suffer, we will only sit there and hoping better luck next time and no one ever come up [sic] to 'fight back.' At least no Chinese activist [sic] are known to ourselves." USENET NEWS SYSTEM, #73171, April 25, 1992, and #73438, April 27, 1992, in news group "soc.culture.china."

8. For example, we know that the Chinese had obtained a good understanding of the American legal system and successfully used their knowledge to protect their rights and interests. See articles by Charles J. McClain, Lucy E. Salyer, and Christian G. Fritz in *Entry Denied*, ed. Chan. See also Christian G. Fritz, *Federal Justice in California: The Court of Ogden Hoffman, 1851–1891* (Lincoln: University of Nebraska Press, 1991); and Charles J. McClain, *In Search of Equality: The Chinese Struggle against Discrimination in Nineteenth-Century America* (Berkeley and Los Angeles: University of California Press, 1994).

9. For example, in 1906, George C. Perkins, U.S. Senator from California, wrote an article, "Reasons for Continued Chinese Exclusion," *North American Review* 183 (July 1906): 16. In this article, he claimed: "The experience of the United States for fifty years. . . . proves conclusively that the Chinese are not assimilable. . . . If they are not assimilative, they can be only a foreign body within our borders, and must either suppress or be suppressed."

10. A typical example is Gunther P. Barth, *Bitter Strength: A History of the Chinese in the United States, 1850–1870* (Cambridge, Mass.: Harvard University Press, 1964).

11. According to a survey completed in 1954, five Chinese students had obtained degrees from American colleges before 1876, one each for 1854 (Yung Wing), 1855, 1856, 1861, and 1876. China Institute in America, Committee on Survey of Chinese Students in American Colleges and Universities, *A Survey of Chinese Students in American Universities and Colleges in the Past One Hundred Years* (New York: China Institute in America, 1954), 38.

12. For further readings on Yung Wing, see his autobiography, *My Life in China and America* (New York: Henry Holt, 1909); Thomas E. LaFargue, *China's First Hundred: Educational Mission Students in the United States, 1872–1881* (Pullman: State College of Washington Press, 1942); Li Zhigang, *Yung Wing yu jindai Zhongguo* [Yung Wing and modern China] (Taipei: Zhongzheng Shuju, 1981); and Chapter 1 of this book.

13. *New York Times*, October 4, 1873, and April 30, 1877.

14. *New York Times*, April 30, 1877.

15. Ibid.

16. Mary R. Coolidge, *Chinese Immigration* (New York: Henry Holt, 1909); Elmer C. Sandmeyer, *The Anti-Chinese Movement in California* (1939; reprint, Urbana: University of Illinois Press, 1973); Alexander Saxton, *The Indispensable Enemy: Labor and the Anti-Chinese Movement in California* (Berkeley and Los Angeles: University of California Press, 1971); Stuart C. Miller, *The Unwelcome Immigrant: The American Image of the Chinese, 1785–1882* (Berkeley and Los Angeles: University of California Press, 1969).

17. *Harper's Weekly*, May 26, 1877, 405.

18. Ibid.

19. *New York Times*, April 30, 1877.

20. Stuart C. Miller followed this view in *The Unwelcome Immigrant*, 187.

21. *New York Times*, April 30, 1877.

22. *New York Times*, April 30, 1877; *New York Herald*, April 30, 1877; *New York Tribune*, May 8, 1877.

23. *Philadelphia Evening Bulletin*, May 1, 1877, and May 2, 1877.

24. "The Heathen among Us. His Horrible Heterodox Views of Christian Missions in China," *New York World*, April 29, 1877, cited in Miller, *The Unwelcome Immigrant*, 187.

25. Wong Chin Foo, "A Heathen's Challenge," *New York Herald*, May 7, 1877.

26. Ibid.

27. Wong Chin Foo, "Why Am I a Heathen?" *North American Review* 145 (August 1887): 169–179.

28. Ibid.

29. Ibid.; in 1877, for example, in an open letter to a newspaper editor, Wong Chin Foo signed himself as "Wong Chin Foo, the Heathen." *New York Herald*, May 7, 1877.

30. See Chinese Consolidated Benevolent Association, California, *Memorial of the Six Chinese Companies: An Address to the Senate and House of Representatives of the United States* (San Francisco, December 8, 1877; reprint, San Francisco: R & E Research Associates, 1970); O[tis] Gibson, *The Chinese in America* (Cincinnati: Hitchcock & Walden, 1877; reprint, New York: Arno Press, 1978).

31. The Act of May 6, 1882, 22 *U.S. Statutes at Large* 58–61.

32. "Chinese Sunday-School (Chicago) Opposes Bill," *Chicago Tribune*, March 21, 1882.

33. "The Chinamen Organizing," *New York Times*, July 30, 1884.

34. Ibid.
35. *New York Times*, July 31, 1884.
36. Ibid.
37. Ibid.
38. The New York Historical Society has the first issue of this paper. See the illustration in Fessler, *Chinese in America*, 242–244.
39. Only three issues of the *Chinese American* published in New York by Wong Chin Foo can be found today, one in the New York Historical Society and two in the Hoover Institution Library, Stanford University. Fessler, *Chinese in America*, 244; Lai, "Shijiu shiji Meiguo Huaren," 349.
40. *New York Times*, January 21, 1884.
41. For Wong's criticism of Chinese gambling habits, see "Three Hundred Chinese Dudes," *New York Times*, January 21, 1884. For his efforts to eliminate prostitution, see *New York Times*, April 30, 1877, and June 10, 1883.
42. Wong Chin Foo, "The Chinese in New York," *Cosmopolitan* 5 (March–October, 1888): 297–311; Wong Chin Foo, "The Chinese in the United States," *The Chautauquan* 9 (October 1888–July 1889): 215–217.
43. Wong Chin Foo, "The Story of San Tszon," *Atlantic Monthly* 56 (August 1885): 256–263; Wong Chin Foo, "Political Honors in China," *Harper's Weekly* 67 (1887): 298–303.
44. Such was his position in the Tom Lee clan dispute in 1883. *New York Times*, April 23, 1883.
45. "Charges against Chinese Editor," *New York Times*, June 13, 1883.
46. "Wong Chin Foo Assaulted," *New York Times*, June 10, 1883. Later, Ching Pong Tip sued Wong Ching [*sic*] Foo for libel, and Wong paid $500 bond to get out of jail. *New York Times*, June 20, 1883, and June 24, 1883.
47. *Chicago Tribune*, June 13, 1883; *New York Times*, June 13, 1883.
48. *New York Times*, July 3 and 7, 1887.
49. Yan Phou Lee, "Why I Am Not a Heathen: A Rejoinder to Wong Chin Foo," *North American Review* 145 (September 1887): 306–312. For a more detailed discussion of this article, see Chapter 1 of this book.
50. Before 1882, the Chinese had been generally regarded as a race ineligible for naturalization because they did not belong to the "white persons" category stipulated in the naturalization laws of the United States. *In re Ah Yup*, 5 Sawyer 155 C.C.D. Cal (1878). In some states, however, the court granted naturalization to some Chinese because no specific laws excluded them from naturalization per se. Wong Chin Foo, for example, was naturalized in Michigan in 1874.
51. As stated by the U.S. Supreme Court in 1893, "[The Chinese] continue to be aliens . . . and therefore remain subject to the power of Congress to expel them, or to order them to be removed and deported from the country, whenever in its judgment their removal is necessary or expedient for the public interests." *Fong Yue Ting* v. *United States*, 149 U.S. 698 (1893).
52. R. Wildman, U.S. Consul in Hong Kong, to David J. Hill, Assistant Secretary of State, March 20, 1899, *Diplomatic Dispatches from U.S. Consuls in Hong Kong* (Washington, D.C.: National Archives Microfilm Publications), microfilm.
53. *New York Times*, September 23, 1892. The report, however, mistakenly called the league the "Chinese Civil Rights League."
54. The Act of May 5, 1892, 27 U.S. *Statutes at Large* 25.
55. *New York Times*, September 22 and 23, 1892.

56. Chinese Equal Rights League, *Appeal of the Chinese Equal Rights League to the People of the United States for Equality of Manhood* (New York: Chinese Equal Rights League, 1892), original in Brown University Library. The pamphlet was most likely the work of Wong Chin Foo, secretary of the League, because among the Chinese he was the most fluent in English.

57. Ibid., 2.

58. Ibid.

59. Ibid., 3; the last sentence is another way of saying why they were opposed to racial discrimination in the naturalization laws.

60. Chinese Six Companies, *Memorial of Chinese Six Companies to the Congress of the United States* (San Francisco: Chinese Six Companies, 1877).

61. *New York Times*, December 18, 1892.

62. *Fong Yue Ting* v. *United States.*

63. Ibid.

64. One issue of the Chicago edition of the *Chinese American* (semimonthly), dated June 24, 1893, is preserved in the Chicago Historical Society. The newspaper reported news about the Chinese community.

65. Thomas W. Chinn, *Bridging the Pacific: San Francisco Chinatown and Its People* (San Francisco: Chinese Historical Society of America, 1989), 90.

66. Ibid.

67. *New York Times*, November 24, 1897.

68. "Equal Rights for Chinese: Chicago Celestials Organize to Demand Citizenship," *New York Times*, November 24, 1897.

69. "Chinese Ask for Rights," *Chicago Tribune*, November 28, 1897.

70. Ibid.

71. *Chicago Tribune*, November 22, 1897.

72. *Congressional Record*, 55th Cong., 1st sess., 1897, 234.

73. "Chinamen as Volunteers," *New York Times*, January 15, 1898.

74. William F. Strobridge, "Chinese in the Spanish American War and Beyond," in *The Chinese American Experience: Papers from the Second National Conference on Chinese American Studies (1980)*, ed. Genny Lim et al. (San Francisco: Chinese Historical Society of America and the Chinese Culture Foundation of San Francisco, 1984), 13–15; Jack Chen, *The Chinese of America* (San Francisco: Harper and Row, 1980), 194.

75. Rupert Hughes, *The Real New York* (New York: Smart Set Publishing Company, 1904), 149.

76. See Fessler, *Chinese in America*, 192–193; Daniels, *Asian America*, 98–99; and Chapter 4 of this book.

77. The National Archives contains a memorial from Hawaiian Chinese that has not been mentioned in other works on the history of the Chinese in Hawaii. Entitled "Memorial and Accompanying Data Presented to the United States Commissioners by Chinese Residents in the Hawaiian Islands, August 17, 1898," the memorial asked Congress not to extend the Chinese exclusion laws to Hawaii. It also demanded that Chinese citizens of Hawaii be granted citizenship in the United States: "B. That all Chinese who have become naturalized under the laws of Hawaii and all children born in Hawaii of parents, in whole or in part, Chinese be eligible to become citizens of the United States of America, on taking an oath of allegiance to the United States of America." "Subject Correspondence," #4315/B86, Segregated Chinese Files, Record Group 85 (Washington, D.C.: National Archives); 31 *U.S. Statutes at Large* 141, Section 4; for an analysis, see Frederick Van Dyne, *A Treatise on*

the Law of Naturalization of the United States (Washington, D.C.: F. Van Dyne, 1907), 318.

78. In 1901, Chinese diplomats in New York actively supported a petition to Congress by Chinese merchants demanding citizenship and repeal of the exclusion laws. *New York Times*, June 16, 1901.

79. Ng Poon Chew came to the United States at age sixteen in 1881, attended a missionary school, and became a Christian minister in San Francisco in the 1890s. After his church was burned in 1898, he began to publish a newspaper, *Chung Sai Yat Po*, which was devoted to China's reform and to obtaining civil rights and citizenship for Chinese in America. In 1901, he organized a "To Become [American] Citizen Society." In 1906, after the earthquake and fire in San Francisco, he led a drive for Americanization. For further information, see Corrine K. Hoexter, *From Canton to California: The Epic of Chinese Immigration* (New York: Four Winds Press, 1976).

80. *Wong Kim Ark* v. *United States*, 169 U.S. 649 (1898).

81. U.S. Bureau of the Census, *16th Census of the United States, 1940: Population*, vol. 2, *Characteristics of the Population*, pt. 1 (Washington, D.C.: Government Printing Office, 1943), 21.

CHAPTER 3

"Exercise Your Sacred Rights": The Experience of New York's Chinese Laundrymen in Practicing Democracy

RENQIU YU

BASED ON AN EXAMINATION OF THE ACTIVITIES OF THE CHINESE Hand Laundry Alliance (CHLA) of New York, this chapter discusses a group of immigrant Chinese laundrymen's understanding and practice of democracy in the 1930s and 1940s. It attempts to elucidate how these laundrymen viewed their position in American society and, as the victims of the various Chinese exclusion acts, how they perceived American democracy.

Although the Chinese were welcomed as reliable and cheap labor when they first arrived in California in the early 1850s, the 1878 *In re Ah Yup* decision deprived them of the right to be naturalized.[1] Then, in 1882, Congress passed the first Chinese Exclusion Act, rendering the Chinese the only ethnic group excluded from the United States on racial grounds and suspending the entry of Chinese laborers, both skilled and unskilled, for ten years. (This provision was extended for another ten years in 1892 and indefinitely in 1904.) The Act also ruled that no Chinese would be granted naturalized citizenship.[2] Because of this act, many Chinese returned to China, while those who remained were excluded from mainstream American society.

In effect, this legislation denied not only Chinese laborers but also their spouses entry into the United States. In two 1884 decisions, the U.S. Circuit Court for California ruled that a Chinese wife held the same legal status as her husband; these decisions deprived most Chinese immigrants, who were mainly male laborers, the right to bring their wives to join them in the United States.

One consequence of the exclusion acts was a great imbalance in the sex ratio in the Chinese American community, which became known as a bachelor society. In New York state, the ratio of Chinese males fifteen years of age and older to Chinese females of the same age group was 3,961 to 100 in 1910, 1,562 to 100 in 1920, 1,402 to 100 in 1930, and 896 to 100 in 1940.[3] Other legal barriers hindered the Chinese from building families in the United States. For instance, during the exclusion period, fourteen states specifically outlawed marriages between whites and Chinese or "Mongolians."[4] Moreover, some U.S. laws specifically discouraged marriages between Chinese male immigrants and women (both Chinese and non-Chinese) who were American citizens; a 1922 federal law, the Cable Act, specified that a woman who married a Chinese alien would automatically lose her U.S. citizenship.[5] Predictably, in view of these legal restrictions, most Chinese immigrants in the United States before the 1950s were unattached males, although some had wives in China.[6] Another result of the Chinese exclusion acts was that the status of many Chinese immigrants was ambiguous; living in constant fear of deportation, they were at a disadvantage in the job market. For many Chinese, the hand laundry business was a self-employment option because it did not require much capital and many rapidly expanding cities needed their cheap labor to fill the least desirable, unskilled jobs, such as washing clothes.[7]

Although for many years the Chinese were mistreated and excluded from American society, which proclaimed that it was founded on the principles of liberty, equality, and democracy, they were not silent about the sharp contrast between American society's basic democratic principles and its mistreatment of Chinese immigrants. From early on, Chinese protested the exclusionary policies and persistently demanded equal treatment.[8] While Chinese diplomats lodged protests with the U.S. government to condemn the anti-Chinese legislation, Chinese immigrant organizations raised funds to hire lawyers to challenge these discriminatory laws in court.[9] Many ordinary Chinese immigrants expressed their frustrations and indignation against the exclusion laws in folk songs and poems written in traditional Chinese forms.[10] One of the most poignant remarks was made by a Chinese American in 1885:

Sir:

A paper was presented to me yesterday for inspection, and I found it to be specially drawn up for subscription among my countrymen toward the Pedestal Fund of the Bartholdi Statue of Liberty. Seeing that the heading is an appeal to American citizens, to their love of country and liberty, I feel that my countrymen and myself are honored in being thus appealed to as citizens in the cause of liberty. But the word liberty makes me think of the fact that this country is the land of liberty for men of all nations except the Chinese. I consider it as an insult to us Chinese to call on us to contribute toward building in this land a pedestal for a statue of liberty. That statue represents liberty holding a torch which lights the passage of those of all nations who come into this country. But are the Chinese allowed to come? As for the Chinese who are here, are they allowed to enjoy liberty as men of all other nationalities enjoy it? Are they allowed to go about everywhere free from the insults, abuses, assaults, wrongs, and injuries from which men of other nationalities are free? . . . Whether this statute against the Chinese or the statue to liberty will be the more lasting monument to tell future ages of the liberty and greatness of this country, will be known to future generations.[11]

Chinese Americans eventually destroyed the discriminatory statutes through persistent protest and struggle; finding the best means to do so was a major theme in Chinese American history. By the late nineteenth century, American-born Chinese realized that they had to organize themselves and become involved in politics to protect their interests. As Chapter 4 of this book indicates, the Native Sons of the Golden State (NSGS) was founded in 1895 (later renamed the Chinese American Citizens Alliance [CACA]) to promote the members' identification with American society and to fight for equal opportunities. Clearly a forerunner in fostering a Chinese American consciousness, the CACA, however, recruited only Chinese Americans with U.S. citizenship and excluded foreign-born Chinese from its membership.[12] This chapter, like Chapter 2, offers another view of Chinese resistance to exclusion, that of the foreign born.

During the 1930s and 1940s, as the antifascist war drastically changed the image of the Chinese in the United States, culminating in the repeal of the anti-Chinese acts, first-generation Chinese immigrants took conscious steps to forge a positive Chinese American identity and to commit themselves to improving their status in the United States. In New York, a group of Chinese laundrymen worked diligently to build their own organization according to democratic principles. While organizing, they conducted serious and revealing discussions on the meaning of democracy. Their discussions and their practice of democracy suggest that although Chinese Americans were subjected to a great deal of abuse under the discriminatory statutes against the Chinese, they did not lose faith in the ideals represented by the Statue of Liberty. Perhaps this faith in Lady Liberty gave them the resilience and courage to endure and ultimately to destroy the exclusionary statutes against the Chinese.

The Background of the CHLA

The CHLA of New York was founded by a group of Chinese laundrymen in response to an imminent crisis caused by a proposed discriminatory city ordinance. The founding of this organization was described by a contemporary Chinese American as "a revolution in New York's overseas Chinese community,"[13] signaling an important development in the labor movement in New York's Chinese community in the 1930s. In the following years, the CHLA became the largest and most influential occupational organization among the New York Chinese, challenging and weakening the patriarchal power structure in Chinatown and making great efforts to improve the laundrymen's political and economic conditions.

According to one account, approximately 30,000 Chinese lived in metropolitan New York during the 1930s.[14] Because they were systematically excluded from many other occupations, most were engaged in either laundry or restaurant work. A typical Chinese laundryman either had his own small hand laundry, as was often the case in the 1930s and 1940s, or shared one with one or two partners. For many years, Chinese laundrymen had no common organization to protect their interests,[15] but they maintained close relations with the traditional district and family (clan) organizations dominated by wealthy merchants. The Chinese Consolidated Benevolent Association (CCBA)—also known as the Chinese Six Companies and traditionally the supreme power within the Chinese community—acted as an arbiter in settling the laundrymen's disputes and conflicts over business or personal issues. To outsiders, the CCBA was known as "the government of Chinatown" because it spoke for the Chinese community as a whole. Claiming to represent and defend the interests of the entire community, the CCBA relied on an annual membership fee that it charged each immigrant before he or she was allowed to depart from the United States and on business transaction fees as its major sources of income.[16]

However, the CCBA and the district and family organizations often failed to provide adequate service to their constituencies. Chinese laundrymen believed that their interests were not well protected by these traditional organizations. Eventually, the Great Depression, racial discrimination, and unequal treatment compelled New York's Chinese laundrymen to organize themselves in 1933. In March of that year, the Council of Aldermen of the City of New York proposed an ordinance charging a license fee of twenty-five dollars per year on all public laundries plus a security bond of one thousand dollars. If passed, the ordinance would have forced most of the Chinese laundries out of existence, because the laundrymen could not afford the exorbitant fees. When the local Chinese-language newspapers reported the effort to pass the ordinance, the whole community was shocked. Facing bankruptcy, the Chinese laundrymen finally acted and founded the CHLA in April 1933.[17]

The CHLA moved immediately to challenge the proposed ordinance of the Council of Aldermen. In May, it sent its representatives and lawyers to present to the Council the laundrymen's opposition to the discriminatory ordinance under consideration. With the support of some sympathetic organizations, and after much maneuvering, the CHLA succeeded in persuading the Council to modify the ordinance significantly: The license fee was reduced to ten dollars a year, and the security bond to one hundred dollars.[18] This tremendous victory demonstrated to the Chinese laundrymen the importance and strength of their collective action. As a result, many Chinese laundrymen enthusiastically joined the CHLA, and by 1934, with an active membership of more than 3,200, the Alliance became the largest occupational organization in the New York Chinese community.[19]

Most Chinese laundrymen who joined the CHLA in the 1930s represented a new generation of Chinese Americans. Unlike the older generations, they had received some education in China before they came to the United States and had been influenced by radical ideas as revolutionary nationalistic movements swept China in the early twentieth century. Like most of the Chinese living in the United States before the 1950s, they were from the Pearl River Delta of Guangdong province in South China. Their hometowns were called "overseas Chinese communities" (qiaoxiang)—communities that sent large numbers of emigrants to Southeast Asia and the Americas and received remittances from these emigrants. Education was highly valued in these communities. From the late nineteenth century on, a substantial portion of the remittances from Southeast Asia and the Americas was designated for establishing schools in these communities. Many Chinese emigrants, with bitter memories of what they had experienced as poor and uneducated laborers in a foreign environment, hoped that their descendants would acquire a decent education and live better lives than their own, avoiding the suffering that they had endured. As a result, many elementary schools flourished in these overseas Chinese communities, and most male children in these areas received some education.[20] After the Chinese Exclusion Act was passed by Congress in 1882, the only Chinese who could immigrate to the United States were those with relatives in the United States. This meant that the bulk of the emigrants continued to be from the "overseas Chinese communities" in Guangdong. Most of these emigrants did not have a chance to learn English before or even after they arrived in the United States, but most of them could read Chinese-language newspapers. Therefore, such newspapers became their basic source of information, a major means of intra-community communication in Chinatowns, and a forum in which Chinese Americans could express their opinions on various subjects. In 1940, the CHLA members founded their own newspaper, the *China Daily News*, through which they expressed their ideas and opinions in various ways, including letters to the editor, poems, commentaries, and short essays.

Growing up in Guangdong, an area greatly influenced by revolutionary thought in the early twentieth century, the "children of overseas Chinese," as the Chinese laundrymen were called before they came to the United States, were influenced by the many revolutionary, radical, anarchical, romantic, and, most important, nationalistic ideas then sweeping across a turbulent China. This new generation had learned the revolutionary vocabulary and imbibed the spirit of the May Fourth Movement and Dr. Sun Yat-sen's revolutionary campaigns, and was ready to make a change. After they joined their fathers, uncles, or cousins in the hand laundry business in the United States, these young people began to think about how they could improve their status in American society and how to make their homeland a better place.

The CHLA's Understanding and Practice of Democracy

In the 1930s and 1940s, the term "democracy" was used in the CHLA members' discussions of political and community affairs as frequently as it was used in international politics and in China's domestic political discourse. Democracy, a concept of Western origin, was publicized in China during the May Fourth New Culture Movement (usually dated 1919, but which actually spanned the 1915–1924 decade). Radical Chinese intellectuals preached in a simplistic way the idea that democratic institutions and the scientific way of thought were the sources of Western power and wealth, and that the lack of them was the cause of China's weakness and humiliating military defeats in modern times. These intellectuals argued that to revive Chinese civilization, the Chinese must internalize modern democratic values and build democratic institutions to replace the traditional, patriarchal, and authoritarian institutions rooted in Chinese society. Some scholars challenged the notion that democracy would cure all of China's ills, but in general, a romantic and optimistic belief in democracy as an alternative to despotism, as a means to rebuild China, and as a vehicle to remold the Chinese national character was maintained.[21] Continuous civil wars and foreign intrusion allowed the Chinese no chance to focus on cultural and economic construction, but they continued to talk about democracy as a guiding principle for rebuilding the country. When Japan occupied Manchuria in 1931, China appealed to world public opinion, calling upon Western countries to support China and to condemn Japan as an aggressor, a militarist state, a member of the fascist club, and, as such, a menace to world peace. China, a victim of Japan's ruthless aggression, was depicted as peace loving and progressive. China's supporters argued that its brave war of resistance against Japan should be seen as "part of the global movement for the survival of democracy." Above all, China had the ability not only to defeat Japan, but also to transform itself according to democratic principles.[22]

Against this historical background, the CHLA members addressed the problems facing them in terms of how to understand, practice, and defend democracy. The Chinese laundrymen's understanding and practice of democracy can be examined from four angles: their efforts to build an organization based on democratic principles; the use of the *China Daily News* to promote political participation; their criticism of the traditional power structure in Chinatown; and their desire to introduce democratic values into Chinese politics.

Efforts to Build a Democratic Organization

The Chinese laundrymen were determined to build an organization based on democratic principles as they understood them. The CHLA established a democratic electoral procedure that met the demands of and was shaped by the experiences of the Chinese laundrymen. From the beginning, "the laundry Alliance is for the laundrymen" was the password among its members.[23] To ensure that the CHLA officials were genuine representatives of the laundrymen, the Alliance adopted a democratic method of electing them. All officials were elected by and from the members, according to the following procedure: New York City (including Manhattan, the Bronx, Queens, and Brooklyn) was divided into about 300 "districts." Each district had six to ten laundries located in the same neighborhood. The members in a given district elected a *quzhang*, or group leader, who served as the representative of his group (or district) and attended the Alliance convention, which was held annually, usually in November. At the convention, the 300 representatives nominated 104 candidates for the executive and supervisory committees. Then, during a membership meeting, 52 of the 104 candidates were elected to these committees. Each year, the new executive and supervisory committees issued an "inaugural statement," which identified the problems facing the laundry business and outlined the major work to be done the following year.[24]

The CHLA bylaws ruled that no one should hold office for more than one year at a time. Because an election was held each year, virtually every member would have a chance to be elected to office. The group leaders constituted a network that linked thousands of CHLA members scattered throughout New York City, and these leaders presented the members' opinions to the headquarters. As a rule, any important issue was decided at the membership meeting. Thus, CHLA members strongly identified with the organization, which they felt to be their own. In contrast, the CCBA, which normally proclaimed that every Chinese in the Greater New York area was automatically a member and obligated to pay dues, denied its members the right to participate in the decision-making process of the organization.

This democratic structure of the CHLA distinguished it from the traditional Chinese organizations in which the elite monopolized all power. Democracy was a new idea in Chinatown, and its appeal can be understood only by looking at the CHLA's struggle against the CCBA's monopoly of power in the community, as well as at the CCBA's ineffectiveness in protecting ordinary Chinese Americans' interests.

The meaning of the CHLA's conception of democracy can be further understood by examining the damaging effects of the notorious "tong wars" on the Chinese community. Tongs, which usually controlled the gambling houses and brothels in Chinatowns, settled their most intransigent problems through violence. From 1933 to the end of 1934, tong wars plagued the Chinese communities on the East Coast. Many people were killed and a large number of innocent Chinese Americans were arrested and deported by the U.S. Immigration and Naturalization Service. Newspaper reports described Chinatowns as dangerous places where the Chinese were killing each other ruthlessly.[25] Against such a background, the CHLA's practice of democracy can be seen as a conscious effort, on the one hand, to break away from the traditional ways of settling disputes in the Chinese community, and on the other, to counter the negative images of the Chinese community.

By the 1940s, CHLA members spoke proudly about the Alliance's "glorious democratic tradition," and each year the elected officials reaffirmed the organization's commitment to democratic principles. The CHLA was able to maintain this democratic system, to a great extent, with the help of Quon Shar members. The Quon Shar (in pinyin, Qun She; literally, the "Mass Club") was founded by the core CHLA members in June 1935 as part of an effort to save the Alliance from an internal conflict. Its members were young, were relatively more educated than most CHLA members and thus more idealistic, and were current or former members of the CHLA's executive and supervisory committees.[26] To strengthen and develop the Alliance, these individuals made tremendous efforts to keep the CHLA annual elections functioning well. Because the CHLA members were scattered throughout New York City and most of them did not have a telephone at home or at work,[27] organizing the elections of the group leaders involved much work. In fact, several years passed before the CHLA managed to institutionalize the democratic election system. Records of Quon Shar meetings show that every year before the CHLA's election of the group leaders, the Quon Shar held a meeting to discuss how to help the Alliance and how to handle such problems as the lack of group leaders (who were responsible for the election of new group leaders) in some districts and some members' noncommittal attitude toward the election. Then, on the date of the election, the Quon Shar members traveled to different districts to help the CHLA members elect the group leaders.

To protect and develop the CHLA, Quon Shar members and CHLA leaders demonstrated a spirit of self-sacrifice. They were all laundrymen working twelve to fifteen hours a day to make a living, but they were willing to sacrifice self-interest for the betterment of the collective organization. This spirit of self-sacrifice, together with the willingness to work for a common cause, was emphasized in every year's inauguration of new officials. One CHLA member praised the Alliance's leaders in 1943 this way:

> Several years ago, when I was in China, I had learned about the CHLA from my friends' correspondences and the CHLA's bulletins. . . . After I

came to New York and I have seen how the officials and members struggle together, I respect them even more. . . . The officials of our Alliance serve the membership without pay. However, I have seen that the officials of every year, when there is a lot of work, always work hard; sometime [sic] they stay up until very late to finish the work, going to bed around 3 or 4 o'clock in the morning.[28]

Probably because of their dedication, spirit of self-sacrifice, and political experience, from 1940 on, the Quon Shar members were frequently elected as CHLA leaders. Although the CHLA bylaws ruled that no one could hold office for more than one year at a time, these people were often reelected in alternate years. Consequently, the CHLA began to have a stable leadership.

Promotion of Political Participation

In the late 1930s, many Chinese Americans in New York City felt that they could not obtain accurate information about the situation in China from the local Chinese-language newspapers subsidized by the Kuomintang (KMT, the Chinese Nationalist Party). At the same time, the CHLA had difficulty making its voice heard in the community. Thus, to "reflect ordinary Chinese Americans' opinions and to get objective information about China's domestic situation, especially about the conditions of the overseas Chinese community [in Guangdong]," [29] CHLA members and their allies raised funds to found the *China Daily News (Meizhou Huaqiao Ribao*—"Americas' Overseas Chinese Daily")* on July 7, 1940, the third anniversary of China's war of resistance against Japan. The paper's introduction made a remarkable observation about Chinese Americans: "This paper is founded by overseas Chinese in the United States. Among the overseas Chinese in this country, many have acquired U.S. citizenship. To them, to love and defend [their] motherland is a bound duty [*tianzhi*], and to be loyal to the United States is an obligation [*yiwu*]."[30]

Three weeks later, an editorial made the same point: "So we regard overseas Chinese concern about their motherland as a natural expression of normal human feelings [*renqing zhi ziran*], and their efforts to permanently develop their settlement [in the U.S.] as a rational development [*shili zhi dangran*]."[31]

This observation is noteworthy because it was perhaps the first elaboration by a Chinese-language newspaper on the dualistic attitude of American citizens of Chinese ancestry toward China and the United

States.[32] It marks the beginning of the awakening of a Chinese American consciousness among a group of first-generation Chinese as they began to think positively of themselves as Americans with a Chinese heritage. In its early issues, the newspaper proclaimed that its sole purpose was "to serve the interests and welfare of the overseas Chinese in America."[33] To inspire, encourage, and help Chinese Americans to understand, obtain, and exercise their political rights became one of its basic forms of service to the community.

Throughout the 1940s, the *China Daily News* persistently encouraged its readers to vote in local, state, and national elections. "Election is the most precious system in a democratic country," one editorial stated. "The most remarkable progress in human political life is that the ballot has replaced the gun to obtain power, and has become the basis of policy-making."[34] The paper urged "the overseas Chinese with franchise . . . not to give up your right to vote," which was seen as a "sacred right and duty of citizens in a democratic country."[35] Moreover, it provided information about the backgrounds and platforms of competing candidates and ran editorials and commentaries analyzing issues and the results of elections to help readers understand the American electoral system. In October 1942, before the New York State elections, the *China Daily News* sent letters to different candidates asking them about their positions on the issues of American aid to China, services for Chinese American communities, the Chinese Exclusion Act, and the elimination of prejudice against Chinese.[36] The replies from the candidates of the Democratic Party, the Republican Party, and the Communist Party were translated into Chinese and published in the paper.[37]

The CHLA's and the *China Daily News*'s view that Chinese Americans should exercise their political rights was shared by many laundrymen. The *China Daily News* offered the CHLA the privilege of regularly publishing a special column (*Yilian Zhengkan*) in the paper. This special column, which appeared monthly, provided information and advice about the hand laundry business to fellow laundrymen, and it served as a forum for the laundrymen to express their political opinions in the form of short articles.[38]

However, although the new ideas espoused by the *China Daily News* and the CHLA members represented remarkable progress in the development of a Chinese American consciousness, the concrete results were limited. In 1940, according to the paper's estimate, the total Chinese population in the United States was about 75,000, among whom fewer than 20,000 were citizens old enough to cast ballots.[39]

Such a small ethnic group had little leverage in American politics. Thus, the candidates' replies to the *China Daily News*'s inquiry into their platforms seemed to be only token gestures rather than pleas to a powerful constituency.

Furthermore, this desire to participate in electoral politics came from and to a certain extent was defined by the CHLA's campaign "to save China, to save ourselves," in which the CHLA consciously linked its patriotic support for China's war against Japan to its struggle for equal treatment in the United States. The *China Daily News*'s editorials and the articles in the CHLA special column indicated a major concern over the candidates' positions on U.S. policy toward China and on issues concerning Chinese Americans, such as the repeal of the Chinese exclusion acts. Only those who promised to support China's war against Japan and to defend the legal rights of Chinese Americans were worth supporting, these editorials and articles suggested. In 1944, for example, Li Chengzhu, an active CHLA member, urged his fellow laundrymen to vote for Franklin D. Roosevelt because FDR "carried out a positive aid-China policy and played a part in abolishing the Chinese exclusion acts."[40] Because the CHLA's attempts to participate in American politics were developed and shaped in their campaign "to save China, to save ourselves," the success of these attempts was, to a great extent, determined by the state of U.S.-China relations and American domestic circumstances related to changes in these relations. In the 1940s, the fact that the United States and China had become allies created a favorable climate in which Chinese Americans could freely express their political opinions; but in the 1950s increasing hostility between the two countries during the Cold War made such free expression extremely difficult. Therefore, if these once politically active Chinese Americans became relatively silent again in the 1950s, their silence was not due to their "inertia" or to the "Chinese cultural heritage" of political apathy, but, rather, to changes in U.S.-China relations.

A scarcity of documents prevents us from knowing not only how many enfranchised Chinese voted (and if they did, for whom in the national, state, and municipal elections in the 1940s), but also how they reflected on the consequences of their voting. *China Daily News* editorials and the CHLA special column articles, however, suggest that the CHLA and its allies had reached a new sophistication in approaching political issues in American society and in seeking solutions to their problems. These Chinese Americans began to think of themselves as an integral part of American society as they set out to consider their franchise as a positive means to improve their conditions. This was a significant development in Chinese American history. Contrary to the conventional stereotypical depictions of Chinese Americans as apolitical and "unassimilable," the CHLA's actions suggest that by the 1940s a group of Chinese Americans had tried diligently to exercise their political rights. Within this context, how much they achieved does not matter (they seemed to have achieved little). What does matter is that this group of Chinese Americans made positive and active efforts to improve their lot, a point usually neglected in most writings in Chinese American history.

Another important aspect of Chinese American history ignored by earlier scholars is the Chinese Americans' efforts to have the unjust Chinese exclusion laws repealed. The repeal of these laws in 1943 had a profound impact on the Chinese American community. All the Chinese exclusion laws were abolished, 105 Chinese immigrants were allowed to enter the United States per year, and they became eligible for naturalized citizenship. While debating the repeal bills, however, Congress and the press, as well as the organizations that vigorously supported the repeal, virtually ignored the Chinese Americans' voices. The fundamental argument for repeal was that it would help end the war, nullify Japanese propaganda, and further U.S. postwar commercial relations with China. The first two concerns were expressed in President Franklin D. Roosevelt's message to Congress on October 11, 1943: "China is our ally. . . . For many long years she stood alone in the fight against aggression. Today we fight at her side. She has continued her gallant struggle against very great odds. . . . By the repeal of the Chinese exclusion laws, we can correct a historic mistake and silence the distorted Japanese propaganda."[41] Some religious and humanitarian groups emphasized "racial equality" and "human rights," but only in a patronizing tone. According to one source, "When Chinese-Americans sought to help the campaign, they were asked to refute the argument that Chinese were inassimilable rather than state their specific group interests."[42] The Citizens Committee to Repeal Chinese Exclusion, an organization founded in New York on May 25, 1943, which played a key role in the campaign, tactically limited its membership "to American citizens not of Asiatic origin so as to give the impression that the demand was completely indigenous and not fostered by the Chinese or anyone with a personal 'axe to grind.'"[43] As a result of this deliberate neglect by both the oppositional and supportive groups, few records exist of how Chinese Americans responded. The editorials and articles published in the *China Daily News*, however, provide glimpses of the strong feelings of Chinese Americans on the issue.

From May to October, when Congress held hearings and debated the bills to repeal the exclusion laws, the *China Daily News* devoted a large amount of space to covering these events. Its special correspondent, Song Feng, sent reports on every development in the process from Washington, D.C., to the paper's New York headquarters each night by long-distance telephone calls.[44] To help readers gain a comprehensive understanding, the paper reported in detail the viewpoints and arguments of both the opponents and the supporters of repeal. The testimony of "friendly American individuals," such as Dr. Arthur Hummel of the U.S. Library of Congress and the writer Pearl S. Buck, and the opinions of some anti-Chinese organizations and individuals were translated into Chinese and published in the paper.[45]

In addition to informing its readers of each development in the hearings, the paper published numerous editorials, letters, and articles to discuss the repeal and to express Chinese American opinions. From the beginning, the *China Daily News* attacked the exclusion laws as racist and counter to the spirit of American democracy. The laws were portrayed as the root of many problems—social, economic, and political—in the Chinese community because these laws institutionalized the discrimination against the Chinese and forced the Chinese to live in ghettos. These laws created a permanent fear among Chinese Americans that they could be investigated and deported at any time, which made them vulnerable to the manipulation and exploitation of both white and Chinese racketeers. Under the exclusion laws, the wives that male Chinese Americans had left behind in China, except those married to "domiciled merchants," were not allowed to join their husbands. As a result, prostitution and gambling became features of a socially impoverished bachelor society. "In short," one editorial asserted, "most of the sorrows, darkness, and various problems in the Chinese community are the products of the Chinese exclusion laws."[46] The day after the House passed the repeal bill, the *China Daily News* ran an editorial to express the delight and hope of Chinese Americans:

> The Chinese in the United States will be affected by the repeal bill the most. After the repeal of the Chinese exclusion laws, we Chinese will be eligible for naturalization and, as taxpayers, will have the right to participate in politics. We then can use the right to vote and to run for

office to present our needs and to express our opinions. This will provide us many direct opportunities and advantages to solve the problems and to promote the welfare of the Chinese community. Furthermore, the Chinese in the United States, now that they can directly participate in all kinds of activities in American society as citizens, will make more contributions to the political, economic, social, and cultural development of the United States, and become more influential. This will benefit both the Chinese themselves and American society as a whole.[47]

These opinions offer insight into how Chinese Americans, or at least a certain group of Chinese Americans, reacted to the successful end of the repeal campaign. Although the repeal bill was passed mainly in consideration of the war effort and of U.S.-China relations, the Chinese Americans who expressed their opinions through the *China Daily News* had based their argument for repeal on the fundamental principles of American democracy and the ideals of the American revolution. They also viewed repeal as vital to the future of Chinese Americans. This attitude suggests that this group of Chinese Americans had come to believe in the promise of American democracy, despite the fact that their experiences in the United States had made a mockery of democratic principles.

Criticism of the Traditional Power Structure in Chinatown

The Chinese laundrymen's understanding of democracy was also reflected in their criticism of the traditional organizations in Chinatown and their desire to change the power structure in the Chinese community. After consolidating itself politically and economically in the Chinese community, the CHLA took initiatives to improve the political conditions in Chinatown. Democratization of the Chinese community was one of the CHLA's primary goals in the 1940s. One important move that it made was its attempt to transform the leading power in Chinatown, the CCBA, through democratic reforms.

The CCBA was founded in the nineteenth century in response to the Chinese immigrants' need for a collective effort to deal with a hostile environment. Founded in the 1860s in San Francisco, it was a loose federation of Chinese organizations in that city. The Chinese consul general, Huang Zunxian, hoped that the CCBA could lead the fight against the anti-Chinese movement.[48] Before the Chinese government set up its first consulate in San Francisco in 1878, the CCBA had acted as the spokesperson of the imperial Qing government in its relations with the Chinese in the United States.[49] The New York branch of the CCBA was founded in 1883. In 1890, the organization registered with the New York State government under the name "The Chinese Consolidated Benevolent Association of the City of New York." From 1894 to 1963, this branch was located at 16 Mott Street; in 1963, it moved to its current location, 62 Mott Street.[50]

The New York CCBA, like its counterparts in other cities, had been established to meet the needs of Chinese immigrants, but it was authoritarian in nature. Its officials were not elected by the membership but were chosen by the merchant elite from the two largest huiguan: the Ning Yang Huiguan (consisting of immigrants from Taishan, dominated by merchants) and the Lian Cheng (Lun Sing) Gongsuo (consisting of all non-Taishan immigrants in New York City). According to the CCBA bylaws, its four officers—president, Chinese secretary, English secretary, and staff member—were to be selected alternately by the Ning Yang Huiguan and the Lian Cheng Gongsuo. For instance, if the president and the Chinese secretary were elected by the Ning Yang Huiguan, the English secretary and the office assistant had to be chosen by the Lian Cheng Gongsuo, and vice versa.[51] Seven permanent members of the CCBA standing committee (consisting of representatives from the Ning Yang Huiguan, Lian Cheng Gongsuo, Chinese Chamber of Commerce, On Leong Association, Hip Sing Association, Mei Chi Party, and Eastern American Branch of the Kuomintang after its founding in China) had the right "to propose and vote for resolutions" and "to help the president handle all affairs."[52]

Those who were chosen to serve as CCBA president before the 1930s were usually Chinese scholars who had earned a degree in the pre-1905 era by passing the traditional civil service examinations in China. These individuals enjoyed considerable prestige in the Chinese immigrant communities in the United States. Yee Wing Yan (Yu Xingjian), for example, was born in Taishan in 1861, earned a *juren* degree (equivalent to an M.A.) in China, and served as president of the San Francisco CCBA in 1904. He returned to China for several years and came back to the United States in 1916 to become president of the New York CCBA.[53] Such Confucian scholars were inefficient administrators in communities as complex as the U.S. Chinatowns; therefore, the wealthy merchants actually controlled the CCBA, the self-styled "highest authority" in the Chinese community.[54]

Although the rank-and-file Chinese immigrants had no right to vote on organization issues, the CCBA bylaws required them to pay various fees to support the association. Every Chinese living in the Greater New York area (including New Jersey and Connecticut) was automatically a member, whether he or she wanted to join or not. A member was required to pay a "foundation fee" of three dollars and an annual membership fee of one dollar, plus a so-called port duty of three dollars before leaving for China. In addition, each laundryman had to pay an extra annual laundry-shop fee of two dollars. Moreover, the CCBA by-laws required all Chinese business transactions to be conducted at the association's headquarters and charged a fee of five dollars each. This regulation was unique to New York.[55] The assertion of such authority over business transactions rendered the official positions in the CCBA profitable; the ownership of Chinese hand laundries, for instance, changed hands often.[56] The CCBA's account books were kept secret, a policy that raised suspicions of corruption and embezzlement.[57]

More than any other Chinese immigrant organization, the CCBA was an American product. Its power stemmed from the historical situation created by anti-Chinese sentiments and legislation and from its connections with the Chinese government. Although it was originally created as an advocate for Chinese immigrants, it became an elite-dominated and repressive organization; its existence largely depended on the ignorance that separated the Chinese community from the larger community.

For years, the CHLA and the *China Daily News* had criticized the CCBA for its lack of democratic election procedures. In 1947, during a drive to raise a large amount of money for building new headquarters, the CCBA began to consider the suggestion from some Chinese Americans to revise its constitution. The CHLA and the *China Daily News* urged the CCBA to adopt a democratic "direct election" system similar to the CHLA's. Citing the American motto, "Taxation without Representation Is Tyranny," the CHLA argued that the right to vote was a basic right of membership, and rejected the view that many Chinese Americans lacked the education to exercise these rights: "Many of us have functioned well in casting our votes in American presidential elections and local governmental elections, why can we not vote in the Chinese community?" Given the increasing political awareness among Chinese Americans, the CHLA asserted, the CCBA must reform itself and introduce the method of direct general elections into its system; otherwise, it would lose its position as a "leading organization" in the community.[58]

The established elite ignored this appeal to democratic principles. The CHLAs and the *China Daily News*'s efforts to change the power structure in Chinatown failed. That such an attempt was made is significant, though. The laundrymen had confidence in the potential of ordinary Chinese Americans to improve their conditions in America by adopting democratic ways. More explicitly, the CHLA hoped that working-class Chinese Americans would have more say in community affairs and that the repressive, arbitrary system through which the CCBA ruled Chinatown for decades would be changed.

The CHLA's and the *China Daily News*'s demand for democratic reforms in the Chinese community was not merely rhetoric. If the principles of democratic elections, such as "one person, one vote," had been introduced into the CCBA's electoral process, each organization would have had equal access to power, and the CCBA would have been a genuine coalition organization instead of a merchant-dominated organ. Consequently, the CHLA, with its large membership and its wide connections with other grassroots organizations, would likely have had a major voice in the CCBA and could have potentially made fundamental changes in the political life of New York's Chinatown.

Desire for a Democratic China

The final aspect of the CHLA's understanding of democracy was reflected in its desire to introduce basic democratic values into politics in China. Being subjected to various forms of discrimination in the United States, many Chinese Americans attributed their miseries to China's weakness and backwardness, so they demonstrated great enthusiasm in promoting political progress in China. Sun Yat-sen's revolutionary movement against the Manchu dynasty gave Chinese Americans their first chance to express strong nationalist feelings. In that period (1890s–1920s), the elites dominated the scene, and the major role of ordinary people was to donate money. Presumably, when Sun's revolution succeeded and a strong Republic of China was founded, Chinese in the United States would return to their homeland, leaving behind all the humiliation that they had suffered in the Gold Mountain. However, Sun's efforts to build a modern, independent, and prosperous China failed. Instead, Sun's successor, Chiang Kai-shek, established an authoritarian government that tolerated no criticism. Chinese Americans were further disappointed by Chiang's failure to launch an efficient military campaign against Japan's invasion of China in the 1930s. They were becoming critical of the dictatorial policies of Chiang's Kuomintang in China and its agents' attempts to control Chinese communities in the United States. In the late 1930s, the CHLA worked with other organizations in New York's Chinatown to form a united anti-Japanese alliance independent of the KMT and consequently became a target of the KMT agents' attacks. From the frustrations and dissatisfactions with Chiang Kai-shek and the KMT regime, the CHLA and other Chinese American organizations began to think of the kind of China that they wanted and the kind of contribution that they could make. They were impelled to reconsider their role in building a new China, and they were no longer satisfied with being mere financial donors, although they contributed almost every spare penny that they had to help the anti-Japanese war. They began to develop political opinions, which reflected both their experiences and their expectations, and they wanted their voices to be heard. Their demands for democratic reforms in China, however, like their demands for democratic reforms in New York's Chinatown, were ignored.

Besides the dictatorial methods of Chiang and the KMT agents, Chinese Americans were alienated by the corruption of the KMT government. They learned of the KMT's corruption in two ways. First, their families were directly affected by the KMT officials' embezzlement of their remittances. Many relatives of Chinese Americans relied entirely on these funds for subsistence, and many starved to death during the war because of delays in delivering the funds or outright embezzlement. Chinese Americans were extremely upset when they received letters reporting such sad stories.[59] Second, Chinese Americans knew about KMT corruption through their observations of KMT officials and these officials' relatives living in the United States. During the war years, many KMT officials sent their family members to the United States, especially to Washington, D.C., and New York City. "They were as numerous as the mice in a slum," one report stated. "From the top KMT officials to third-class politicians, almost no one has not sent relatives to the United States. Some even manage to get the whole family out here, having bought a house or invested in something." These people reportedly brought to the United States huge amounts of money, which were believed to have been squeezed from the Chinese people or accumulated through currency speculation in the black market. Ordinary Chinese Americans resented these people and called them "high-class refugees."[60] These wealthy newcomers looked down on Chinese American laundrymen and restaurant workers. One KMT official's wife reportedly called Chinese American restaurant workers "inferior people," and another official's wife was surprised to find that many Chinese Americans worked in hand laundry shops: "My God! They work in those [kinds of] jobs!"[61]

The extravagant lifestyle of the high-class refugees in the United States and the starvation of the Chinese Americans' relatives in China constituted a striking contrast. Angry and sorrowful, Chinese Americans attacked the KMT regime and tried to find a solution to the problem that this regime caused or was unable to solve. In the New York Chinese community, the CHLA became a spokesperson for ordinary Chinese Americans in criticizing the KMT's corruption and demanding democratic reforms, while the *China Daily News* became the essential instrument through which ordinary Chinese Americans shared information and expressed their opinions on China's politics. In 1943, the CHLA passed a resolution to hold a "Sunday Discussion on Current Events" twice a month. Some summaries of the discussions were published in the CHLA special column in the *China Daily News*.[62] How to eliminate the corruption in Chinese politics and how to build a democratic government in China became the two major themes that dominated these discussions in the years to come.

The first two Sunday discussion sessions focused on the Taishan famine and on corruption in the Chinese government. The Taishan famine of 1943 was catastrophic. About 100,000 people (from a population of 860,000) died of starvation or diseases caused by malnutrition. Many of the victims relied on overseas remittances from Chinese American relatives for survival, but the remittances were cut off by the war and much of the money that did reach Taishan was embezzled by local officials.[63] Angry Chinese laundrymen insisted that the tragedy was caused more by human failure—the corruption and black-market speculation of government officials and unscrupulous merchants—than by natural calamity. Zhong Huitang, a member of the CHLA executive committee, summed up the discussions on the issue: "The corruption of the motherland's politics and the unfair exchange rate between the dollar and yuan were the root of the famine. So, if we want to save China and to save our families, we have to be concerned with reforming China's politics."[64]

The CHLA's criticism of the KMT government bore distinctive Chinese American characteristics. The Alliance criticized the KMT regime from the perspective of ordinary Chinese Americans, on the basis of their deep concern for their relatives at home. Moreover, the CHLA used the democratic principles that its members had learned in the United States as yardsticks against which to measure the KMT's performance and to demand political reforms. Interestingly, from these criticisms of the KMT, a positive identification with some basic values of American democracy developed.

In September 1943, to mitigate the increasing demand for democracy, the KMT government announced that a national constitutional convention would be held within the first year after China won the war against Japan. The Association to Promote the Implementation of the Constitution was set up in Chongqing (Chungking), the wartime capital of China, with a stated purpose to solicit opinions and suggestions from Chinese at home and abroad. Some overseas Chinese organizations, including the CHLA, were excited about this move. After several months of discussion, the CHLA submitted to the Association a long "Opinion Letter," which examined line by line the constitution drafted by the KMT and suggested numerous changes. It is interesting to note that the CHLA desired to introduce American democratic ideas to China. In the brief preface of its letter, the CHLA stated:

> We, the overseas Chinese in the United States, are living in a democratic and free country. What we see and hear here is the politics of the people and for the people; we not only have long been admiring the excellence and efficiency of [American] political institutions, as well as the ways the government functions, but also desire that our motherland build institutions after this pattern so as to become a wealthy and powerful nation.[65]

This identification with basic American values has many meanings in Chinese American history. In 1943, the CHLA and the *China Daily News* criticized the Chinese exclusion acts from the perspective of American democratic principles. However, it was in their criticisms of the KMT government that the CHLA members applied these values most frequently. To these Chinese laundrymen, the fundamental principles of democracy were simple, direct, and, even more important, applicable to China. The words of a CHLA member are representative:

> China belongs to Chinese, and the Kuomintang must end its one-party dictatorship. To understand the essence of democracy, we don't have to talk about abstract theories. We can just take a look at some plain facts. Living in the democratic United States, it's not difficult for us to know the effectiveness of democracy through what we see and hear. For example, if there is a problem in a local community, any citizen can write to [his/her] Representatives and Senators, and in most cases, Representatives and Senators respond quickly. Why? Because they are elected by local people. . . . They are obligated to serve the people. Now let's examine the situation in China. Does any Chinese official have to be responsible

to the people? They all have a contemptuous attitude to the people. We saw much of this when we were in China. Even a minor official always strutted about in front of people. . . . Recently, every newspaper [in the New York Chinese community] ran reports on the problems in [overseas Chinese] remittances. But our protests met the deaf ear of the Bank of China. Why? Because the Bank is run by the government, and its managers are officials of the ruling dictatorial party that is not responsible to the people.[66]

The CHLA members addressed these issues not for the sake of flaunting their knowledge of democracy, but because they were compelled by their relatives' sufferings to do so and because they believed that "China politics has a direct influence on their economic conditions and social status in the United States." Also, they felt obligated to express support for the "people's zealous struggle for democracy at home."[67] Furthermore, their criticisms of the KMT government were related to their attacks on Chinatown's established forces.

The CHLA's criticisms of the KMT regime in China and of the CCBA's monopoly of power in Chinatown were based on the same point—neither organization represented the people because both were not elected by the people. Implicit in these criticisms was a strong desire to acquire and exercise political rights and power. Such a desire indicated that this group of Chinese Americans was determined to practice and protect their rights. Because the depressing situation in China discouraged them from returning to their homeland, improving their conditions in the land of their settlement became their primary concern. Therefore, the CHLA's criticism of the KMT regime must be read alongside its criticisms of the CCBA and vice versa. Their discussions of democracy were part and parcel of their criticism of the realities in China and Chinatown, not just theoretical debates about abstract principles.

Conclusion

The CHLA's activities, when examined in a broad historical context, suggest some new ways to think about the meaning of Chinese American experiences. John Higham, one of the leading scholars of American history, argues that the different experiences of ethnic groups in the United States involved a process of "pluralistic integration." Despite their diversities, all these immigrant groups shared a culture in the United States.[68]

However, one fundamental difference existed between the Chinese and other ethnic groups: Only the Chinese were excluded explicitly by name from the United States from 1882 to 1943. Every aspect of Chinese life in the United States was influenced by the exclusion acts, thus any comparative study must give serious consideration to this fact. Compared with the "alienation" experienced by other ethnic groups in the migratory process, as defined by Oscar Handlin,[69] the Chinese immigrants' story was far more complex. From the beginning, however, the Chinese protested the exclusionary policies and persistently demanded equal treatment. The CHLA carried on that tradition of protest. A basic pattern in the CHLA's response to Chinese exclusion and isolation was to hold American society to the democratic values and principles embodied in the Declaration of Independence and the U.S. Constitution. Eugene Moy, editor-in-chief of the *China Daily News*, once characterized the nature of the Chinese American struggle in the United States by a single phrase: "I am a human being too."[70] The CHLA's and the *China Daily News*'s call for repeal of the Chinese exclusion acts expressed a deep desire to be treated as equal members in American society, a right that these Chinese Americans believed they were entitled to on the basis of their understanding of fundamental democratic values.

If one accepts John Higham's notion of "pluralistic integration," in which all ethnic groups develop a common culture, of which democratic values are a part, then one may say that the CHLA's identification with basic democratic values is a significant expression of its members' integration. In that sense, protesting against exclusion and discrimination was the beginning of their integration into American society.

The CHLA's praise for American political institutions and how they work is one of the great ironies in Chinese American history. If the CHLA's suggestion, made in 1944, that American democracy should be the model for China is juxtaposed against its criticisms of U.S. anti-Chinese legislation, as expressed in 1943 in the campaign to repeal the Chinese exclusion acts and in its comments on U.S. policy toward China a few years later, one cannot help but think that the CHLA's understanding of U.S. politics was full of contradictions. On the one hand, the CHLA criticized the United States for the injustices that the Chinese had been subjected to; on the other, it held up American democracy as an ideal model for China to follow.

Precisely this kind of ambivalent attitude characterized the true feelings of the Chinese laundrymen regarding the United States. These contradictions were a reflection of the contradictions in U.S. society itself, especially those in the laundrymen's experiences. The

United States claimed to be a free and equal society, but the Chinese experienced severe racial discrimination and exclusion. Nevertheless, when the Chinese stood up to fight against injustices and to defend their interests, they appealed to American democratic principles and legal procedures. Although many times the laundrymen failed in their struggle for equality and felt disillusioned about the way in which American democracy actually worked, sometimes they won, as in the CHLA's struggle against New York City's discriminatory laundry ordinance in 1933. Most significant, the repeal of the Chinese exclusion acts in 1943 provided a new atmosphere in which some Chinese Americans, such as the CHLA members, could affirm their experiences of fighting injustice within American society and could identify more positively with the basic values and principles embodied in the U.S. Constitution.

Nevertheless, the historical reality is that, while the CHLA—whether philosophically and ideologically or for political expediency—chose to identify positively with the basic democratic values generally upheld in American society, its members were physically, politically, socially, and economically kept on the periphery of that society. Before 1943, the legal system denied them the right to be naturalized, whereas the social and political conditions in the larger society rendered their demands for equal rights isolated voices. The Chinese laundrymen's marginal position limited the scope of their efforts and accomplishments. Their voices were ignored in the past, just as the voices of black slaves were ignored; nevertheless, what can be recovered of their testimony through historical research can make a constructive and instructive contribution to a more nuanced and sophisticated understanding of American democracy.

Notes

Acknowledgments: This chapter elaborates on one of the major themes of my book, *To Save China, To Save Ourselves: The Chinese Hand Laundry Alliance of New York* (Philadelphia: Temple University Press, 1992). I have borrowed sentences, paragraphs, and long quotations from that book. I want to thank Sucheng Chan for her help in editing that book and this chapter.

1. See Sucheng Chan, *Asian Americans: An Interpretive History* (Boston: Twayne Publishers, 1991), 47, 54.
2. For the full text of the Act, see 22 *U.S. Statutes at Large* 58–61; or Cheng-Tsu Wu, ed., *"Chink!" A Documentary History of Anti-Chinese Prejudice in America* (New York: World Publishing Company, 1972), 70–75. For analyses

of these exclusion acts and their impact on Chinese Americans, see Bill Ong
Hing, *Making and Remaking Asian America through Immigration Policy,
1850–1990* (Stanford: Stanford University Press, 1993), 44–53; Benjamin B.
Ringer, *"We the People" and Others: Duality and America's Treatment of Its
Racial Minorities* (New York: Tavistock Publications, 1983), 629–680; Stan-
ford M. Lyman, *Chinese Americans* (New York: Random House, 1974), 63–69;
and Shih-shan Henry Tsai, *The Chinese Experience in America* (Bloomington:
Indiana University Press, 1986), 62–67.

3. Shepard Schwartz, "Mate-Selection among New York City's Chinese Males,
   1931–38," *American Journal of Sociology* 56 (May 1951): 562–568; for the statistics, see page 564.

4. Fowler V. Harper and Jerome H. Skolnick, *Problems of the Family*, rev. ed.
   (New York: Bobbs-Merrill, 1962), 96–99. The fourteen states were Arizona,
   California, Georgia, Idaho, Mississippi, Missouri, Montana, Nebraska,
   Nevada, Oregon, South Dakota, Utah, Virginia, and Wyoming.

5. Sucheng Chan, "The Exclusion of Chinese Women 1870–1943," in *Entry Denied: Exclusion and the Chinese Community in America, 1882–1943*, ed.
   Sucheng Chan (Philadelphia: Temple University Press, 1991), 128.

6. Lyman, *Chinese Americans*, 89–90.

7. See Paul C. P. Siu, *The Chinese Laundryman: A Study of Social Isolation*, ed.
   John K. W. Tchen (New York: New York University Press, 1987), 44–55.

8. Alexander McLeod, *Pigtails and Gold Dust* (Caldwell, Idaho: The Caxton
   Printers, 1947), 220–21; Liu Pei Chi, *Meiguo Huaqiao shi* [A history of the
   Chinese in the United States, 1848–1911] (Taipei: Limin Wenhua Shiye
   Gongsi, 1976), 575–586.

9. Charles J. McClain and Laurene Wu McClain, "The Chinese Contribution to
   the Development of American Law," in *Entry Denied*, ed. Chan, 3–24; Shih-
   shan Henry Tsai, *China and the Overseas Chinese in the United States,
   1868–1911* (Fayetteville: University of Arkansas Press, 1983), 96–97.

10. See Him Mark Lai, Genny Lim, and Judy Yung, eds., *Island: Poetry and His-
    tory of Chinese Immigrants on Angel Island, 1910–1940* (Seattle: University
    of Washington Press, 1991); Marlon Hom, ed. and trans., *Songs of Gold Moun-
    tain: Cantonese Rhymes from San Francisco Chinatown* (Berkeley and Los
    Angeles: University of California Press, 1987).

11. This letter was written by Saum Song Bo, published in *American Missionary*,
    39 (October 1885), no. 10, 290 and reprinted in *East/West Chinese American
    Journal* (San Francisco), June 26, 1986, and in *Bu Gao Ban* (New York China-
    town History Project), Summer/Fall issue, 1986, 2.

12. Sue Fawn Chung, "The Chinese American Citizens Alliance: An Effort in As-
    similation, 1895–1965," in *Chinese America: History and Perspectives*, 1988
    (San Francisco: Chinese Historical Society of America, 1988), 30–57; and
    Chapter 4 of this book.

13. Lei Zhuofeng, "1933-nian Niuyue Huaren Xiyiguan Lianhehui chengli qian-
    hou" [Before and after the establishment of the Chinese Hand Laundry Alliance
    of New York in 1933], in *Huaqiao shi lunwen ji* [Essays on overseas Chinese
    history], vol. 1 (Guangzhou: Ji'nan Daxue Huaqiao Yanjiusuo, 1981), 333–339.

14. Leong Gor Yun, *Chinatown Inside Out* (New York: Barrows Mussey, 1936),
    133. For various reasons, great differences exist between the number of the
    Chinese listed in the U.S. census and the estimates given by observers and the
    Chinese themselves. Usually, the Chinese estimate was larger than the num-
    ber given in the U.S. census. This is especially true in the case of New York,

a port of entry and departure. The 1930 U.S. census listed 75,000 Chinese in the United States, but the Chinese's estimate of themselves was between 100,000 and 150,000. See Ibid., 126.

15. According to Louis Beck, author of *New York's Chinatown*, two Chinese laundrymen's guilds existed in metropolitan New York in the nineteenth century, the Chop Sing Hong and the Sing Me Hong. These two hongs fixed service prices, defined each hand laundry shop's "district" to prevent encroachment, and supervised the selling and purchasing transactions of the laundry shops. In exercising their power, the two hongs cooperated closely with the "highest authority" in Chinatown—the Chinese Consolidated Benevolent Association, or CCBA. In fact, the CCBA's headquarters and the Sing Me Hong's were at the same location, 16 Mott Street. See Louis Beck, *New York's Chinatown: An Historical Presentation of Its People and Places* (New York: Bohemia Publishers, 1898), 59–61. This is the only brief account of the two hongs; we do not know when and why they ceased to exist. In any event, by the early 1930s they were gone, and the Chinese laundrymen in New York City had no organization of their own. According to a contemporary Chinese journalist, "If you were looking for the least organized class of workers before 1933, you could find no better example than the Chinese laundrymen." See Leong, *Chinatown Inside Out*, 86.

16. Leong, *Chinatown Inside Out*, 49–50.

17. *Minqi Ribao* [The *Chinese Nationalist Daily*] (New York City), April 10, 1933, 1; Y. K. Chu, *Meiguo Huaqiao gaishi* [History of the Chinese people in America] (New York: China Times, 1975), 115.

18. Lei Zhuofeng, "Niuyue Huaqiao xiyiguan lianhehui chengli jingguo" [The founding of the Chinese Hand Laundry Alliance of New York], *Guangzhou Wenshi Ziliao Xuanji* [Guangzhou Committee on Historical Materials] 22, no. 4 (1984): 216–222.

19. Leong, *Chinatown Inside Out*, 103.

20. For example, in Taishan county, which contributed almost half the Chinese emigrants to the United States in the nineteenth century, about 90 percent of the adult males were estimated to be more or less literate in 1910. See Liu Xiaoyun, "Chongjian Taishan zhi jihua" [The plan to rebuild Taishan], *Xinning Zazhi* [Xinning Magazine] 12 (1912); and Renqiu Yu, "Chinese American Contributions to the Educational Development of Toisan, 1910–1940," *Amerasia Journal*, 10, no. 1 (1983): 49–72.

21. Lin Yu-sheng, *The Crisis of Chinese Consciousness: Radical Antitraditionalism in the May Fourth Era* (Madison: University of Wisconsin Press, 1979); and Lloyd Eastman, *The Abortive Revolution: China under Nationalist Rule, 1927–1937* (Cambridge, Mass.: Harvard University Press, 1974).

22. See Akira Iriye, *China and Japan in the Global Setting* (Cambridge, Mass.: Harvard University Press, 1992). The quotation is from page 85.

23. Leong, *Chinatown Inside Out*, 95.

24. Ibid., 96–97; and *China Daily News* [*Meizhou Huaqiao Ribao*] (New York City), December 6, 1940, 7; January 15, 1941, 7; November 15, 1941, 7.

25. *Xianfeng Bao* [The *Chinese Vanguard*] (New York City), December 15, 1934, 1; December 22, 1934, 1; and the leaflet *All Overseas Chinese in New York City, Rise to Resist the Tong War!* distributed by the Su Zhaozheng branch of the International Labor Defense, November 24, 1934.

26. For details, see Yu, *To Save China, To Save Ourselves*, 71–76.

27. Interview with Mr. C., Chinatown, New York City, February 21, 1988.

28. Jinjian, "Fuwu jingshen yu zhandou jingshen" [The spirit of serving and the spirit of fighting], *China Daily News*, December 21–22, 1943, 6.

29. *China Daily News*, January 1, 1941, 2; August 25, 1941, 2.

30. *China Daily News*, July 8, 1940, 1.

31. *China Daily News*, July 31, 1940, 2.

32. A leading scholar in Chinese American history, Him Mark Lai, comments that "this is the opinion rarely heard in the Chinese communities in that time period." See Lai, "Meiguo Huaren jianshi" [A brief history of the Chinese in the United States], *Shi Dai Bao* [San Francisco Journal], December 30, 1981, 2. Further research may benefit from a comprehensive comparison of the *China Daily News*'s opinion with that of others.

33. *China Daily News*, July 8, 1940, 1.

34. *China Daily News*, November 3, 1942, 7.

35. *China Daily News*, November 1, 1942, 2.

36. *China Daily News*, October 24, 1942, 7.

37. *China Daily News*, November 2, 1942, 2.

38. This observation is based on a reading of the CHLA special column in the *China Daily News* from 1940 to 1948.

39. *China Daily News*, July 10, 1943, 6.

40. *China Daily News*, October 30, 1944, 6.

41. Fred W. Riggs, *Pressures on Congress: A Study of the Repeal of Chinese Exclusion* (New York: King's Crown Press, 1950), appendix, 210–211.

42. Ibid., 129.

43. Ibid., 113.

44. *China Daily News*, May 20, 1943, 7.

45. Dr. Arthur Hummel's testimony was published in the paper on May 21, 1943, 2; Pearl S. Buck's, on May 24, 1943, 3.

46. *China Daily News*, May 4, 1943, 2.

47. *China Daily News*, October 23, 1943, 2.

48. Him Mark Lai, "Historical Development of the Chinese Consolidated Benevolent Association/Huiguan System," in *Chinese America: History and Perspectives, 1987* (San Francisco: Chinese Historical Society of America, 1987), 13–51.

49. Gunther Barth, *Bitter Strength: A History of the Chinese in the United States, 1850–1870* (Cambridge, Mass.: Harvard University Press, 1964), 100.

50. Liu, *Meiguo Huaqiao shi*, 182, 191.

51. CCBA bylaws, article 7, sections (a) and (b). Liu Pei Chi, *Meiguo Huaqiao shi, xubian* [A history of the Chinese in the United States of America, II] (Taipei: Limin Wenhua Shiye Gongsi, 1981), 185.

52. Ibid., 184, 186.

53. Warner Van Norden, *Who's Who of the Chinese in New York* (New York: n.p., 1918), 84.

54. For a criticism of the CCBA's inefficiency, see Liang Qichao, *Xindalu youji* [Diary of traveling in the New World] (Japan: Xinmincongbao, 1904; reprint, Changsha: Hunan Renmin Chubanshe, 1981).

55. Liu, *Meiguo Huaqiao shi, xubian*, 189.

56. Ibid., 188.

57. Ibid., 189; Leong, *Chinatown Inside Out*, 35–37.

58. "Promoting the Democratization of the Overseas Chinese Community," *China Daily News*, June 23, 1947, 2.

59. Some letters were published in the *China Daily News*. For a sample, see "Xielei jiashu baogao Taishan jihuang canxiang" [A blood-and-tears letter from home reporting Taishan famine], *China Daily News*, October 16, 1942, 2.

60. Lu Ming, "Gaodeng nanmin zai Meiguo suozuo heshi?" [What are the high-class refugees doing in the U.S.?] *China Daily News*, December 4, 1944, 3. Earlier reports on the high-class refugees include one *China Daily News* editorial, "Zhenzhi shang de tanwu bixu gengjue" [Political corruption must end], *China Daily News*, October 27, 1942, 2.

61. *China Daily News*, August 14, 1945, 6.

62. *China Daily News*, November 17, 1943, 7.

63. *Taishan Xianzi* [The Taishan Gazetteer] (comp. Taishan Archives, Taishan, Guangdong, 1985), 76–90. During the 1943 Taishan famine, many atrocities were committed, including cannibalism. The story of these events, reported in the United States, deeply distressed many Chinese Americans. For example, see *China Daily News*, July 31, 1944, 6.

64. *China Daily News*, November 11, 1943, 7.

65. *China Daily News*, April 3, 1944, 2–3.

66. Li Yan, "Comments on the Political Consultant Conference," *China Daily News*, January 29, 1946, 6.

67. Wu Yushu, "Inaugural Address," *China Daily News*, December 30, 1944, 6.

68. John Higham, *Send These to Me: Jews and Other Immigrants in Urban America* (New York: Atheneum, 1975), 237, 241–242.

69. Oscar Handlin, *The Uprooted: The Epic Story of the Great Migrations That Made the American People*, 2d enl. ed. (Boston: Little, Brown, 1973).

70. *China Daily News*, September 18, 1955.

PART II

THE AMERICAN-BORN
GENERATIONS

Fighting for Their American Rights: A History of the Chinese American Citizens Alliance

SUE FAWN CHUNG

BY THE 1890S MANY AMERICAN-BORN CHINESE EDUCATED IN the American public school system had become adults. Their numbers had risen from a mere one percent of the total Chinese-ancestry population in the United States in 1870 to eleven percent in 1900 (see Table 4.1). In San Francisco, the proportion was even higher: the 4,767 American-born Chinese represented 34 percent of the Chinese-ancestry population in that city.[1] Fluent in English, these young men and women coming of age had greater potential for contact with the surrounding Euro-American community. Brought up in the United States, they also had a greater desire to interact with the majority society and to participate in the American political process. Some had acculturated to such a degree that they felt uncomfortable with the conservative, China-oriented segment of the population; others, raised among Euro-Americans, could not even identify with the other Chinese.[2] The latter, for their part, often referred to the new generation derisively as "ABCs" (literally "American-born Chinese" but implying "brainless" or *juk sing* [in Cantonese, literally the hollow part of a bamboo stalk but meaning "empty" or "useless"]).[3] A generation gap consequently developed between the immigrant generation and their progeny.

Members of the two generations, however, had encountered one thing in common: racial discrimination. Though Americans by birthright, fluent in English, and familiar with American culture, most, if not all, of the native-born Chinese Americans had nevertheless experienced some form of racial discrimination. The effects of the anti-Chinese movement

TABLE 4.1. Nativity of Chinese Males in the United States, 1850–1950

Year	Total Population	Foreign Born (%)	Native Born (%)	Total Males	Percent	Native Born	Percent	Foreign Born	Percent
1850	758	—	—	—	—	—	—	—	—
1860	34,933	—	—	33,149	95	—	—	—	—
1870	63,199	99	1	58,633	93	308	1	58,325	92
1880	105,465	98	2	100,686	95.5	648	1	100,038	95
1890	107,488	—	—	103,620	96	—	—	—	—
1900	89,863	89	11	85,341	95	6,657	7	78,684	88
1910	71,531	79	21	66,856	94	11,921	17	54,935	77
1920	61,639	70	30	53,891	87	13,318	22	40,573	66
1930	74,954	59	41	59,802	80	20,693	28	39,109	52
1940	77,504	48	52	57,389	74	25,702	33	31,687	41
1950	117,629	46	54	77,008	66	36,399	31	40,609	35

— = No separate figures available.

Sources: Data calculated from the tables on the characteristics of the population on race, nativity, and sex from the following sources:

U.S. Superintendent of the United States Census, *The Seventh Census of the United States: 1850* (Washington, D.C.: Robert Armstrong, 1853), Table 15, 758.

U.S. Department of the Interior, Census Office, *The Ninth Census, Vol. 1: The Statistics of the Population of the United States* (Washington, D.C.: Government Printing Office, 1872), 8.

U.S. Department of the Interior, Census Office, *The Tenth Census: Compendium, Part I* (Washington, D.C.: Government Printing Office, 1883), 3, 334. 557 covering 1860–1880.

U.S. Department of the Interior, Census Office, *Compendium of the Eleventh Census: 1890,* (Washington, D.C.: Government Printing Office, 1894), Part I, 474, 516–524, 580–581; Part II, 603, 653.

U.S. Census Office, *Twelfth Census of the United States Taken in the Year 1900, Vol. 1: Census Reports, Part I: Population* (Washington, D.C.: U.S. Census Office, 1901), cxxii, 483, 487.

U.S. Department of Commerce, Bureau of the Census, *Thirteenth Census of the United States Taken in the Year 1910, Vol. 1: Population, 1910* (Washington, D.C.: Government Printing Office, 1913), 128, 132, 146, 273, 789.

U.S. Department of Commerce, Bureau of the Census, *The Fourteenth Census of the United States, Vol. 2: Population, 1920* (Washington, D.C.: Government Printing Office, 1922), 29, 101–103.

U.S. Department of Commerce, Bureau of the Census, *The Fifteenth Census of the United States: 1930, Population, Vol. 2: General Report, Statistics by Subjects* (Washington, D.C.: Government Printing Office, 1933), 34, 101 covering 1900–1930.

U.S. Department of Commerce, Bureau of the Census, *The Sixteenth Census of the United States: 1940, Population, Vol. 2: Characteristics of the Population of the United States* (Washington, D.C.: Government Printing Office, 1943), 19, 21.

U.S. Department of Commerce, Bureau of the Census, *A Report of the Seventeenth Decennial Census of the United States: Census of the Population: 1950, Vol. 2: Characteristics of the Population of the United States, Part I: United States Summary* (Washington, D.C.: Government Printing Office, 1953), 88, 106.

of the 1870s and early 1880s, which culminated in the passage of the 1882 Chinese Exclusion Act, were still keenly felt within the Chinese American communities.[4] In particular, a small group of native-born Chinese Americans in San Francisco believed that the 1892 Geary Act, which renewed the 1882 Chinese Exclusion Act and made it far more stringent, violated the rights not only of the immigrant generation but also of themselves as American citizens. In their opinion, political action by American citizens was required because the Chinese Six Companies (also known as the Chinese Consolidated Benevolent Association, or CCBA) and the Chinese minister to the United States could only make ineffective written protests to the U.S. government about the Geary Act. Another group of Chinese Americans, in New York City, founded the Chinese Equal Rights League and appeared before the U.S. House of Representatives Committee on Foreign Affairs. The League also assisted in the preparation of a test case that was eventually brought before the U.S. Supreme Court. Its members participated in other political activities as well.[5] (See Chapter 2 of this book.) All of these Chinese efforts came to naught when the Supreme Court upheld the constitutionality of the Geary Act on May 15, 1893 in *Fong Yue Ting* v. *United States* (149 U.S. 698). The failure of the Chinese Six Companies, the activities of the New York Chinese Equal Rights League, growing anti-Chinese sentiment, and the increasing number of Chinese Americans prompted several young Chinese Americans in San Francisco to establish an organization to defend their rights as American citizens.

Formative Years

On May 4, 1895, the small group of Chinese Americans mentioned in the previous section, encouraged by an unidentified Euro-American attorney, met at 753 Clay Street in San Francisco's Chinatown to discuss the creation of a fraternal organization through which they could exercise their civil rights, express their patriotism, and promote American social and cultural activities. They would elevate their position so that the foreign-born Chinese would respect them, fight discrimination, and accelerate their process of assimilation into American society.[6] They chose the name United Parlor of the Native Sons of the Golden State (NSGS), which was later changed to the Chinese American Citizens Alliance (CACA). Their stated purpose was "to fully enjoy and defend our American citizenship; to cultivate the mind through the exchange of knowledge; to effect a higher character among the members; and to fully observe and practice the principles of Brotherly Love and mutual help."[7]

The group elected seven men as officers: Chun Dick, president; Sue Lock, vice president; Ng Gunn, secretary; Li Tai Wing, treasurer; Leong Sing, marshal; and Leong Chung and Lan J. Foy, inside sentinel and outside sentinel, respectively. On May 10, 1895, they filed the Articles of Incorporation for their organization with the county clerk of the city and county of San Francisco.

The NSGS members had conscientiously modeled their organization after the politically powerful and influential but virulently anti-Asian Native Sons of the Golden West (NSGW).[8] The NSGW was a guild founded in 1875 by and for native-born Euro-Americans primarily of English, Irish, German, French, and Italian descent, who were "unparalleled in physical development and mental vigor and unsurpassed in pride and enthusiasm for the land that gave them birth."[9] By 1895, the San Francisco–based NSGW had expanded into many parts of California, and by 1897, two hundred parlors had been formed. At first, the NSGS tried to affiliate with the NSGW because of their identical birthplace requirements and their similar objectives and organizational structure; however, this effort failed. The NSGW objected to the similarity of the two names. After exhausting legal remedies, however, the NSGW could not force the NSGS to change its name.

The NSGS created a political-social structure in which Chinese Americans could achieve some degree of communitywide recognition. The early leaders were usually professionals or white-collar workers with at least an American high school education, and more commonly some college education or a college degree. Little is known about Chun Dick other than that he came from a wealthy San Francisco mercantile family and eventually moved to New York. In 1896, the presidency of the organization went to Robert Leon Park, also known as Leong Qui Pak and Len Pak,[10] who had graduated from a San Francisco high school; attended the University of California, Berkeley; and was a charter member.[11] The group expressed its opinion about the upcoming U.S. presidential election and tried to persuade other Chinese Americans to vote. Some members of the older generation scoffed at these young men's efforts, and the generational differences in attitudes about the organization's potential political effectiveness created a chasm. Apparently the leadership was not strong enough to hold the organization together. The NSGS gradually became inactive, but Robert Leon Park, who worked for the U.S. Immigration and Naturalization Service, left his imprint on the organization because the NSGS/CACA, which was subsequently revived, continues to this day to work on Chinese immigration issues.

Problems related to Chinese immigration prompted the revival of the organization. In 1902, the U.S. Senate Committee on Immigration conducted more hearings on Chinese exclusion and, according to Xiao Yishan, the Chinese were poorly represented.[12] Chinese minister to the United States Wu Tingfang complained about the unreasonable application of the 1894 Gresham-Yang Treaty and the discriminatory treatment of the Chinese, but his speeches fell upon deaf ears.[13] In January 1904, the Chinese government refused to renew the 1894 Treaty. This refusal did not prevent Congress from reenacting and continuing all exclusion legislation indefinitely and unconditionally. At this juncture, Walter Uriah Lum (1882–1961), Joseph K. Lum, and Ng Gunn, one of the original founders, revived the NSGS under its original charter.[14]

Walter U. Lum's background was characteristic of many of the young male NSGS members. His parents, Lum Guey Yue[15] and Yan Lan, and older sister, Lum Choy Fung, then aged five or so, had emigrated from Xinhui in the Siyi area of Guangdong province in the 1860s.[16] His father's brother, Lum Guey Yee, had paved the way and sent home stories of the riches to be made in mining. However, instead of mining, the Lum brothers, in keeping with a typical Xinhui tradition, opened a grocery store in the Sacramento River area, catering to Chinese and Euro-American miners until 1879, when they moved to San Francisco to open another grocery store. In 1882, Walter, the fourth child and only son, was born in San Francisco. His parents believed that he would be teased in the American school system because of his Chinese-style clothing and Manchu-required queue, so he was taught by private American and Chinese tutors. Realizing the importance of English in this country, his parents stressed his English-language studies. In 1899, he met and married Lee Gum Yung (1885–1939), who eventually gave birth to seven children. By the mid-1900s, he was working as a clerk in Look Yuen Hing's Sing Chong Bazaar on Grant Avenue in San Francisco's Chinatown. One day in 1904, while Lum was playing billiards with his closest friends, Joseph Lum and Ng Gunn, the young men decided that Chinese Americans needed to be protected from the abuses of the times and to fight for their rights, so they revived the NSGS.

These men were not alone in wanting to demand an end to the discriminatory practices of Euro-Americans against Chinese immigrants. In 1905, protestors in China launched an anti-American boycott to express their anger over the 1904 Chinese Exclusion Act.[17] Lum and his friends persuaded other young Chinese Americans to join, and they gradually gained the respect of the community for speaking out against discrimination.[18] Walter Lum became the president of the local organization and held the grand presidency in 1912, 1914, 1915–1917, 1923–1929, and 1933–1935.[19] Under his leadership and that of those who followed, the organization developed and expanded.

The revival of the NSGS occurred at a time of rising political consciousness in San Francisco's Chinatown. Leaders of the Empire Reform Party (Baohuanghui) and the Revolutionary Party (Tongmenghui) were wooing overseas Chinese in an effort to bring about political change in China. In 1908, Huang Boyao, who headed the NSGS, committed the organization to support the Empire Reform Party.[20] Around 1910, however, Huang found himself in an awkward position because he was also a member of the Zhigongtang, an organization then supporting the Revolutionary Party of Sun Yat-sen. In the end, he sided with the more radical group. In the winter of 1910, the Revolutionary Party began its daily newspaper, *Young China* (Shaonian Zhongguo chenbao) and Huang became one of its four editors.[21] Between 1910 and 1912, Chinese Americans and Chinese immigrants followed the political developments in China through Chinese-language newspapers and American newspapers. In 1912, Sun Yat-sen established the Republic of China. The revolutionaries had overthrown the Manchu rulers and for many Chinese Americans, the promise of a stronger, more modernized Chinese government seemed bright. Numerous news stories about China appeared in the English-language press in the western United States. Also in 1912, Walter U. Lum, while holding his NSGS presidency, joined the staff of *Young China*, working as a reporter, a translator, and later an editor.[22] This was the beginning of his thirty-five years as a newsman.

The excitement over China spilled over into political concern about the civil rights of the Chinese in America. Because of the initial success of the NSGS, others outside San Francisco also wanted to join the organization, and other Asian Americans tried to establish similar associations. The Articles of Incorporation permitted the organization "to establish subordinate lodges, parlors, or branches with such members, officers, authorities, and powers as the society may determine . . . " In 1912, local lodges were founded in San Francisco (incorporated May 15, 1912), Los Angeles (same date), and Oakland (June 21, 1912). The original parlor became the Grand Lodge, with Walter U. Lum as its president. When a lodge in Fresno was opened on January 18, 1914, and one in San Diego soon followed, the organization became statewide.[23] This growth prompted the leaders to plan for the construction of a head-quarters for the Grand Lodge. Like the NSGW, the NSGS had the power to sell, rent, lease, mortgage, improve, and otherwise dispose of and deal in real estate and personal property. Despite discriminatory real estate practices, the NSGS was able to purchase a lot and construct a head-quarters at 1044 Stockton Street, San Francisco. It was completed on August 10, 1921, at a cost of $135,000 and stands at the same location today.[24] The funds came from a bank loan and a building fund of $40 levied upon each member. By the mid–twentieth century, the loan had been paid off and the organization had complete ownership.[25] The increasing visibility of the organization prompted Chinese Americans outside California to ask to affiliate with the NSGS, but because they did not reside in the Golden State, the name could not be used. To expand outside California, the name of the organization had to be changed.

To become a national organization, at its third annual convention held in Los Angeles in 1915, the NSGS proposed a new name to be adopted some time in the future: Chinese American Citizens Alliance. Local lodges were formed in Chicago (March 28, 1917), Detroit, Boston, Pittsburgh, and Portland (February 24, 1921). Table 4.2 shows the Chinese population in these cities and the number of members in each city. Some attempts were made to bring New York into the organization, but by 1923, New York had established its own Chinese American Citizens Alliance, and although the English name was the same, the Chinese name was different.[26] The Chinese in New York, originating from a wider geographic area in China, would not link up with the CACA until after 1965.

Because the organization had expanded to ten lodges by 1927, the old Articles of Incorporation and the constitution were considered to be too vague. In addition, the name identification with the anti-Asian NSGW was no longer desirable. Young NSGS members resented the leadership role of NSGW members in the anti-Japanese agitation of the 1910s and 1920s that resulted in numerous discriminatory laws. Moreover, some of the NSGS members also belonged to the Ancient Arabic Order of the Nobles of the Mystic Shrine for North America, popularly called the Shriners, and believed that the new Articles of Incorporation and constitution should be modeled after the respective documents of the Shriners. Therefore, in 1927, changes, many of which had been proposed in 1915, began to be made. At a special convention held in San Francisco from November 15 to December 4, 1928, a new Articles of Incorporation, constitution, and name were adopted; they were filed in

TABLE 4.2. Chinese Population in Cities with NSGS/CACA Lodges, 1910–1930

City and State	1910			1920			1930		
	No. of Chinese	No. of Members	% Who Were Members	No. of Chinese	No. of Members	% Who Were Members	No. of Chinese	No. of Members	% Who Were Members
San Francisco, Calif.	10,582	3,675	35	7,744	3,294	43	16,303	7,754	48
Oakland, Calif.	3,609	1,086	30	3,821	1,225	32	3,048	1,682	55
Fresno, Calif.	975	—		617	—		747	—	
Los Angeles, Calif.	1,954	476	24	2,062	802	39	3,009	1,421	47
San Diego, Calif.	348	51	15	254	83	33	509	214	42
Portland, Oreg.	5,699	613	11	1,846	609	33	1,416	786	56
Chicago, Ill.	1,778	455	26	2,353	708	30	2,757	933	34
Detroit, Mich.	28	4	14	438	169	39	710	273	38
Pittsburgh, Pa.	236	41	17	306	93	30	296	100	34
Boston, Mass.	1,192	376	32	1,192	333	28	1,595	636	40

—No separate figures available.

Sources: Statistics of number of Chinese calculated from the tables on the characteristics of the population on race from the following sources:

U.S. Department of Commerce, Bureau of the Census, *Thirteenth Census of the United States Taken in the Year 1910, Vol. 1: Population, 1910,* (Washington, D.C.: Government Printing Office, 1913), 128, 132, 146, 273, 789.

U.S. Department of Commerce, Bureau of the Census, *The Fourteenth Census of the United States, Vol. 2: Population, 1920,* (Washington, D.C.: Government Printing office, 1922), 29, 101–103.

U.S. Department of Commerce, Bureau of the Census, *The Fifteenth Census of the United States: 1930, Population, Vol. 2: General Report, Statistics by Subjects* (Washington, D.C.: Government Printing Office, 1933), 34, 101, covering 1900–1930.

Statistics on membership were reported in the Chinese American Citizens Alliance, *Mei-chou t'ung-yuan tsung-hui chih ch'eng ti shih chieh shuang chou ken-chin-tai-hui pao-kao-lu* [Proceedings of the Biennial Convention of the Chinese American Citizens Alliance, Grand Lodge] (San Francisco: Chinese American Citizens Alliance Grand Lodge, 1923, 1925, 1927, 1929, 1931], "Reports on Membership," n.p.

San Francisco on December 14, 1928, and became effective after the 1929 convention in Boston. Thus, the Chinese American Citizens Alliance was born.

The new Articles of Incorporation were more specific and sophisticated; the purpose of the organization was now

> To unite citizens of the United States of Chinese descent into close bonds, to elevate the moral standard among its members, to disseminate among them the true ideas of personal and public morality as well as principles of political rights and liberties and the duties of true citizenship; to promote the general welfare and happiness of its members and the Chinese communities in America; to quicken the spirit of American patriotism and to encourage and promote education; to use every effort to have its members perform their duties as American citizens; to insure and protect the legal rights of its members and to secure equal economic and political opportunities for them; to promote social intercourse and friendly feeling among the members.... To establish, maintain, manage, and control newspapers and other enterprises in conjunction with and for the purpose of carrying out the objects of this corporation, provided, however, that such newspapers or enterprises shall not be conducted or operated in any way for any gain or profit, but solely for the purpose of better carrying out the objects of this corporation. To organize auxiliaries [such as the Mandarins and Bears, younger groups], to affiliate with other associations, and make rules for the regulation of the same.[27]

The cardinal principles, however, were derived from the original Articles:

> To fully enjoy and defend our American citizenship; to cultivate the mind through the exchange of knowledge; to effect a higher character among the members; and to fully observe and practice the principles of Brotherly Love and mutual help. It is imperative that no member have sectional, clannish, tong, or party prejudices against one another, or to use such influences to oppress fellow members.[28]

Thus, the organization had a new name and delineated its aims, which would be executed through the Grand Lodge and the local lodges. The interest in establishing a newspaper was the result of Walter U. Lum's experience at the *Young China* office. Themselves young men when the organization was started, the leaders recognized the need to channel the next generation's energies and thus made provisions for a younger group. Moreover, because of Lum's experience with the controversies over the Chinese political parties and "fighting tongs" in Chinatown, during which his life was threatened,[29] the last sentence was added to the cardinal principles.

Members

The members of the CACA were usually born and raised in the United States and had little knowledge about old or contemporary China. The Chinatowns had preserved many of the Old World customs, but not in their complete form. Some of the adaptations bore little resemblance to anything found in South China, whereas others preserved older traditions that had already been forgotten in China with the passage of time.[30] These adaptations of traditions were passed on from the first immigrant generation to the second generation, who selected only the customs and practices that it considered useful and practical. The same process was repeated by the next generation. In many respects, Winifred Raushenbush was correct when she wrote in May 1926, "The native-born, who have Chinese Native Sons' Parlors up and down the Coast, know little about either old China or the new. . . ."[31] They were different from the older, first-generation Chinese immigrants because their orientation was toward the United States, their birthplace.

At the same time, because of the high visibility of the Chinese in the United States and the discrimination that they experienced, the Chinese Americans were acutely aware of their racial differences and cultural heritage.[32] As described by Kit King Louis in 1932:

> While the American-born Chinese are in grammar schools, they are proud of their citizenship. As they advance in the schools and have more contact with the American community, they begin to feel discrimination against them and race-consciousness develops. They wake up from an illusion; many feel disappointed and pass through a period of emotional disturbance. Some find satisfaction in returning to their own group . . . and some maintain the attitude that they should organize themselves to struggle for citizenship rights.[33]

Chinese Americans who came of age during the 1920s and who had been educated in the American public school system provided the foundation for the CACA. They differed from the men of Walter U. Lum's and Huang Boyao's generation in that they did not know the Chinese language as well as Lum and Huang did, even though most of them had been sent to daily Chinese-language school after the regular American school session. Their parents sent them to such classes in the belief that these young people's future occupations would involve working with Chinese-speaking people, given the limited opportunities in the Euro-American community.[34] The emphasis of these Chinese-language schools was on oral communication, with some elementary reading, an introduction to Chinese culture, and socialization to Chinese norms. The bilingualism of the CACA members was taken for granted, but with each passing decade, more and more of the members had little, if any, Chinese-language education. Although the monthly lodge meetings were conducted in English, the minutes of the meetings were kept in Chinese until the Grand Lodge passed resolutions in 1953 to record all proceedings in both English and Chinese. Beginning in 1957, all bookkeeping and correspondence was in English only.

Being a member of the organization established a person as a Chinese American community leader. From its inception until 1976, when the CACA first admitted women, the membership was restricted to American male citizens of Chinese ancestry who were twenty-one years of age or older, of good character, and capable of self-support. Beginning in the 1930s, some men younger than twenty-one years old were able to affiliate with the organization in recognition of the youthfulness of the original charter members. A prospective member had to be sponsored by two members in good standing, and his application was reviewed by a screening committee, which made its recommendation to the lodge members at the next monthly meeting. Three members in good standing could blackball an applicant from that lodge or any other local lodge for two years. According to Y. C. Hong, grand president of the CACA from 1949–1953, "An invitation to join the Alliance is and has always been regarded as recognition of one's intellectual achievement, ability, and dedication to help better the lives of his fellowmen as well as become better Americans."[35] There was, and continues to be, a large percentage of professional men, especially lawyers, medical doctors, dentists, newsmen, federal and state government employees, and businessmen, in the CACA. This upper stratum, or elite, of Chinese American society certainly had the potential to assimilate into American society should the barriers of discrimination be lowered. However, because this was not the case during the early years of the organization, the members had to work within the Chinese community. They nonetheless gained satisfaction from this work.[36]

Membership expanded throughout the first three decades of the twentieth century because of the growing number of U.S.-born Chinese in America. From 11 percent of the total Chinese population in 1900, Chinese Americans increased to 21 percent in 1910, 30 percent in 1920, 41 percent in 1930, and 52 percent in 1940 (see Table 4.1). By the 1930s, in some cities, the CACA members represented a majority of the Chinese Americans who were U.S. citizens in those localities with lodges. Unfortunately, no statistics are available on how many had gained citizenship through naturalization (this number would be extremely small anyway because naturalization was prohibited by law, although rare exceptions were made) or by derivation. Derivative citizens were born in China to fathers who were American citizens.

The number of lodges and the size of the membership shifted during the next several decades. After 1950, interest in expanding the organization nationally revived in response to the anticipated changes in immigration laws. During the 1950s, lodges were established in Salinas (1952), Houston (1954), San Antonio (1955), and Albuquerque (1961). In 1993, fifteen lodges existed, one each in San Francisco, Oakland, Los Angeles, Portland, Chicago, Salinas, Houston, San Antonio, Albuquerque, New York, Washington, D.C., Tucson, Phoenix, Sacramento, and Peninsula (California). The CACA's success in increasing its membership was due to its political, economic, and social activities. In the cities where membership declined, the main cause was the establishment and growth of other American-oriented political and social organizations that rivaled the CACA's goals and purposes.

Political Activities

In the spirit of the founding members of the NSGS, CACA members used their rights as citizens to try to redress many of the existing discriminatory policies and acts, especially with regard to immigration, imposed upon the Chinese in the United States. Robert Leon Park, with his connection to the U.S. Immigration and Naturalization Service, undoubtedly had a great interest in this topic. He left a legacy of serving as an "immigration watchdog." Following that tradition, Walter Lum went beyond local and state political bodies to the federal government when he and his brother-in-law, Wong Bock Yue, fought for fairer laws for the Chinese. One of the early political efforts focused upon repealing the Act of March 2, 1907, which stated "that any American woman who marries a foreigner shall take the nationality of her husband."[37] This effort was unsuccessful. Lum and Wong opposed the proposed laws forbidding families left behind in China from joining the men in the United States and permitting the deportation of Chinese because of minor ailments and other trivial causes.[38] When they could not get satisfaction from officials in Sacramento, they went to Washington, D.C., but experienced great frustration. At this point, Walter Lum decided to appeal directly to President Woodrow Wilson during the latter's first term in office to help end injustices against Chinese Americans, though to no avail. Today, the CACA continues that tradition of lobbying and appealing to government officials and agencies on behalf of Chinese Americans and their families.

One of the early political activities that brought the NSGS prestige was its apparent success in 1913 in blocking the proposal by California State Senator Anthony Caminetti (who represented the Tenth District of Alpine, Amador, Calaveras, El Dorado, and Mono from 1907 to 1913) to disenfranchise Chinese Americans.[39] Through their success, NSGS members showed the Chinese community that they, as Americans, could effect change for the benefit of the community while simultaneously making a name for themselves among Euro-Americans.

The NSGS also gained national fame in its efforts against the 1924 Immigration Act, sometimes also called the National Origins Quota Act of 1924, sections 4 and 13.[40] At its 1925 convention, the grand council decided to present its grievances to Congress and appointed as the organization's spokesman Y. C. Hong, who had been born in San Francisco in 1899, worked for the U. S. Immigration and Naturalization Service from 1918 to 1928, and received his law degree from the University of Southern California in 1925. On behalf of the NSGS, Hong wrote a letter to Congress charging that the 1924 Act was contrary to Americanism and that the U. S. government was not fulfilling its responsibility to protect and help all American citizens. He pleaded for major revisions. Several NSGS representatives—including Hong and Peter Soo Hoo of the Los Angeles lodge; Kenneth Fung, Peter Lum, and Walter U. Lum of the San Francisco lodge; Wu Lai Sun of the Portland lodge; and George Fong of the Detroit lodge—appeared before the U.S. Senate Subcommittee on Immigration several times regarding this matter. The nonaffiliated organization in New York and other Chinese American community organizations supported the group. Hong wrote a pamphlet entitled *A Plea for Relief Together with a Supplement Containing Some Arguments in Support Thereof,* and testified on February 6, 1928 at the Senate Subcommittee hearing: "The right of a man to have his wife with him in this country . . . is a fundamental right recognized, not only in civilized society, but even among savages . . . . But this right is denied to us who are American citizens."[41] He pointed out that 80 percent of the Chinese population in the United States was male; therefore, the only ways in which a Chinese American male could marry were to marry outside the race, which was prohibited in many states; to marry a foreigner outside the race who could enter as a nonquota immigrant; or to go to China and marry a woman whom he might not see but once every ten years. An articulate speaker, Hong made an impact. A compromise was finally reached, and on June 13, 1930, the 1924 Act was amended to permit alien wives married before May 26, 1924, to enter the United States. When the Judd Bill (H.R. 199), passed by the House of Representatives on March 1, 1946, eliminated the nonquota status of Chinese wives, the CACA lobbyists persuaded U.S. senators to kill the bill in the Senate. Final victory was attained only on August 9, 1946, when Chinese wives of American citizens were granted nonquota status. Albert and William Jack Chow, immigration attorneys who worked with Y. C. Hong and Peter Soo Hoo, Sr., and who were members of the CACA, related the story of how the bill to place the Chinese alien wives on a nonquota basis was languishing in committee because of the powerful chair's somewhat obvious hostility against Chinese, but the Chow brothers, through a friendly interaction, managed to persuade him to get the bill passed.[42] A similar privilege was extended to husbands of American citizens in the McCarran-Walter Act of 1952. The CACA tenaciously fought against other discriminatory legislation by lobbying in this manner and by testifying before Congress.

As mentioned previously, because several CACA leaders had worked for or were employed by the U.S. Immigration and Naturalization Service, immigration issues were of great concern to them. Many Chinese American citizens appealed to them for assistance, and they handled large and small cases. An example of this was the case of Chin Bow (Chen Bao), who arrived in Seattle, Washington, on July 9, 1924, at the age of ten. His grandfather was born in the United States and his father, although born in China, gained derivative American citizenship through Chin Bow's grandfather.[43] In 1922, Chin Bow's father came to the United States and established his residency. Chin Bow followed but was not permitted to enter because he was an alien. When his case was taken to the U. S. District Court in Seattle, he won, but Commissioner Weedin of the Immigration and Naturalization Service appealed the decision in the U.S. Ninth Circuit Court of Appeals in San Francisco. Chin Bow's father turned to the CACA for help, and the Grand Lodge assisted him in hiring an attorney and contributed $250 to defray his legal fees. The court decided in favor of Chin Bow, but Commissioner Weedin was adamant and took the case to the U.S. Supreme Court. The Grand Lodge gave more legal and financial assistance to the Chin family. However, this time, on June 6, 1927, the Supreme Court reversed the decision of the lower courts and declared that Chin Bow was not a citizen because his father had not resided in the United States prior to the boy's birth. The final decision was a blow to the numerous separated Chinese families, but it spurred the CACA to be even more active in other similar cases.

The CACA was involved in other national legislation as well. The leaders recognized that many seemingly innocuous bills were subtly directed against the Chinese. One example was the 1925 "Cinch Bill" to regulate the manufacture, sale, and use of herbs, roots, and other natural products used in the treatment of disease, which would have adversely affected Chinese doctors who were practicing traditional medicine. The CACA successfully worked to defeat the bill.

In another example, some CACA members worked informally for the repeal of the Chinese exclusion acts—a repeal signed into law by President Franklin D. Roosevelt on December 17, 1943. However, Fred Riggs, who studied the repeal process, thought that most of the credit for ending the 1882 Act should go to the Citizens Committee to Repeal Chinese Exclusion, an Euro-American group.[44] Political pressures that arose because China had become a U.S. ally during World War II and speculation that China could still be a great market for American goods and a source of raw materials contributed to the passage of the Repeal Act of 1943. This act gave the right of naturalization to Chinese who had lawfully entered the United States, thus expanding the potential membership of the CACA, and allowed, in accordance with the formula contained in the 1924 Immigration Act, a quota of 105 Chinese immigrants annually.

Members of the CACA likewise were active during the hearings on the McCarran-Walter Act of 1952, which was passed when the Cold War was at its height.[45] This act gave the right of naturalization and property ownership to all Asians and accorded a nonquota status to wives of Asians who were permanent residents, but it retained the national origins quota system of 1924. The CACA criticized the absence of judicial review of consular discretion and decisions and the arbitrary administration of the law by American consular officials in Hong Kong. In 1955, the Grand Council voted to send representatives to Washington, D.C., to participate in the hearings for revisions of the act in November of that year. Then in 1957, the CACA published and widely distributed a pamphlet entitled *Current Report by San Francisco Lodge on Changes in Immigration and Nationality Act,* which described in detail the CACA's position and recommendations. The organization's vigilance in this matter continued during the next few years. At its 1963 convention, the Grand Council supported the amendment of section 249 of the McCarran-Walter Act, which changed the date from June 28, 1940, to December 24, 1952, for the admission of Chinese aliens to the United States and had a bearing upon the granting of permanent resident status to Chinese aliens as well as other foreigners. The CACA also supported President John F. Kennedy's proposal on immigration and H.R. 7903, "Amending and Revising the Immigration and Nationality Act." Not only did the CACA send representatives and lobbyists to Washington, D.C., but the organization also asked members to urge other Chinese Americans to support its position through letters to Congress and to create a greater interest in these matters in Chinese American communities. In recent years, the CACA has joined with organizations representing other minority groups to fight in Congress and in the courts against injustices.

Another political activity of the CACA has been to encourage its members and other Chinese Americans to vote. Members must vote or they are fined.[46] In the 1944 election, for example, the Los Angeles lodge had 270 members who were eligible to vote and these members persuaded 700 other Chinese Americans to register to vote at the lodge.[47] In 1992, after twenty-two months of volunteer work to determine voter eligibility, the San Francisco lodge proudly announced that 90 percent (774) of its members were registered voters.[48] In this way, Chinese Americans earned the reputation of political activism during election campaigns.

The lodges also have supported measures that protected the interests and welfare of the Chinese American community and have sponsored informative programs about candidates and election issues for members and the general public.[49] For example, in 1992, the San Francisco lodge hosted the candidates for the Board of Education and questioned them about new immigrant students in middle schools where no special transitional assistance was provided, the alienation of new immigrant students, parent involvement in education, racial tensions in the schools, bilingual teachers, and interaction with the Asian community.[50] The effect of this kind of activity was related by Samuel E. Yee, grand secretary in 1964–1965 and former president of the San Francisco lodge, who also served as deputy city attorney of the city and county of San Francisco: "Our survey that is made by the San Francisco Lodge each year shows that our recommendations and endorsements invariably are followed by the general electorate among Chinese-American voters."[51] The CACA recommendations have been followed more closely by older Chinese Americans who are not as fluent in English as the younger generations.

When American women acquired the right to vote in 1920, the CACA members considered establishing auxiliaries for members' wives, to encourage all U.S.-born Chinese women, who had outnumbered foreign-born Chinese women since 1900, to vote,[52] but no formal organization materialized. Some lodges, including those in Los Angeles and San Francisco, established unofficial women's auxiliaries for members' wives, with their own officers, beginning in the 1940s. Responding to the criticism that the CACA membership might be more effective if, like the Japanese-American Citizens League, men and women could join and participate on an equal basis, the Portland lodge of the CACA proposed the inclusion of women as full members. At first the proposal was defeated, but after much lobbying, the CACA decided to include female members. In 1976, Mrs. Noel Lim became the first female member. Another landmark was reached in 1991 when Virginia C. Gee was elected the first female president of the San Francisco lodge. The next year, Joyce Chen followed as president of the Oakland lodge. According to one anonymous interviewee, women have not yet attained full equality in terms of power and influence in the organization. However, a foundation has been laid with the two female local lodge presidencies. More women with leadership abilities are needed to strengthen the role of women in the organization.

CACA members have participated in other types of local, state, and national political activities. A few members have run for local offices and some, like Samuel E. Yee or Judge Delbert Wong of Los Angeles, have held government positions by appointment. These prominent members have enhanced the status of the organization and paved the way for other members to follow in their footsteps. However, the CACA has not been just a political organization; it has participated in extensive economic and social activities as well.

Economic and Social Activities

Besides being politically active, from early on CACA members became involved in economic activities and social and community service. The NSGS/CACA provided some economic benefits to its members through an insurance program and aided the wider Chinese community not only in its creation of a Chinese American newspaper and educational programs, but also in the fight against defamatory literature in an effort to fulfill its goal "to promote the general welfare and happiness of its members and the Chinese communities." Although the local lodges had more varied programs of activities, the Grand Lodge and the San Francisco lodge served as the leaders and basic models.

Many NSGS/CACA members had a concern about death benefits. In 1920, because of the numerous discriminatory practices of American insurance companies, the NSGS leaders instituted an insurance, or death benefits, program, which had been in the planning stages for years and was important not only to those without families, with regard to burial, but also to those with families who would suffer when the major wage earner died. Death benefits had been one of the main attractions of joining the Chinese Six Companies and other Chinatown associations, so in offering these benefits, the NSGS/CACA increased Chinese Americans' enthusiasm about joining the group. In trying to fill this void in the lives of its members, the NSGS/CACA ran into a financial crisis, and by 1947, because American insurance regulations had been sufficiently liberalized, the Grand Council decided to end the program.

The leaders also believed that establishing lines of communication to the community was important. At the eighth Biennial Convention held in Oakland in August 1921, the United Publishing Company, Inc., was proposed as the organization's official organ and means of publishing books, pamphlets, and stationery. The company opened for business in San Francisco on November 1, 1921, and changed its name to the Chinese Times Publishing Company in 1926. It had a shaky beginning until the membership decided to increase the company's capitalization so that a daily newspaper could be published. On July 5, 1924, the *Chinese Times* made its debut as the first successful Chinese daily newspaper owned, edited, and published by American citizens of Chinese ancestry. The other Chinese daily newspapers in San Francisco and New York were supported and owned by the Chinese government's political party, the Guomindang (Kuomintang), or other groups in China.

Walter U. Lum was the prime mover in this endeavor and served as editor, managing editor, vice president, and finally president of the publishing company during the next thirty-five years. The newspaper's policy was to publish only authentic news and to provide a bridge for

TABLE 4.3. Three San Francisco Chinese Dailies: Circulation Figures

Newspaper	1925	1926	1927	1928	1929	1930	1964
Chinese Times	3,870	6,268	6,268	7,105	7,953	7,953	9,650
Chinese World	7,562	7,562	7,562	7,200	7,000	7,557	7,200
Young China	6,800	6,800	6,800	6,800	5,510	7,490	6,345

Source: Ayer Directory of Newspapers and Periodicals, 97th edition (NewYork: N.W. Ayer & Sons, 1965 edition), "California, San Francisco Newpapers," 222–230.

understanding between democratic ideals and Chinese cultural traditions. The CACA leaders believed that a bilingual publication would have been ideal, but they did not have the capital or the writing talent to support an English press along with their Chinese press and were fearful that an English-language newspaper would go the way of the short-lived Oriental and Occidental Press, an English-language weekly, that had been established on June 9, 1900, in San Francisco.[53] Like other Chinese dailies, the circulation of the Chinese Times was not limited to San Francisco or California, but extended throughout the United States. By 1929, it had the largest circulation among the Chinese newspapers in San Francisco.[54] A comparison of the circulation figures demonstrates this in Table 4.3.

When the Chinese World began its English section on December 1, 1949, and Young China followed suit in 1961, the Chinese Times likewise considered the bilingual possibilities, but decided to remain a Chinese-language newspaper to continue to fulfill its original aim of being "dedicated to the service and betterment of the Chinese community in America" and to realize its goal of "arousing its readers to their civic duty."[55] By the 1950s, Chinese Americans who were fluent in English were making up their own minds about political issues and current events. The group that still needed help consisted of the Chinese Americans who felt more comfortable with the Chinese language than with English. In 1977 the newspaper moved to larger quarters on Sacramento Street and in the 1980s became an independent body; thus it severed its connection with the CACA.

The CACA, most of whose membership had attended or graduated from college, also became known as a promoter of equal educational opportunities and educational endeavors. As early as 1915, the organization donated gifts for the reconstructed Oriental School (later renamed Commodore Stockton School) in San Francisco's Chinatown.[56] When the new Oriental School could not house the growing number of

Chinese American students in the early 1920s, the organization pushed for an expansion of the facilities, and eventually an annex was constructed.[57] The NSGS also worked toward renaming the school to eliminate the racial overtones and proposed that the school be called the "Harding School," but the San Francisco Board of Education rejected that name in favor of "Commodore Stockton" in 1924.[58] In 1925, when the Board of Education created a segregated secondary school, Francisco Junior High School, in the North Beach area adjacent to Chinatown, the NSGS appealed to the Board to allow the students of Commodore Stockton to attend the seventh and eighth grades there. Supported by the Northern Federation of Civic Organizations, a group of clubs located in the northern part of San Francisco, the Board yielded despite protests from white parents and organizations such as the Northern Federation of Civic and Improvement Clubs.[59] Attorney Kenneth Fung, an officer of the NSGS/CACA, was active in the fight for desegregation from the 1920s to the early 1930s, and told the school board in 1934: "Segregation does not make for good American citizenship. Our children, born here, should be given American training comparable with that of other American students and should not be subjected to a humiliation which would only breed discontent. This would start a prejudice against our children."[60] Along with others, such as the Cathay Post of the American Legion, the CACA succeeded in defeating segregation in the San Francisco schools by the mid-1930s.

In addition to fighting for equal educational opportunities, the CACA worked toward offering English-language classes and practical Chinese-language classes for its members and the general Chinese community. Walter U. Lum, assisted financially by multimillionaire Joe Shoong of the Oakland lodge, Tom Chan of the Chicago lodge, and Y.C. Hong of the Los Angeles lodge, even worked out a basic course of study that gave the students a vocabulary of three thousand to four thousand Chinese characters, to be taught in a manner that was closer to the Western approach to language learning than to traditional Chinese-language training.[61] Although the programs lasted for several years, many of the lodges had to abandon them because of a lack of community support, dwindling funds, and the filling of this void by other, often more professional, organizations offering Chinese-language instruction. Instead, the CACA gave scholarships to encourage students to attend Chinese-language schools and in 1991 initiated Chinese-language "Teachers Recognition Awards." The educational goals of the organization include supporting activities that "offer Chinese American students an opportunity to enhance their personal, educational, and career growth," said Virginia C. Gee, 1991–1992 president of the San Francisco lodge. Toward this end, the CACA instituted programs that encouraged native-born and foreign-born Chinese Americans to develop the necessary leadership skills, such as critical thinking, communication skills, problem solving, and planning and organizational skills.

The CACA has also been concerned about the image of the Chinese in America. When Charles R. Shepherd wrote his book *The Ways of Ah Sin* (New York, 1923), the judiciary committee of the NSGS decided to take a stand against this type of literature, which had been produced since the late nineteenth century. The committee members undoubtedly recalled some of the sensational anti-Chinese works such as P. W. Dooner's *Last Days of the Republic* (1880), which included a picture of a Chinese as governor of California and a picture of a group of Chinese drinking tea, subtitled "Chinese Mandarins in Washington," both of which hinted at the possible takeover of the United States by the Chinese, or Robert Woltor's *A Short and Truthful History of the Taking of California and Oregon by the Chinese in the Year A.D. 1899* (1882), the content of which is reflected in the title. The committee, at the 1923 convention, asked for a condemnation of Shepherd's book because it created prejudice and ill feelings between the races and presented erroneous and defamatory statements about the Chinese. Although unsuccessful in getting the book suppressed, the CACA managed to call the attention of federal and state officials and postal authorities to the book's content and obscenities. Throughout the years, the NSGS/CACA has worked toward fostering a more positive image of the Chinese in the United States and has condemned literary works and television or movie programs that portray the Chinese in an unfavorable and untruthful manner.

A major turning point in the process of assimilation occurred during and after World War II. In 1942, when the California State Military Reserve called for volunteer militia units, many patriotic Chinese Americans formed groups. In Los Angeles, CACA member Peter Soo Hoo, Sr., commanded a sixty-man force and they practiced drilling at the Los Angeles CACA lodge, at that time located at 415½ North Los Angeles Street. Within a year, the unit disbanded because many members had joined the national service. The war gave some Chinese Americans the opportunity to interact closely with Euro-Americans and to assume leadership positions as sergeants, corporals, and officers of other ranks. After the war and the repeal of the Chinese exclusion acts, Chinese Americans found more opportunities for greater acculturation and assimilation. When barriers appeared, they fought more diligently for their political, social, and economic rights as Americans. As mentioned previously, the CACA expanded in the 1950s as more lodges became affiliated with the national organization.

Most of the CACA's social and economic activities resembled those found in the Euro-American community. For example, the CACA sponsored "Miss Chinatown" beauty contests, established Chinatown community health information programs, awarded scholarships to meritorious students, provided federal tax information, and worked with other Chinatown organizations, such as the YMCA and YWCA, Cameron House, Friends of the Chinatown Library, and the Chinese Historical Society, to promote worthwhile community projects. In response to the McCarthyism hysteria of the 1950s, and the need to reassert their loyalty to the United States with the establishment of Mao Zedong's communist government in China, the CACA initiated a program to promote good citizenship through the "I Am an American Day" from 1952 to 1959 and through patriotic essay contests after that. Since the 1950s the organization has joined African American, Hispanic, and Asian Pacific coalitions to fight job discrimination and resolve labor disputes in an effort to achieve equality in the workplace.

Before the 1950s, Chinese Americans were forbidden to attend many social affairs in the Euro-American community. In response to this discriminatory practice, the CACA sponsored its own social functions, including athletic tournaments, picnics, dinners, and dances, most notably the New Year's Eve dance at the San Francisco lodge and the St. Valentine's Day dance at the Los Angeles lodge.[62] All these social activities were departures from nineteenth-century Chinese traditions and had American themes, such as "Western Barbecue Night." Young CACA members participated in athletics, such as baseball and tennis, which were completely foreign to their parents. The *Chinese World*, a San Francisco daily, praised the Los Angeles Mandarins' sponsorship of a softball league, basketball team, and other youth activities by saying, "They are constantly striving to better the lot of the Chinese youth in the Los Angeles area." All these social activities reinforced the members' efforts toward assimilation. "The CACA was," as Shangying Wu commented, "a link between the East and the West."[63]

Conclusion

The early CACA members were American citizens of Chinese ancestry. In 1895, these Chinese Americans rebelled against the Chinese culture of Chinatown that stressed conformity to the old ways, but neither were they accepted into Euro-American society. Therefore, they created their own niche, with one foot in each tradition. Wanting to emphasize simultaneously their American citizenship, their Chinese and American heritages, and their patriotism toward the United States, they worked to resolve injustices through peaceful and legal means.

At the turn of the twentieth century, the Chinese Six Companies had been the spokesperson of the Chinese communities in the United States, but as the years passed, the NSGS/CACA played an increasingly important role. Its members had several distinctive advantages: They were American citizens; most of them had at least a high school, if not a college, education; most were fluent in English; most were professionals who could interact with the Euro-American community with relative ease; and many had training in the legal profession so that they could represent their own positions on various matters. These advantages were especially evident during the height of the organization's development from the 1920s through the 1940s as members appeared before Congress on immigration issues or protested discriminatory educational practices. The successes of the NSGS/CACA showed other Chinese in the United States that they could be effective. Thus, more Chinese Americans became interested in joining the organizations and, consequently, the membership grew nationally.

In the post–World War II years, there has been a greater acceptance of Chinese Americans in all areas of life, including political and social activities, educational institutions, housing, and jobs, and greater social interaction with the majority community. Ironically, instead of stimulating growth in the CACA, this acceptance has led to a slow decline in its membership and activities because potential members could move into other, larger community organizations with a more focused agenda and greater visibility. Thus, for example, the 1954 formation of the Chinese American Democratic Club in San Francisco and other similar organizations in other cities eroded the CACA's strength. In the 1970s through 1990s, pan–Asian American groups were established in an effort to be a more effective numerical and political force; to fight for the right to belong to American society; and to be treated with respect. The Asian Americans for Equality in New York is one such organization.[64] The CACA works with these groups on specific issues and common causes.

As early as the late 1940s, the CACA leadership recognized the need to have a broader appeal to potential members and created independent junior organizations, like the Mandarins in Los Angeles and the Bears in San Francisco, which could attract men between the ages of twenty-one and thirty-nine who were young professionals and businessmen and increasingly more comfortable in the larger American society. At the same time, the CACA became active in local politics. Kung-Lee Wang, founder of the Organization of Chinese Americans, believes that since the mid-1950s, one of CACA's weaknesses has been its involvement with local, rather than national, issues.[65] Another writer, Jack Chen, in 1980 criticized the CACA for its "elitist character," Republican orientation, and failure to gain a wider constituency.[66] Many Chinese community leaders saw the CACA as a conservative political force that did not adequately serve the needs of the entire Chinese American community. Following changes in the 1965 immigration laws, the influx of new immigrants, who in general were better educated and came from many parts of China, increased dramatically, with a growth rate of 6.2 percent annually between 1970 and 1980 and 7.1 percent annually between 1980 and 1990, resulting in a total population of 1,645,472 by 1990.[67] These newcomers, who in the 1980s made up two-thirds of the Chinese population of the United States, had different goals and aims from the older, predominantly southern Chinese immigrants. Some wanted to begin participating in the American political system and society as soon as possible and turned to the CACA as a means of bridging the gap between their old and new lives. The CACA solved the problem of their foreign birth by offering them associate memberships. The leadership recognized the problem of trying to find a common ground among the interests and activities of third-, fourth-, and fifth-generation Chinese Americans; descendants of immigrants from South China; and first- and second-generation Chinese Americans from other parts of China. Recent leaders have turned to social activities as a means to unite these diverse generations while continuing to offer political informational programs.

Despite these difficulties, the CACA leaders continue to work toward improving the position of Chinese Americans, toward their assimilation into the majority society, toward equal rights and opportunities, and toward more equitable immigration laws. The CACA has learned to work with others in the fight for equality, for example, by becoming plaintiffs with other organizations and challenging in court immigration policies that may be unconstitutional.[68] As an organization that has existed for more than a century, the CACA has attracted local, state, and occasionally national political candidates to their political forums. This outside recognition has given them status within the Chinese American community and outside it.

The CACA has made many contributions to the improvement of Chinese communities in the United States and raised the political consciousness of Chinese Americans continuously since 1895. With an increasing number of new, often well-educated Chinese immigrants since 1965, and especially in the aftermath of the 1989 Tiananmen Massacre in Beijing, the CACA continues to serve as a bridge between East and West, helping newcomers in their adjustment to their new homeland, and preparing future generations to become productive American citizens. In some cities, such as San Francisco and Los Angeles, the CACA still plays an important role in politics and is recognized for doing so by the larger community; this enables the organization to nominate members and other Chinese Americans for appointed positions in local, state, and federal governments. As long as the CACA provides a service to local communities, remains flexible in its approach to fulfilling its goals, has a strong leadership dedicated to improving the political and economic welfare of these communities, unites with other historically disenfranchised groups in common causes, and can recruit new members, this more-than-a-century-old organization will be a mainstay in fighting for the American rights of its members.

Notes

Acknowledgments: I am indebted to the following CACA officers (all now deceased) who generously gave their time and memorabilia to me and participated in formal, taped (*) interviews (deposited at UCLA) or informal interviews: Walter K. Chung, president of the CACA Mandarins, 1948–1949; Albert L. Hing, first president of the CACA Mandarins, 1946–1947; *Y. C. Hong, grand president of the CACA, 1949–1953; William Lem, past president of the Oakland lodge; *Samuel E. Yee, grand secretary of the CACA, 1964–1965; several more recent members of the CACA who wanted to remain anonymous; and Virginia Gee, first woman president of a CACA lodge. Assistance for this project was also given by Albert C. Lim, past president of the Chinese Consolidated Benevolent Association; Thomas Chinn, historian, newsman, and civic leader; and H. K. Wong, newsman and civic leader, all of San Francisco. I began studying the CACA in 1964 under the guidance of Roger Daniels at the University of California, Los Angeles and received travel support funds from that institution.

1. U. S. Bureau of the Census, *1900 Census of the Population,* vol. 1, *Characteristics of the Population* (Washington, D.C.: Government Printing Office, 1901).
2. This sentiment was expressed to a Euro-American newspaper reporter by a Chinese American who was born in Fiddletown, California, in 1855 and became more pervasive as the number of Chinese Americans increased around the turn of the twentieth century. *Carson City Morning Appeal,* June 18, 1882.

3. Interview with Y. C. Hong, grand president of the CACA (1949–1953) in 1965; tape deposited with the Oral History Project, University of California, Los Angeles. See also Bernard Wong, *Patronage, Brokerage, Entrepreneurship and the Chinese Community of New York* (New York: AMS Press, 1988), 67.

4. For a general background on the 1882 Exclusion Act, see Shirley Hune, "Politics of Chinese Exclusion: Legislative-Executive Conflict, 1876–1882," *Amerasia* 9, no. 1 (1982): 5–27.

5. Elmer C. Sandmeyer, *The Anti-Chinese Movement in California* (Urbana: University of Illinois Press, 1939), 104; Walter Fong, "The Chinese Six Companies," *Overland Monthly,* 2d ser., 23 (May 1894): 525; and Stanford M. Lyman, "The Structure of Chinese Society in Nineteenth Century America" (Ph.D. dissertation, University of California, Berkeley, 1961), 409–412.

6. Y. C. Hong, *A Brief History of the Chinese American Citizens Alliance* (San Francisco: Chinese American Citizens Alliance, November 1955), 1. See also Lim P. Lee, "The Political Rights of the American Citizens of Chinese Ancestry," *Chinese Digest* 2 (October 1936): 11; and Lim P. Lee, "The Chinese American Citizens Alliance, Its Activities and History," *Chinese Digest* 2 (October 1936), 11, 15.

7. Nowland C. Hong, President, Los Angeles lodge, CACA, to *East/West Chinese American Journal* (San Francisco) February 17, 1971; reprinted in Cheng-Tsu Wu, ed., *"Chink!" A Documentary History of Anti-Chinese Prejudice in America* (New York: World Publishing Company, 1972), 156.

8. See Franklin Ng, ed., *Asian American Encyclopedia* (New York: Marshall Cavendish, 1995), entry on Native Sons of the Golden State.

9. Theodore Hittell, *History of California* (San Francisco: N. J. Stone and Company, 1897), 536–537.

10. Chinese names in the United States present serious problems to the scholar. In China, a person has several names; in the United States names become even more complicated because of the inability to transliterate the person's name accurately, the frequent confusion between the last name and the first name, honorific forms of address, the Chinese practice of having three or more first names, and other problems. Often, three or more versions of Robert Leon Park's name were used.

11. He was probably Leong Sing, the marshal, or Leong Chung, the inside sentinel. See Sandy Lydon, *Chinese Gold: The Chinese in the Monterey Bay Region* (Capitola, Calif.: Capitola Book Company, 1985), 77.

12. Xiao Yishan, *Qingdai tongshi* [History of the Qing dynasty], vol. 2 (Shanghai: Commercial Press, 1928), 46. See also Fred W. Riggs, *Pressures on Congress: A Study of the Repeal of Chinese Exclusion* (New York: King's Crown Press, 1950), 4–5 and Shien-woo Kung, *Chinese in American Life: Some Aspects of Their History, Status, Problems, and Contributions* (Seattle: University of Washington Press, 1962), 7–8, 48.

13. Charles F. Remer, *A Study of Chinese Boycotts, with Special Reference to Their Economic Effectiveness* (Baltimore: Johns Hopkins University Press, 1933), 30–39 and Tien-lu Li, *Congressional Policy of Chinese Immigration* (Nashville, Tenn.: Methodist Episcopal Church, 1916), 102–103.

14. Much of the information about the organization was acquired through the following CACA documents, some of which are in Chinese and others in English or English and Chinese: *Application for Permit to the Commissioner of Corporations of the State of California,* (Sacramento, Calif.: Chinese Times

Publishing Company, 1926); *Articles of Incorporation of the United Parlor of the Native Sons of the Golden State,* May 1895; *Articles of Incorporation of the Chinese American Citizens Alliance,* December 1928; *Report on Changing the Alien Wives Act, 1925–1930; Proceedings of the Biennial Convention of the Chinese American Citizens Alliance, Grand Lodge,* 1923, 1925, 1927, 1929, 1931, 1935, 1937, 1939, 1951, 1953, 1955, 1957, 1959, 1961, and 1963; *Constitution of the Chinese American Citizens Alliance,* 1928; *Bylaws of the Chinese American Citizens Alliance,* rev., 1955; National Biennial Convention books, various dates; *Statutes of the San Francisco Lodge,* 1949; miscellaneous pamphlets and publications; San Francisco Lodge *Survey,* 1991–1993. A more complete history of the organization is possible only when all the CACA records can be examined.

15. In the Chinese tradition, the family name, in this case, Lum, is given first. This practice caused much confusion for U.S. immigration officials, who made the person's family name part of his or her first name and the last part of the two-character first name the person's new last name.

16. Information about Walter U. Lum and his family is from his oldest daughter, Mabel Lum Lew. This information was published by the Chinese Historical Society of Southern California in the *Gum Saan Journal* 1, no. 1 (August 1977): 2–4, and 2, no. 1 (July 1978): 1–3.

17. 33 *U.S. Statutes at Large* 428; see Bill Ong Hing, *Making and Remaking Asian America through Immigration Policy, 1850–1990* (Stanford: Stanford University Press, 1993), 206; Shirley Hune, "The Issue of Chinese Immigration in the Federal Government, 1875–1882" (Ph.D. dissertation, George Washington University, 1979); Chester L. Jones, "The Legislative History of Exclusion Legislation, "*Annals of the American Association of Political and Social Science* 34, no. 2 (September 1909): 351–359. For a general summary of the boycott, see Jonathan D. Spence, *The Search for Modern China* (New York: W. W. Norton, 1990), 238; Yen Ching-hwang, "Wu T'ing-fang and the Protection of the Overseas Chinese in the United States, 1897–1903" working paper no. 12, University of Adelaide, Centre for Asian Studies, Adelaide, Australia, 1981, 16–23; Linda P. Shin, "China in Transition: The Role of Wu T'ing-fang (1842–1922)" (Ph. D. dissertation, University of California, Los Angeles, 1970); and Delber L. McKee, "The Chinese Boycott of 1905–1906 Reconsidered: The Role of Chinese Americans," *Pacific Historical Review* 55, no. 2 (May 1986): 165–191.

18. Thomas W. Chinn, *Bridging the Pacific: San Francisco Chinatown and Its People* (San Francisco: Chinese Historical Society of America, 1989), 111.

19. Other grand presidents and their occupations between 1917 and 1965 were as follows: Leong Kow (1917–1923), San Francisco, newspaperman and immigration interpreter; S.K. Lai (1929–1931, 1935–1947), San Francisco, accountant for the Southern Pacific Railroad Company and president of the *Chinese Times;* Harry T. Yip (1931–1933), Los Angeles, assistant to the president of National Dollar Stores, Inc.; Kenneth Y. Fung (1947–1949), San Francisco, attorney; Y. C. Hong (1949–1953), Los Angeles, attorney; Henry Lem (1953–1959, 1961–1963), San Francisco, newspaperman; George Chew (1959–1961), Oakland, Department of Motor Vehicles employee; and Wilbur Woo (1963–1965), Los Angeles, produce businessman and banker. Other past grand presidents (dates of term unknown unless noted) include Nowland C. Hong (Los Angeles, attorney), Leonard Louie (San Francisco, judge), Irvin R. Lai (Los Angeles, community leader and businessman), Francis Louie (San Francisco, gift shop

owner), Harold Y. G. Fong (San Francisco, city employee), and Harry W. Low (San Francisco, judge, 1991–1993).

20. L. Eve Armentrout-Ma, *Revolutionaries, Monarchists, and Chinatowns: Chinese Politics in the Americas and the 1911 Revolution* (Honolulu: University of Hawaii Press, 1990), 130, and 193, note 11. See also L. Eve Armentrout-Ma, "A Chinese Association in North America: Pao-huang Hui from 1899 to 1904," *Ch'ing-shih wen-t'i* 3 (1978): 91–111.

21. Ma, *Revolutionaries*, 133.

22. Lew, *Gum Saan Journal* 1, no. 1 (August 1977): 2–4, and 2, no. 1 (July 1978): 1–3.

23. Incorporation dates are omitted from local lodges that became inactive before 1961. See Gustave K. Lee, "The Purpose and Aim," in *26th Biennial National Convention* (San Francisco: Chinese American Citizens Alliance, 1961), 9.

24. Julius Su Tow, *The Real Chinese in America* (New York: Academy Press, 1923), 113.

25. Interview with Samuel E. Yee, grand secretary of the CACA, in 1964. Tape on deposit with the Oral History Project, University of California, Los Angeles.

26. Tow, *The Real Chinese*, 113; and Ruzhou Zhen, ed., *Meiguo Huaqiao nian jian* [Handbook of the Chinese in America] (New York: People's Foreign Relations Association of China, 1946), 574. The Chinese American Citizens Alliance's Chinese name is *Meizhou tongyuan zong hui*; the one in New York is *Huaren doushen hui*.

27. *Articles of Incorporation of the Chinese American Citizens Alliance*, December 1928.

28. Nowland C. Hong, *East/West, Chinese American Journal*; reprinted in Wu, "*Chink!*" 256. See also *Articles of Incorporation of the United Parlor of the Native Sons of the Golden State*, May 1895.

29. Lew, *Gum Saan Journal* 1, no. 1 and 2, no. 1. In the 1920s, Walter U. Lum was vice president and managing director of the Chinese-owned China Mail Steamship Line. When financial difficulties arose, he received death threats from one of the "fighting tongs" and had to hire bodyguards. Eventually he resigned from this post.

30. An example of this can be seen in the use of kinship terminology. See Elizabeth Cheng, "Some Features of the Kinship Terminology Used in New York Chinatown," *Southwestern Journal of Anthropology* 8 (Spring 1952): 97–107. This process with regard to language and culture has been described in Lornita Yuen-Fan Wong, *Education of Chinese Children in Britain and the USA* (Clevedon, England: Multilingual Matters Ltd., 1992).

31. Winifred Raushenbush, "The Great Wall of Chinatown," *Survey* LVI (May 1926): 154–155.

32. Generational differences and interactions between Chinese and persons of European ancestry have been discussed in Ching-chao Wu, "Chinatowns: A Study of Symbiosis and Assimilation" (Ph.D. dissertation, University of Chicago, 1928), 287; and Ng Bickleen Fong, *Chinese in New Zealand: A Study in Assimilation* (Hong Kong: Hong Kong University Press, 1959).

33. Kit King Louis, "Problems of Second Generation Chinese," *Sociology and Social Research* 16 (January–February 1932): 256; and Kit King Louis, "Program for Second Generation Chinese," *Sociology and Social Research* 16 (May–June 1932): 455–462.

34. See Lornita Wong, *Education of Chinese Children.*

35. Y. C. Hong, "Milestones of the Chinese American Citizens Alliance," in *27th Biennial National Convention* (Los Angeles: Chinese American Citizens Alliance, 1963), 16.

36. See N. B. Fong, *Chinese in New Zealand*, 7-8 and Kian-moon Kwan, "Assimilation of the Chinese in the United States: An Exploratory Study in California" (Ph.D. dissertation, University of California, Berkeley, 1958), 139–141.

37. Hing, *Making and Remaking*, 206, 213. The 1922 Cable Act expanded upon this by specifying "that any woman citizen who marries an alien ineligible to citizenship [such as a person of Chinese ancestry] shall cease to be a citizen of the United States." The act remained in effect until a 1931 amendment modified the law. The Cable Act was repealed in 1936. See Sucheng Chan, *Asian Americans: An Interpretative History* (Boston: Twayne Publishers, 1991), 105–106.

38. Lew, *Gum Saan Journal.*

39. Jack Chen, *The Chinese of America* (San Francisco: Harper and Row, 1980), 201 and Shih-shan Henry Tsai, *The Chinese Experience in America* (Bloomington: Indiana University Press, 1986), 97. I do not have any CACA records of their activities prior to 1924. This proposal could not be located in California Legislature, *Senate Journal*, 40th sess., 1913, or any of the earlier sessions because it was not brought to a vote on the senate floor. In June 1913, Caminetti was appointed commissioner of the U.S. Immigration and Naturalization Service, but when he tried to interfere with the prosecution of his son Drew in a white slavery case later that month, his political career declined rapidly. See report by John Hall Stephens (D-Texas) in 63rd Cong., 1st sess., *Congressional Record*, 50 (JUNE 17–AUGUST 2, 1913): 2532–2533; and the *San Francisco Chronicle*, June–August 1913.

40. For more details of this act, see Hing, *Making and Remaking*, 212; Helen Chen, "Chinese Immigration into the United States: An Analysis of Changes in Immigration Policies," in *The Chinese American Experience: Papers from the Second National Conference on Chinese American Studies (1980)*, ed. Genny Lim (San Francisco: Chinese Historical Society of America and Chinese Culture Foundation of San Francisco, 1984), 44–45.

41. U. S. Congress, Senate, Committee on Immigration, *Admission as Nonquota Immigrants of Certain Alien Wives and Children of United States Citizens: Hearings on S. 2771* (Washington, D.C.: Government Printing Office, 1928), 4–15. See also U. S. Congress, House of Representatives Committee on Immigration and Naturalization, *Wives of American Citizens of Oriental Race: Hearings on H.R. 6974* (Washington, D.C.: Government Printing Office, 1928).

42. Munson Kwok, nephew of William Jack Chow, related this tale in "The Fine Art of Lobbying," *Gum Saan Journal* 16, no. 2 (December 1993): 37. See also Susie Ling, "Repeal of the Chinese Exclusion Act: A Contradiction," *Gum Saan Journal* 16, no. 2 (December 1993): 21–31.

43. *Weedin v. Chin Bow*, 274 U.S. 657 (1926) and 47 Sup. Ct. 772 (1926).

44. Kim Fong Tom, in "The Participation of the Chinese in the Community Life of Los Angeles" (M.A. thesis, University of Southern California, 1944), 68–70, mentions the work of the CACA in passing, but Fred W. Riggs attributes this repeal to the Caucasian group, Citizens Committee to Repeal Chinese Exclusion, in *Riggs Pressures on Congress: A Study of the Repeal of Chinese Exclusion* (New York: King Crown's Press, 1950), 43, 118. CACA convention proceedings and other materials were not available for the war years.

45. Helen Chen, "Chinese Immigration," 45.
46. Charles Kasreal Ferguson, "Political Problems and Activities of the Oriental Residents in Los Angeles and Vicinity" (M.A. thesis, University of California, Los Angeles, 1942), 77.
47. Tom, "The Participation of the Chinese," 68–69.
48. CACA, *San Francisco Lodge, Survey* 2, no. 8 (October 1992): 1, 6. I am indebted to Virginia C. Gee, San Francisco lodge president, for giving me numerous issues of this publication and granting me several interviews in California and Nevada, 1990–1994.
49. *1992 President's Annual Report*, San Francisco lodge.
50. CACA San Francisco Lodge, *Survey* 2, no. 8 (October 1992).
51. Interview with Samuel Yee, 1964–1965. Tape deposited with the Oral History Project, University of California, Los Angeles.
52. In 1900, 52 percent (2,353) of the 4,522 Chinese women in the United States were born in this country; by 1910, 64 percent (3,014 of 4,675) were; by 1920, the figure rose to 67 percent (5,214 of 7,749) and remained at that percentage in 1930 (10,175 of 15,152); and by 1940, it reached a high of 72 percent (14,560 of 20,115). U. S. Department of Commerce, Bureau of the Census, *Sixteenth Census of the United States: 1940, Population, Vol. 2: Characteristics of the Population, Part I: United States Summary* (Washington, D.C.: Government Printing office, 1943), 21.
53. Yuk Ow, "A Selected List of Published and Unpublished Materials Written by the California Chinese with Brief Biographical Sketches of the Authors and Comments on the Works," Bancroft Library, University of California, Berkeley, typeset manuscript.
54. Jack Chen, *This Chinese of America*, 201.
55. Application for permit from the State Corporation Department of the State of California.
56. *San Francisco Call and Post*, January 21, 1915. See also Victor Low, *The Unimpressible Race: A Century of Educational Struggle by the Chinese in San Francisco* (San Francisco: East/West Publishing Company, 1982).
57. Low, *The Unimpressible Race*, 113.
58. Ibid., 115.
59. Ibid., 116–119.
60. *San Francisco News*, November 21, 1934. See Low, *The Unimpressible Race*, 130. The NSGS officially became the CACA in 1929.
61. Y. C. Hong, "Milestones," 15.
62. Y. C. Hong, *A Brief History*, 4. On the need for social activities, see Kwan, "Assimilation of the Chinese," 143; and Louis, "Problems of Second Generation Chinese," 252, 254.
63. Shangying Wu, *Meiguo huaqiao bainian jishi: Jianada fu* [One Hundred Years of the Chinese in the United States and Canada] (Hong Kong: n.p., 1954), 236.
64. Peter Kwong, *The New Chinatown* (New York: Hill and Wang, 1987), 160–173.
65. Kung-Lee Wang, "The Changing Chinese Americans: Trends in Political Awareness and Involvement Since 1950," in *The Chinese American Experience*, ed. Lim, 304.
66. Jack Chen, *The Chinese of America*, 201.
67. Herbert R. Barringer, Robert W. Gardner, and Michael J. Levin, *Asians and Pacific Islanders in the United States* (New York: Russell Sage Foundation, 1993), 37–38. See also Leon F. Bouvier and Anthony J. Agresta, "The Future

Asian Population of the United States," in *Pacific Bridges: The New Immigration from Asia and the Pacific Islands,* ed. James T. Fawcett and Benjamin V. Carino (Staten Island, N.Y.: Center for Migration Studies, 1987).

68. See, for example, *Chinese American Citizens Alliance et al. v. Immigration and Naturalization Service,* 976 F. 2d 1198 (1192) (U.S. Ct. Appeals 1992); LEXIS 22879.

CHAPTER 5

Race, Ethnic Culture, and Gender in the Construction of Identities among Second-Generation Chinese Americans, 1880s to 1930s

SUCHENG CHAN

IN 1870, TWO DECADES AFTER CHINESE IMMIGRATION BEGAN, census takers counted only about five hundred American-born children (less than 1 percent) among the sixty-three thousand persons of Chinese ancestry living in the United States. Three decades later, the American born numbered some nine thousand (approximately 10 percent) among the almost ninety thousand persons of Chinese ancestry in the country. By 1920, approximately eighteen thousand (29 percent) of the sixty-two thousand persons of Chinese ancestry were listed in the census as American citizens.[1] Not all eighteen thousand had been born in the United States, however, because an unknown number of Chinese with derivative U.S. citizenship had arrived by that date.[2] Only in 1940 did the number of Chinese with American citizenship—a significant proportion American born—exceed the number of foreign born.

Second-generation Chinese Americans comprised a minority of the Chinese-ancestry population in the United States during the first nine decades of Chinese immigration because few Chinese women came to the United States. Chinese tradition deemed it more important for daughters and daughters-in-law to stay home to serve their parents or parents-in-law than to accompany their menfolk abroad, especially if the men intended to return to China after working overseas. Even if no cultural constraints had existed, the cost of passage for one's family was a hurdle that few peasants and laborers could surmount. Also, frontier conditions and anti-Chinese hostility in the American West made living there unsafe for Chinese women. Finally, restrictive laws passed by Congress from 1875 onward kept Chinese women away from America's shores.[3] The paucity of women meant that few children of Chinese ancestry were conceived, born, and raised on American soil.

Despite their relatively late appearance and small numbers, Chinese American children have played a significant, although unacknowledged, role in Chinese American history: They have served as one of the most important socializing agents in Chinese American communities. This statement may sound strange, because socialization usually refers to the process by which adults teach children the beliefs, values, and norms of the culture into which they are born. The socialization of children, however, is not the only kind of socialization that occurs: When individuals emigrate from their homelands to other countries, they undergo a second round of socialization—a process more commonly called "acculturation." In the latter instance, the immigrants' neighbors, coworkers, bosses, English teachers, and social workers, as well as the mass media, all teach them—both directly and indirectly— new ways to behave in their adopted land. What is less often recognized is that the immigrants' children also play a significant role in socializing their parents to a different behavioral pattern.

The children of immigrants can perform this crucial function because they can learn a new language—in this instance, English—faster than adults can. Thus, they acquire the ability to communicate with members of the host society much sooner and consequently are often called upon to serve as interpreters and translators when their parents deal with the outside world. These children thereby become mediators between two cultures. Such a role reversal upsets the balance of power within immigrant families. When children see how ignorant or helpless their parents may be in relationship to the world at large, they begin to question their parents' authority within the home. Parental authority is further eroded when the children begin attending schools where they come into close contact with American teachers and schoolmates who unwittingly become competing authority figures or role models vis-à-vis the parents. The teachers introduce them to a different set of values, whereas the other schoolchildren show them how American youngsters, who enjoy greater freedom of movement and expression than children in many other societies, are allowed to act. As the progeny of immigrants bring these American notions home—notions that clash with what is deemed appropriate in their parents' cultures of origin—severe intergenerational conflicts almost inevitably result. To maintain family harmony or out of sheer frustration, some immigrant parents acquiesce to their offsprings' demands and modify their expectations, in the process becoming, however reluctantly, more Americanized themselves. As this happens, sojourners become immigrants, and immigrants, in turn, become members of American ethnic groups. Family formation on American soil, therefore, has greatly affected the identities of immigrant groups. Chinese Americans have been no exception.

In this chapter, to explore the evolution of Chinese American identities, I draw upon twenty-eight extant autobiographies written by Chinese Americans who grew up along the Pacific Coast between the 1880s and 1930s. These works include three books, *Father and Glorious Descendant,* by Pardee Lowe, and *Fifth Chinese Daughter* and *No Chinese Stranger,* both by Jade Snow Wong; seventeen life histories written in the first-person singular and collected by the Survey of Race Relations Project in the mid-1920s;[4] four reminiscences in *Longtime Californ': A Documentary Study of an American Chinatown,* by Victor G. and Brett de Bary Nee; three autobiographical essays in *Bridging the Pacific: San Francisco Chinatown and Its People,* by Thomas W. Chinn; and one autobiographical statement in *Ting: Chinese Art and Identity in San Francisco,* edited by Nick Harvey. Although twenty-eight is not a large number and the sample is not representative in a scientific sense, the fact that certain themes were stated repeatedly allows us to assume that the thoughts and sentiments expressed in these accounts were prevalent among Chinese Americans during the late nineteenth and early twentieth centuries. These documents preserved more than the unique voices of individuals; they likely captured the consciousness of sizable numbers of Chinese Americans during the historical period that these documents covered. Before analyzing these available life stories, I review briefly the different conceptual frameworks that scholars have used to study ethnic identities.

Approaches to the Study of Ethnic Identities

Such terms as "identity," "ethnicity," "culture," and "assimilation" are now widely used in academic discourse as well as in everyday conversation, but their meaning remains ambiguous. One reason for their lack of conceptual clarity is that scholars in different disciplines have used them in divergent ways. Historians, psychologists, sociologists, and anthropologists have all written about ethnic identity, but they have focused on different aspects of the phenomenon. Moreover, within each discipline, competing schools of thought have arisen.

Historians have been interested mainly in the nature of American national identity, which, as Philip Gleason persuasively argued, has been based more on a set of ideological principles than on any sense of common ethnic or cultural origins.[5] In the early period of U.S. history, relatively little concern was expressed over the loyalties of various ethnic groups and how such homeland ties or intragroup affiliations might influence the "character" of the nation. However, as an increasing number of European immigrants started arriving from the 1840s onward, political leaders, social commentators, and scholars all began worrying about how well and how fast these immigrants would assimilate, on the one hand, and what impact their presence might have on American political institutions, social relations, cultural practices, and religious beliefs, on the other hand. The voluminous amount of historical literature that has been published about ethnic life in the United States has focused largely on the experiences of European immigrants.[6] Until the 1970s, little attention was paid to newcomers from other continents. So, attempts to apply the European-immigrant model to other immigrant groups, such as Chinese Americans, can sometimes lead to questionable conclusions.

Among psychologists, the pioneering work on how a sense of identity develops in the successive stages of an individual's life was done by Erik H. Erikson. In several seminal works on Martin Luther, Adolph Hitler, Mohandas Gandhi, and other famous historical figures, Erikson demonstrated how biography intersects history. (The idea of "intersection," however, was popularized not by Erikson but by the sociologist C. Wright Mills.[7]) Although as a psychoanalyst Erikson was initially concerned primarily with childhood, his most influential ideas have come from his studies of adolescence, adulthood, and old age. In a conceptual scheme based on clinical case histories that he called the "eight ages of man," he posited that at each stage of an individual's maturation, a specific sociopsychological task must be performed, the successful completion of which endows that person with the strength to cope with the challenges in the next phase of his or her life.[8] He argued that identity development involves two kinds of time: a *developmental stage* in the life of the individual, and a *period* in history. "[T]here is," as he stated, "a complementarity of life history and history," of "identity and ideology."[9] Although Erikson's theories have not been widely applied to the study of ethnic identities because he paid little attention to the impact of culture on identity formation, a number of his insights, particularly those on the adolescent phase of human development, can help us better understand the evolution of Chinese American identities.[10]

In contrast to psychoanalysts such as Erikson, sociologists, anthropologists, and social psychologists have been more interested in how
culture—particularly the interaction or conflict of cultures—affects
the identities of individuals.[11] These social scientists may be broadly
divided into two schools of thought. One group of scholars asserts that
members of immigrant groups possess ethnic identities because they
cling to the cultural baggage that they brought with them. So-called
hyphenated Americans experience conflicts because American culture
differs in fundamental ways from these people's ancestral cultures.
Within this "cultural legacy" school of thought, the scholars who favor
assimilation believe that as soon as the immigrants and their children
learn the ways of the new society and stop following the dictates of the
old, cultural conflicts will automatically disappear. In contrast, those
who advocate pluralism argue that no conflicts would arise in the first
place if members of the majority society would accept people from
other lands as their cultural equals. In the 1970s, William Yancey and
his associates departed from the "cultural legacy" mode of analysis by
proposing that ethnic identities are not cultural residues or sediments
transplanted from other countries but are, rather, the products of structural conditions encountered *in the United States*.[12] In their view, ethnicity is an emergent or situational phenomenon because ethnic
solidarity crystallizes only under certain specific conditions. For this
reason, not all persons with the same national origin possess the same
degree of ethnic identification.

None of the previously mentioned conceptual frameworks is fully
adequate for understanding the historical development of Chinese
American identities because, important as immigrant adaptation, individual psychology, and cultural differences may be, they were not always the most powerful factors determining the consciousness of
Chinese American youth in the late nineteenth and early twentieth
centuries. These young people's racial origin, as manifested in visible
characteristics of their bodies—their skin color, the color and texture of
their hair, the shape of their eyes, the flare of their noses—often im-
pinged on their lives in even more potent ways. Like other nonwhite
groups in the United States, Chinese Americans endured social segregation, economic discrimination, political disenfranchisement, and legal
handicaps as a result of their physical and biological differences, regardless of whether these differences were putative or real. Gender, too, was
a vital force shaping the experiences of Chinese Americans, as I discuss
later in this chapter. No doubt, class was a crucial consideration as well.
However, many of the available autobiographical accounts contain no

information on the socioeconomic standing of the narrators' families. In the life stories where the fathers' occupations were revealed, almost all the fathers were merchants. That so many second-generation Chinese Americans were the children of merchants is not surprising, given that merchants' wives and daughters were the only Chinese females allowed to enter the country with relative ease during the sixty-one years of Chinese exclusion. In light of this lack of diversity in the narrators' class backgrounds, nothing definitive can be said about how class differences might have affected identity formation.

Can Chinese Be Americans?

Almost all the Chinese American narrators believed strongly that they were, and should be treated as, "Americans,"[13] but the young men and women differed in what they considered to be the markers of their American identity. To the men, being American meant having certain rights—the right to be in the United States, the right to vote, the right to own property. Ying Foy of Seattle stated, "I born here... I have a right to be here."[14] Chin Yen, who was born in California in 1876, related "I am a son of the Golden West. . . . The United States, we feel, is our home. . . . I got property here. I pay taxes. I vote. . . . I feel like a Chinese descendant and American citizen, because I am an American. I represent American; that is Chinese American."[15] Bong Chin, who was born in Seattle in the 1880s, stated, "Yes, I vote. . . . I consider myself American."[16] Chin Cheung, a native of San Francisco, declared, "I own my home. They have to let me own my own home because [I am] American born."[17]

These Chinese American young men recognized that when they could not enjoy the rights that other American citizens enjoyed, Euro-American discrimination (a discrimination based on race), and not Chinese culture, constrained them. The message that they were not accepted, that they did not belong, that they were not equal, was conveyed to them at a young age and was repeated in multiple ways as they grew older. When David Young, who grew up in San Francisco and eventually became the Chinese vice consul of Seattle, became old enough to attend school, his teacher at the Chinese Baptist Mission took him to be enrolled at a grammar school, but

> . . . they refused to take me in because I was a Chinese. Finally we went
> in one and went to see the principal, and I think she must have taken

me for a Filipino or something and I entered the fourth grade. . . . A month before I graduated from the grammar school, during lunch, I was talking to the other Chinese boy. We both had been taken for Japanese or Filipino, so the American boys went and reported us to the principal. I was called up to his office and asked if I were Chinese. Naturally, I told him yes, and he said I would have to leave the school, as there was a school for Orientals in Chinatown and I must go back there.[18]

Although Chinese American children living in other places along the Pacific Coast were not forced to attend segregated schools, as Chinese American children in San Francisco were, some nevertheless chose not to go to the public schools because, as Bong Chin of Seattle recalled, "Very few Chinese go to public school. Chinese at that time have cue [sic]. Boys make fun then. Make lots of fun. No like to go public school."[19]

Outside the classroom, Chinese American young people were deprived of certain kinds of recreation. They were forbidden to sit in the better sections of movie theaters or to use public swimming pools. For instance, David Young once tried to buy tickets at a theater, "they would only sell me tickets in certain parts of the show. . . . We were forced to go up-stairs, when the lower floor was only half full. We were so much disgusted, we came down and got our money back and I have never gone to a show since," he said.[20] Like African Americans, Chinese Americans were forbidden to use public swimming pools lest they somehow "contaminate" the water. Thomas Chinn was an accomplished athlete who excelled in many sports. The exceptions were swimming and other water sports "for the simple reason that when I was young there was no pool in Chinatown, and Chinese were not welcomed at any of the pools outside of Chinatown."[21] Another young man who

> . . . had registered in a swimming class which met at the Y.M.C.A. in town . . . had no fears of being "turned down," especially since he was with the university class. What was his surprise and indignation to learn from the secretary of the Y that Orientals were not allowed the use of the pool! This astonishing statement was made unperturbably by the secretary, just as though he were not violating in one breath every principle for which his organization stood.[22]

The most devastating blow came, however, when Chinese American youth began looking for jobs. Pardee Lowe had his first encounter with

job discrimination when he was thirteen. When he rebelled against going to Chinese-language school, his father explained to him that learning Chinese would be "good job insurance"[23] in the future. However,
Pardee did not understand what his father meant. Instead, he decided to
prove his father wrong. So, he applied to one company after another for
a position as an office boy. To his dismay, he discovered that

> . . . everywhere I was greeted with perturbation, amusement, pity or ir-
> ritation—and always with identically the same answer. "Sorry," they
> invariably said, "the position has just been filled." My jaunty self-con-
> fidence soon wilted. . . . Suspicion began to dawn. What had Father
> said? "American firms do not customarily employ Chinese.". . . I broke
> down and wept. For the first time I admitted to myself the cruel truth—
> I didn't have a "Chinaman's chance."[24]

Years later, as he encountered great difficulty in finding work—any
kind of work—to pay his way through Stanford University, the harsh
truth again hit home. One potential employer he approached "stared at
me and blurted a whole conversation in pidgin English. I was thunder-
struck. . . . the tenor of her long and embarrassed message . . . was perfectly clear. It was, 'Me no likee, me no wantee Chinee boy!' "[25] He
finally had to admit to himself, "My employment problem was entirely conditioned by one fact: I was Chinese."[26]

Prejudice was encountered even when Chinese Americans were trying only to be polite. Once, David Young was in a crowded streetcar,
"An old lady came into the car, and I went and offered her my se[a]t,"
he recalled. "She never said a word, but just looked at me, so I went and
sat down again. Afterwards, another fellow (a white man) offered her a
seat. She said, 'All right' and sat down. That made me feel bad."[27]

Yet another form of discrimination that irked some Chinese American young men was the attitude of the police, who either declined to
protect the Chinese or pressured the Chinese to give them bribes or
free meals for protection. As Bong Chin of Seattle related, "No police-
man never going to help Chinese unless you give him good feed every
day. . . . They won't pay any attention to me. You Chinese, that what
they say. You're not white, we are white. No help you." Bong Chin
deeply resented this attitude because, as he said, "I pay taxes just the
same for protection."[28] Speaking about the "tong wars" that raged in
American Chinatowns during the early part of the twentieth century,
Lew Kay observed: "The officials don't care, they look upon it as a Chinaman killing Chinaman, and let them go, saves money for the State as
they don't have to take care of them." Then Lew Kay lamented bit-

terly: "We contribute every year to the Community Fund, but share no benefits at all. . . . We get no help from the Community Fund."[29]

In contrast to their male peers, Chinese American young women thought that being American meant having certain freedoms—the freedom to *not* behave according to Chinese customs, to choose their own mates, to work, and to be recognized for their individual achievements. Lillie Leung of Los Angeles spoke for many other young Chinese American women when she said:

> I am American-born of Chinese parentage, and because of my American training I feel the restraints imposed by the Chinese traditions. I feel the restrictions imposed upon the girls: we are not permitted to go out to socials or to have good times as the American girls have. . . . I have wanted to work—just do any kind of work to feel that I was doing something and making my own way—but my parents would not listen to it because it might appear that they could not support their children. . . . My parents wanted to hold to the old idea of selecting a husband for me, but I did not care for them and would not marry them.[30]

Flora Belle Jan of Fresno, whom the Survey of Race Relations researchers called a flapper because of how she dressed and whom they considered an exemplar of Americanized Chinese (see Chapter 7 of this book for more information on this woman), had this to say: "When I was a little girl, I grew to dislike the conventionality and rules of Chinese life. . . . My parents have wanted me to grow up a good Chinese girl, but I am an American and I can't accept all the old Chinese ways and ideas."[31]

A third young woman resented that her parents would not allow her to go away to college. They believed that because all Chinese girls were expected to marry, sending her to a college in another town would be a waste of money, when there was a college in their town. Neither would they allow her to work because, like Lillie Leung's parents, they feared "it would seem that they were unable to support me." After graduation, she planned to go to China to work, but she said, "I will feel that America is home, and to me, there is 'no place like home.' "[32]

One Chinese American girl was even bolder in defying her father's wishes. Raised by her older sister who was married to a cook in a lumber camp, she did not trust her father when he wanted to take her to China, ostensibly to get an education:

> One of my older sisters had been married in China, against her will, after she had been just a very short time in school. I felt that if I went back with him I would very shortly be married, and that I would not

have anything to say about it. . . . My father brought me to San Francisco, and bought my ticket to China. But I had been away from my father for so long that I was not much afraid of him. . . . The night before the boat sailed, I told him . . . I would go to the Mission and throw myself on their protection. . . . I was resolved not to marry, to have an education instead. . . . If I once consented to go, I would be lost. There would be no police, one could not telephone for help, the American consul could not help me.[33]

She managed to find her way to the Presbyterian Mission Home for Chinese Girls, even though she had last visited it when she was only six years old. When she explained her plight to Donaldina Cameron, a missionary who spent many years rescuing Chinese prostitutes, Cameron took her to see a judge. He decided that because she was American born, she could not be forced to go to China.[34] In time, this spirited young woman became president of her high school class and the first vice president of the Association of Women Students at her junior college. Her goal was to become a medical missionary because, as she said, "I think I feel more American really, than Chinese, but still what I want to do is to help my own people."[35]

For Jade Snow Wong, who wrote the most widely read Asian American autobiography ever published, being American meant being recognized as an individual. She prayed to God that she would become "a person respected and honored by my family when I grow up."[36] Her wish did not come true until years later, after her book had been published and was being translated into several languages. Even then, her father expressed his admiration for her only in an indirect way when he said the following prayer:

We are gathered here because of a book about which fellow villagers, merchants, and friends on the street have been congratulating me. For this book was written in America by a Chinese, not only a Chinese but a Chinese from San Francisco, not only a Chinese from San Francisco but a Wong, not only a Wong but a Wong from this house, not only a Wong from this house but a daughter, Jade Snow. Heavenly Father, this accomplishment was not mine, but Yours! From Your many blessings, this girl, raised according to Your commandments, was able to do this work.[37]

Although Jade Snow personally received no credit for her achievement, she was touched because, she wrote, "[i]t was the first and only time the family heard what he thought about the book, and one of the few times a daughter was complimented in prayer. . . . The prayer had rewarded Jade Snow in a way which the most flattering review from an astute critic could not."[38]

Thus, whereas Chinese American young men felt the sting of racism in the public arena most keenly, Chinese American young women were more concerned with escaping the constrictions of Chinese cultural practices within the private sphere of their lives. This did not mean that they experienced no racism, however, for racial discrimination did not separate its victims according to gender. The childhood memories of Chinese American girls were laced with just as many unpleasant experiences as the recollections of boys. "At times I have been called a 'Chink' and I have resented it bitterly and would at times answer back, but recently I have not replied," reported Lillie Leung of Los Angeles.[39] A Chinese American young woman who had been brought up in Hawaii "found Americans staring at me as though I were a strange being" when she came to the mainland to attend college.[40] She could not become accustomed to such stares, having grown up in a place where people of Asian ancestry formed a majority of the population. "I was very, very lonesome; I had no friends," she confessed.[41] Another Chinese American young woman was chagrined when her teacher said in class, "You belong to a dirty race, that spit at missionaries."[42]

The contents of textbooks also sometimes caused Chinese American students great embarrassment. As one Chinese American woman recalled,

In grade school I was fairly successful in being admitted to the "inner circles," as it were. . . . It was only during geography and history that I became in any way race-conscious. When we came to the study of China, the other children would turn and stare at me as though I were Exhibit A of the lesson. . . . I remember one particularly terrible ancient history lesson; it told in awful detail about "queer little Chinamen, with pigtails and slanting eyes"—and went on to describe the people as though they were inhuman, and at best, uncivilized.[43]

Even the children who had Euro-American friends when they were young eventually were ostracized as they grew older. According to Lillie Leung, who had "never lived in Chinatown, but ha[d] always lived in an American neighborhood," she experienced no problems until she reached puberty. "I have always had a number of American friends. I mingled with all the children quite freely, but when I was about twelve years old they began to turn away from me and I felt this keenly. Up to that time I never realized that I was in any way different, but then I began to think about it."[44] When another Chinese American young woman entered high school, the relationship between her and her schoolmates also changed. "High school made my sense of race-consciousness keener," she said. "I received a few snubs from former 'friends,' which really shocked and amazed me."[45]

Why did Euro-American children begin to treat their Chinese American peers so much more negatively when they all became teenagers? Erikson's observations about adolescence offer an explanation:

> The danger of this stage is role confusion. . . . To keep themselves together they temporarily overidentify, to the point of apparent complete loss of identity, with the heroes of cliques and crowds. . . . Young people can . . . be remarkably clannish and cruel in their exclusion of all those who are "different," in skin color or cultural background, in tastes and gifts, and often in such petty aspects as dress and gesture as have been temporarily selected as *the* signs of an in-grouper or out-grouper. For adolescents not only help one another temporarily through much discomfort by forming cliques and by stereotyping themselves, their ideals, and their enemies; they also perversely test each other's capacity to pledge fidelity. . . . the adolescent . . . is eager to be affirmed by his peers, and is ready to be confirmed by rituals, creeds, and programs which at the same time define what is evil, uncanny, and inimical.[46]

Adolescence was the most painful period in the lives of Chinese Americans because several processes were occuring simultaneously. According to Erikson, adolescents often go through a psychosocial "moratorium," during which they set aside many other concerns as they attempt to resolve their "identity crisis." Adolescence was the period when Chinese Americans became the most self-conscious about being pulled in opposite directions by "Chinese" and "American" cultures. Their identity crisis manifested mainly as a cultural conflict, so rebelling against their parents was synonymous with rejecting Chinese culture. Meanwhile, their Euro-American peers, in also trying to come to terms with who *they* were, felt compelled to draw clear boundaries between themselves, the in-group, and those whom they consigned to out-groups. Their cliquish behavior—expressed in this case in racial terms—was validated by the widespread anti-Chinese discrimination during this era in U.S. history. Indeed, a "complementarity" existed between the psychosocial demands inherent in the developmental stage called adolescence and the ethos of an entire society during this particular historical period. Unfortunately for Chinese Americans, what they experienced during their adolescence was not simply a passing phase. Instead, the rejection that they encountered as teenagers became a permanent feature in their adult lives because the era of Chinese exclusion in which they lived lasted far longer than their own adolescence.

Their experiences with racism notwithstanding, some Chinese American young women still thought that Chinese culture was a more binding force because the rules that many Chinese American girls were expected to follow reached into every nook and cranny of their daily lives. For example, Jade Snow Wong was scolded by her father for daring to wear slippers in the family's living room. Her father had always insisted that all members of the family be fully dressed outside their bedrooms. In his eyes, to have "bedroom attire flaunted publicly" was "indecorous conduct." He reprimanded his daughter for turning the "organization of [his] household into chaos."[47]

Not only did Chinese American girls suffer from their parents' strict expectations, but some of them did not even have friends to tell their troubles to. The only confidante Jade Snow Wong had was her second oldest sister. After the latter married and moved out of the family home,

> Her [Jade Snow's] visits to her sister were surreptitious, for Jade Snow knew that the reason her parents did not invite confidences was that they disapproved of them; they did not encourage companionship because it might undermine their respect, or offer understanding because it might conflict with obedience. Besides, Second Older Sister had married into and belonged to another family, and Jade Snow should not be seeking comfort from one who was thus an "outsider."[48]

Chinese American young women especially resented the favoritism shown their brothers. Louise Leung said, "Chinese parents tend to restrict their daughters. I want to go to Stanford University and have been accepted there, but my father is opposed to my going. He is in favor of education for girls, but adds that there is no need of spending so much money since we will soon be married anyway."[49] Likewise, the most bitter passages in Jade Snow Wong's autobiography concerned the differential treatment that she and her sisters, on the one hand, and her brothers, on the other hand, received. The Wong family celebrated joyously when her younger brother was born: "Because he was a brother, [he] was more important to Mama and Daddy than dear baby sister . . . who was only a girl. But even more uncomfortable was the realization that she herself [Jade Snow] was a girl and, like her younger sister, unalterably less significant than the new son in their family." [50]

Although Jade Snow's father had repeatedly urged her to get an education, he refused to help her financially when she decided to go to college. She was stunned. He told her: "You have been given an above-average Chinese education for an American-born Chinese girl. You now have an average education for an American girl. I must still provide with all my powers for your Older Brother's advanced medical training. . . . If you have the talent, you can provide for your own college education." [51] Hearing this answer, "a new and sudden bitterness" welled up in Jade Snow, who cried to herself, "I can't help being born a girl. . . . I am a person, besides being a female! Don't the Chinese admit that women also have feelings and minds?" [52] With no other recourse, Jade Snow earned her way through college by working as a live-in maid. Years later, after *Fifth Chinese Daughter* had become a best-seller, she sought her father's help when the book was being translated into Chinese. When they came to passages about how he had treated his sons and daughters unequally, he asked her sternly, "Did this really happen?" "Yes, it did," Jade Snow insisted. "I have not put in this book anything which did not happen." [53]

In families without sons, daughters faced contradictory expectations from their parents. On the one hand, they had to assume heavy responsibilities—responsibilities that boys would have shouldered had there been sons in the family—while on the other hand their lives were still strictly controlled. One Chinese American female college student recalled that she not only had to work in her father's sewing factory from a very young age onward, but

The strange thing about my early factory work was not so much the long hours, but the responsibility. When I was twelve my father gave me the oversight of 25 men; I was to give out material, see that their work was right, see that the factory was kept clean, etc. My father, at that time, had no boys, and he started in to train me as if I was a boy. . . . When I was 13 my brother was born and then he lost interest in us girls. . . . My brother has a great deal of spending money and a bank account of his own and can do just about as he likes. We girls were expected to do everything and to pay for our room and board. . . . If my father should die, everything would go to my brother, except perhaps a little to my step-mother and the children. If they had nothing, it would be the duty of my sister and myself to support them, as we are older than my brother, although he would have all the property.[54]

This situation was obviously unfair, but the narrator could do little about it. Her only consolation was that the burdens that she had borne since childhood stood her in good stead as she grew up. She managed to break away from her family to live and work independently and to put herself through college.

Overall, although race and ethnic culture shaped the identities of both the male and female Chinese Americans who came of age during the six decades of Chinese exclusion, race was a more salient feature in the young men's experiences, whereas ethnic culture (and the constraints that it imposed) played a more dominant role in the young women's lives. In short, gender refracted race as well as ethnicity. One result was that the male and female narrators often ascribed different meanings to experiences that, on the surface, seemed similar.

Sources of Cultural Knowledge

Simple dichotomies are now widely disparaged by scholars, especially feminists with a postmodernist bent, but the available life stories show clearly that what is now called "essentialist thinking" was common among young Chinese Americans in the period under study. They believed that compelling differences existed between "American" and "Chinese" cultures, they thought that the two were irreconcilable, and they agonized over how to choose between them. As Esther Wong of San Francisco explained, "For many years I struggled between the two different ways of doing things, the way my parents brought me up and the way that I became acquainted with in college. I really feel that I have had the chance to know the best in conservative Chinese bringing up and in American life, but for a long time I tried to decide which of the two was better and which I should follow."[55]

Moving at will among one's various "subject positions"—a stance advocated by scholars such as the literary critic Lisa Lowe—was a freedom that Chinese Americans and other peoples of color simply did not enjoy until recently, if they do even now.[56] Nonetheless, even when Chinese exclusion was in effect, neither "Chinese" culture nor "American" culture was static or monolithic. Internal contradictions characterized both. Like all other cultures, each was contantly being interpreted by its bearers. Such a process of negotiation is apparent when we ask where Chinese American youngsters got their ideas about what being an "American" or a "Chinese" meant. During the exclusion era, public schools, Christian institutions, and employment as domestic servants in Euro-American homes were the most common sources of information about American culture, whereas Chinese immigrant parents and Chinese-language schools were the chief repositories of Chinese cultural knowledge.

Of the American socializing agents, the most important was the public school. Pardee Lowe not only learned self-reliance at school, but developed "Presidential fever" after hearing his teacher tell the class that "every single one of you can be President of the United States someday!"[57] Pardee could take such a statement to heart because the principles encapsuled in the American creed are couched in universalistic terms—all men, and not just some men, are created equal . . . didn't his teacher tell him so? And wasn't she his most reliable American cultural authority?

Pardee explained why his teacher had such a profound impact on the children of immigrants like himself:

Coming mainly from immigrant homes where parents were too preoccupied with earning a living to devote much time to their children, we transferred our youthful affections to this one person who had both the time and the disposition to mother us. We showered upon our white-haired teacher the blind, wholehearted loyalty of the young. Our studies we readily absorbed, not because we particularly liked them so much as because it was "she" who taught us. . . . Thus, . . . she whom we staunchly enshrined in our hearts laid the rudimentary but firm foundation of our personal brand of American culture.[58]

To Pardee, the American public school was the "institution in which I was free to indulge my own most un-Chinese inclinations."[59] For this reason, when his father proposed sending him to a boarding school in China, he burst out vehemently, "I want to stay in America!" He explained his reaction as follows: "I loved America, . . . why would I wish to go to China? All the things I had learned from our kinfolk about the old country were bad, with no redeeming features. After all, I added as my clinching argument, if this were not so, why should our kinsmen wish to come to the United States?"[60]

Admittedly, the last sentence does ring with ironic logic.

Jade Snow Wong also first became aware of the differences between Chinese culture and American culture during an incident at school.

One day, while she was playing in the school yard, one of her classmates accidentally hit her hand with a baseball bat.

> As Jade Snow cried out, the teacher was there. She leaned down and held Jade Snow closely, rubbing her fingers, wiping the tears which fell involuntarily as the pain gradually flowed into her numb hand. It was a very strange feeling to be held to a grown-up foreign lady's bosom. She could not remember when Mama had held her to give comfort. Daddy occasionally picked her up as a matter of necessity, but he never embraced her impulsively when she required consolation. . . . [It was] wonderful to be embraced by Miss Mullohand. But suddenly the comfort changed to embarrassment. What was one supposed to do now in response? The embarrassment turned to panic. . . .[S]he was now conscious that "foreign" American ways were not only generally and vaguely different from their Chinese ways, but that they were specifically different, and the specific differences would involve a choice of action.[61]

Although its influence was less pervasive than that of the public schools, the Christian church—and its offshoots, such as the YMCA and the YWCA— likewise served as a source of American cultural knowledge, even though Chinese were treated as foreigners by the church and had to use segregated facilities. (When the various Protestant denominations established churches in Chinatowns, they called them "missions," which were supported by the denominations' boards of *foreign* missions. The YMCA and YWCA, meanwhile, set up special branches for Chinese Americans.[62]) Pardee Lowe became active in church because he thought that it provided a "spot in which to exercise all my American proclivities."[63] However, the hypocrisy of certain Euro-American Christians, such as the YMCA secretary described previously who refused to allow a Chinese American young man to use the organization's swimming pool, turned some Chinese Americans away from the Christian faith. As Lew Kay of Seattle noted, "Many are very much against Christianity, because they say Americans are Christians. . . . Chinese don't believe that Americans live up to what they preach."[64] Even Pardee Lowe, who had fervently embraced the religion, became disillusioned when Christians defended their religion and their ideals in the same breath as they refused to hire him: "If that was the type of religious conduct practiced by pillars of [the] church, I concluded in my despair, I would have none of it."[65]

Besides the public schools and Protestant churches, only a few other settings existed in which Chinese American young people could come into close contact with Euro-Americans. Becoming domestic servants in Euro-American homes provided one such venue. When Jade Snow Wong was a teenager, she started working as a maid in Euro-American families to earn pocket money. There, she had a chance to observe social relationships within what she assumed to be a typical American home—relations that seemed the opposite of those in her own family.

> It was a home where children were heard as well as seen; where parents considered who was right or wrong, rather than who should be respected; . . . where the husband kissed his wife and the parents kissed their children; . . . where the family was actually concerned with having fun together and going out to play together; where the problems and difficulties of domestic life and children's discipline were untangled, perhaps after tears, but also after explanations; . . . where, above all, each member, even down to and including the dog, appeared to have the inalienable right to assert his individuality . . . in an atmosphere of natural affection.[66]

It is poignant how Jade Snow Wong lamented what seemed lacking in her own home environment more than she did the menial position to which she had been relegated in American society.

Making these kinds of comparisons between their own families and those of Euro-Americans, Chinese American children and youth often felt deprived. Chinese culture and social relations seemed rigid and restrictive, whereas American culture and social relations seemed warm and affectionate. In the late nineteenth and early twentieth centuries, the ideology of assimilation ruled supreme in American society. Cultural pluralism was not an available option. Therefore, Chinese Americans found that drawing strength from both their heritages was difficult. Rather, they thought that they always had to make choices, because, in the words of Pardee Lowe, "it was difficult to be a filial Chinese son and a good American citizen at one and the same time."[67]

In virtually all instances, during their childhood Chinese Americans showed a strong preference for the American part of their legacy because in American society children can speak freely and express themselves in other ways with exuberance. They are allowed to "be themselves." As Chinese American children reached puberty, however, and as their Euro-American peers began to reject and ostracize them, they became painfully aware that no real choice was possible. Regardless of where they were born, how they behaved, or how well they spoke English, they, like their immigrant parents, were considered unassimilable aliens and perpetual foreigners. As the young woman from Hawaii recalled,

> I realized very soon that I was not an American in spite of the fact that I had citizenship privileges. At the university, I was referred to as a *foreign* student; I objected to being called such at first; I insisted that I was an American—born on American soil and coming from an American . . . state. But soon, I learned that I was laughed at, mocked at my contention that I was an American and should be treated as such. . . . I gradually learned that I am a foreigner—a Chinese—that I would be wiser to admit it and to disclaim my American citizenship.[68]

Then, when they began to enter the labor market, the full force of prejudice and racial discrimination hit them: Regardless of how they might have perceived themselves, other Americans did not consider them to be "real" Americans. Sadly, this was only half the dilemma that faced, for they were not "real" Chinese, either. This was so because the manner in which Chinese cultural knowledge was transmitted to them was shot through with ambiguities.

Although Chinese immigrant parents, in the eyes of their American-born children, were the fount from which all things Chinese flowed, they were, in fact, not always paragons of Chinese propriety. In the Chinese American life stories that have been passed down to us, many parents were not stereotypically Chinese in either outward appearance or inner thoughts. In Thomas Chinn's family, although his mother spoke no English, she managed to communicate well with her Euro-American neighbors, who spoke no Chinese. She learned to make American desserts that her children loved. And, most significant, at the age of forty-three, she decided to unbind her feet—a painful process that took years, during which the bandages were loosened bit by bit.[69]

According to Lillie Leung of Los Angeles, her parents, "contrary to the Chinese custom," wanted both their sons and their daughters to secure a good education. Her father even urged her to study medicine.[70] Another young Chinese American woman growing up in Los Angeles said, "Father . . . believes in the old Chinese idea that all girls must eventually be launched into matrimony. He is modern enough to allow me to launch myself, but that I will be launched he seems very sure."[71] Such attitudes deviated from those commonly found in pre-1911 China (that is, before the Qing dynasty was overthrown and a republic was established), where girls were not sent to school and were given away in arranged marriages soon after they became nubile.

In the case of Jade Snow Wong's father, his outlook was "revolution-ized" after he converted to Christianity. Arriving as a youth in San Francisco, he had attended the English classes offered by the Cumber-land Presbyterian Chinese Mission. The Chinese pastor at that mission not only taught him English but also "educated him in a new doctrine of individual dignity and eternal personal salvation." He then wrote his wife who was still in China with their two daughters: "Do not bind our daughters' feet. Here in America is an entirely different set of stan-dards, which does not require that women sway helplessly on little feet to qualify them for good matches as well-born women who do not have to work. Here in Golden Mountains [America], the people, and even women, have individual dignity and rights of their own."[72]

After a few years, Mr. Wong brought his wife and two daughters to the United States because "here my wife will have opportunity to do honest work and my daughters will enjoy an education."[73] He wanted his children to attend both the American public school and the Chi-nese-language school. However, because the latter did not accept girls until the late 1920s, he tutored his daughters himself to help them master the Chinese language. He justified his efforts to educate his daughters as follows:

> Since sons and their education are of primary importance, we must have intelligent mothers. If nobody educates his daughters, how can we have intelligent mothers for our sons? . . . The peace and stability of a nation depend upon the proper relationships established in the home; and to a great extent, the maintenance of proper relations within the home depends on intelligent mothers.[74]

His reasoning, although still sexist from a contemporary perspec-tive, was a far cry from the beliefs that were prevalent in most of China (except possibly such large cities as Canton or Shanghai, where West-ern influences had penetrated) and in American Chinatowns during that period. Wanting his daughters to become educated was not the only way in which he differed from his peers. When Jade Snow reached marriageable age, her parents made some desultory attempts to find her a suitor. However, when one of her father's fellow villagers indi-cated that he "would like very much to have a daughter-in-law [from the Wong family] live with us and help around the house," Mr. Wong replied, "Very difficult. That will make a problem with these Ameri-can-born girls."[75] By declining this marriage offer, he was looking out for Jade Snow's welfare; he did not want to put her into a situation where she might have to suffer at the hands of her parents-in-law. These aspects of Mr. Wong's behavior are worth pointing out because more often than not, *Fifth Chinese Daughter* has been read as a chronicle of an American-born daughter's rebellion against her China-born "patriarchal" father. In fact, Mr. Wong's efforts to "liberate" women extended beyond his own family: he personally delivered cut denim, to be sewn into overalls, to Chinese women who wanted to work but whose husbands would not allow them to leave home to earn money.[76] (Of course, a more cynical interpretation of his actions is also possible: He could not have exploited the labor of these women had he not delivered the fabric to their homes.)

Pardee Lowe's father likewise was no patriarch avidly upholding Chinese tradition. He had cut off his queue long before it was legal to do so in China. At his wedding, he refused to put on a cap to which a fake queue had been attached. "I am not a slave!" he proclaimed angrily.[77] (The Manchus, who founded the Qing dynasty [1644–1911], forced all Chinese men to wear a queue. Many Chinese thus considered the queue a symbol of their subservience.) As his children were born, he, like Thomas Chinn's father, gave them American first names. He did not simply choose names he liked, though; he made his children the namesakes of famous Americans. Pardee was named after Governor George C. Pardee of California; his sisters, Alice and Helen, were named after family members of Presidents Theodore Roosevelt and William Howard Taft (Alice Roosevelt and Helen Taft); and his twin brothers, Wilson and Marshall, were named after President Woodrow Wilson and Wilson's vice president, Thomas Riley Marshall. When Mr. Lowe's Euro-American friends alerted reporters to the christening of Pardee's twin brothers, the event was duly noted in some of San Francisco's newspapers. Pardee commented, "I think Father liked the idea that in the eyes of the Barbarian Press we had . . . been accepted as Americans."[78] Pardee's mother, meanwhile, learned to cook turkey for Thanksgiving. "We share the holiday of our American neighbors . . . because we wish to live in peace and harmony with them and because I do not wish you children to grow wicked with envy of others," she explained.[79]

Because cultural boundaries are permeable and meanings can change even as cultural forms remain the same, the interplay of Chinese and American cultures within Chinese immigrant families sometimes led to unusual outcomes. After Pardee Lowe's mother died, the skillful manner in which she had managed to bridge the gulf between her husband and her children suddenly became apparent. Once she was gone,

Pardee and his siblings began quarreling more often with their father. The most bitter disagreement between the two generations arose over Mr. Lowe's reluctance to move the family into better quarters. When he claimed that he could not afford to do so, Pardee burst out angrily: "It's possible for you to buy a one-thousand-acre fruit ranch, but it is not possible for you to satisfy our family with a home!" His father refused to yield, however. The impasse lasted for two years, until Pardee's stepmother found a way to change her husband's mind by asking him, "What are dollars compared with family harmony?" [80] She had cleverly used something greatly valued in *Chinese* culture—family harmony—to persuade him to give in to his children's *American* desires.

Given the immigrant parents' own ambivalent and changing stances as they negotiated between their Chinese legacy and the American milieu in which they now lived, some Chinese American children predictably found their childhood world confusing. Lisa Mar [pseudonym], who grew up in an apartment above a bar in the Mission District in San Francisco in the 1930s, recalled that her parents gave her mixed messages about the outside world:

> I never knew certain things . . . that you would think I should know, because my parents never would explain enough to me. . . . What my parents told me about being Chinese, and the outside world, was a very mixed thing. . . . When my parents would talk about the outside being a bad place, they would refer sort of generally to "the whites out there," they always called them *sai yen.* To me, of course, that meant the whites right around us. . . . The same people who would vomit and pee on our doorstep, were the people who had the power to take our home away from us. We had to do a little placating of them. . . . But there were other things my family would tell me. Like when my mother got locked out of the house, she would go down to the bar and one of these men would go around back, climb up some steps, crawl across a ledge and in through the window to open the door for her. And my mother would tell me, "You know, only a *sai yen* would do that for you." [81]

Confusion also characterized Jade Snow Wong's childhood. "[L]ife was a constant puzzle," she wrote. "No one ever troubled to explain. Only through punishment did she learn that what was proper was right and what was improper was wrong. . . . The daughters of the Wong family were born to requirements exacting beyond their understanding. These requirements were not always made clear, until a step out of bounds brought the parents' swift and drastic correction." [82]

Victor Wong, who also grew up in San Francisco's Chinatown in the 1930s, was stymied not so much by his parents' failure to explain things to him, but by the gap between their words and their actions. He recalled:

> The thing that is so puzzling is not to know what Chinese culture *is*. I mean, I'm taught by my parents what it means to be Chinese, and then I watch their actions, and there's so much discrepancy. They say one thing and then they act another way entirely, and so you wonder which *is* the Chinese culture, the way they're actually performing or what they're trying to transmit by word of mouth.[83]

These accounts reveal that although Chinese immigrant parents tried their best to pass on to their children the *ideals* they had learned from their own childhoods in China, they did not always follow those guiding principles after they arrived in the United States.

The traditional idea of how children should be raised was not the only reason that Chinese immigrant parents did not explain things to their young. Two other considerations were perhaps even more important. First, in Chinese immigrant communities in late-nineteenth- and early-twentieth-century America, telling children too much was often unsafe, given the harsh treatment that the Chinese received from tax collectors, policemen, and immigration officials. After the Chinese Exclusion Act was passed in 1882, some Chinese managed to get themselves smuggled into the country, whereas others entered as "paper sons," having purchased documents and assumed the identities of individuals who were eligible for entry. All Chinese attempting to enter the United States during the six decades of exclusion were subjected to detailed interrogation and grueling confinement. Between 1882 and 1910, the aspiring immigrants or returning residents were held in a shed on the wharf in San Francisco. From 1910 to 1940, they were confined in the immigration station on Angel Island in the middle of San Francisco Bay. Even after individuals were allowed to land, they could still be arrested at any time. Those found without the registration cards required by the 1892 Geary Act could be arrested, imprisoned, and deported. During these terrifying years, the Chinese community lived in constant fear. In such an intimidating atmosphere, adults could not afford to tell children anything, lest the little ones unwittingly reveal secrets that might jeopardize other family members.

Second, parents sometimes gave conflicting signals because they often felt torn over how to rear their young. Many immigrant parents changed their attitudes and behavior as time passed. In general, the longer they remained in the United States, the more "liberal" and less "old-fashioned" they became. Commonly, the younger children in a family grew up with far fewer restrictions than their older siblings had been subjected to. These changes in the parents' behavior made them seem inconsistent and, worse, unfair, from the older children's viewpoint. But such, unfortunately, were the hard facts of life in many an immigrant family.

Given their own uncertainty about their adequacy as cultural authorities, almost all Chinese immigrant parents insisted that their children attend Chinese-language school—at least in the localities with such schools. Thomas Chinn's family, for example, felt so strongly about having their children attend Chinese-language school that they moved from a small town in Oregon, where they had lived comfortably, to San Francisco to make such enrollment possible.[84] The parents who could afford to do so kept their children in Chinese-language school as long as possible. Years of schooling were required not only because Chinese is such a difficult language to learn, but also because, teaching children to show respect to their elders, in particular their parents and teachers, takes time and repeated lessons. When Pardee Lowe protested that going to Chinese-language school was a waste of time, he missed the point because he was thinking in purely utilitarian terms. He declared, "I wrote no Chinese letters to our relatives in China. Only the simplest phrases were used in Chinatown. In our home I spoke mostly pidgin Chinese or English." The adult members of his family had a more compelling reason for sending him to Chinese-language school, however; they wanted to "neutralize" his "excessive Americanism."[85]

Even American-born men of Chinese ancestry, who may not have enjoyed going to Chinese-language school during their youth, believed that sending their own children there was imperative. The reason is that, apart from teaching the Chinese language, the Chinese-school teachers were also expected to instill social decorum into their wards. As Chin Cheung of Seattle related, "I want my children to get Chinese education first; they must have Chinese custom and understand Chinese language because they always be Chinese. . . . If they don't have this old country education they no good."[86]

What did he mean by "no good"? His main criticism centered on the liberties allowed American-born girls: "This country you know, girl too independent. Go out in the evening, dance, spend money, don't like stay home much. . . . Girls this country don't make so good wives as girls in China. Girls in China have more respect I think for husband. They look after husband better; look after children better; have more children."[87]

His sentiments were echoed by other men, all American born. Bong Chin confirmed, "Chinese generally prefer to marry women in China. Born this country to [sic] much American. . . . Too freedom this country, the women."[88] Ying Foy explained why he had returned to China to marry: "I go back China get girl to marry. Over here all girl born in this country no good. Spend too much money, no like to have too many children. . . . I think women got too much freedom, too much power over here. I think divorce very bad. Break up lots of families. These customs U.S. very, very bad."[89]

The broader social functions performed by Chinese-language schools help explain why some Chinese immigrants did not always support their children's desire for a college education, the extraordinary value that Chinese have traditionally placed on education notwithstanding: They feared that their children's acquisition of an *American* higher education might prove subversive. The ideas learned in college, even more so than those absorbed in elementary, junior high, and high schools, might erode some of the fundamental tenets of Chinese culture.

When Pardee Lowe was about to graduate from high school, he not only wanted to go to college, but also desired to enroll specifically at Stanford University, then, as now, an expensive institution. When his father asked him who had suggested that he apply to Stanford, Pardee replied that it was his favorite teacher in high school. "Who is this woman," his father asked irritably, "whom you would set above your father?"[90]

Jade Snow Wong offended her father in a similar way. She had taken what her college sociology teacher said to heart when he declared: "Today we recognize that children are individuals, and that parents can no longer demand their unquestioning obedience. Parents should do their best to understand their children, because young people also have their rights." Soon thereafter, when her father stopped her as she was stepping out the front door to go on a date, she responded verbatim with the passage she had heard in her sociology class. "Where," demanded her father, "did you learn such unfilial theory?" "From my teacher . . . who you taught me is supreme after you, and whose judgment I am not to question," Jade Snow replied. In furor, her father shouted, "A little learning has gone to your head! How can you permit a foreigner's theory to put aside the practical experience of the Chinese, who for thousands of years have preserved a most superior family pattern?"[91]

In both instances, the Chinese immigrant parents obviously felt threatened by the existence of alternative authority figures to whom their American-born children could turn. The dilemma that these parents faced was that although they were pleased to see their children respect their teachers' opinions, they did not want their progeny to follow the counterexamples set by these instructors whose teachings undermined the two key organizing principles in traditional Chinese society—showing respect and obedience to those who are older than oneself, regardless of whether they are right or wrong, and upholding the dominance of males over females.

Some Chinese parents opposed their offsprings' desire to go to the university for more pragmatic reason as well. For one thing, few immigrant families eking out a meager living in early-twentieth-century America could afford the tuition. In the case of Pardee Lowe, if he were allowed to go to Stanford University as he desired, not only would he use a large portion of his father's earnings, but he would also deprive his family of the money that he could have earned had he gone to work instead.[92] Even more important, in the years before World War II, immigrant parents were acutely aware that persons of Chinese ancestry— regardless of where they had been born, what citizenship they held, and what level of education they had attained—were barred from a wide variety of jobs. Therefore, even though these parents might have prized education per se, they hesitated to pay tuition for additional years of schooling that promised no economic or social returns in America. James Low, who was born in 1925 in San Francisco, recounted, "My father used to tell me, 'Look at your boss, he was going to be an engineer, look what happened to him! What are you studying engineering for?' At the time I was working for a man who had trained to be a mining engineer, but he ended up running a sewing factory. This was one of the reasons my father really disapproved of my going to school."[93]

However desperately members of the American-born second generation tried to prove that they were Americans, in time they did learn to reconcile themselves to their Chinese origins. Ironically, neither their parents nor their Chinese-language school teachers effected this change. Rather, the racial discrimination that they encountered in the larger society as they grew up, finished school, and tried to find jobs finally forced them to make peace with their Chinese heritage.

Becoming Chinese Americans

Anti-Chinese prejudice and discrimination expressed themselves in myriad ways during the first century of Chinese settlement in America. Being called names, being stoned in the streets, having to at-

tend a segregated "Oriental" school in San Francisco, and often being
ostracized by their Euro-American classmates in towns where Chinese
American pupils could attend integrated public schools were all common experiences. So were being forbidden to use public recreational facilities, having to live within the confines of a ghetto, being perceived
as foreigners even when they were born as Americans, and not having
police protection. How, then, did Chinese Americans deal with the
hostility that confronted them at every turn? Some avoided situations
where they knew that they would be singled out for maltreatment, others tried to repress their upset feelings, a few worked to combat the
negative stereotypes imposed up on them, and a handful resisted, while
a large number began identifying with China.

Avoidance and repression were forms of behavior that many Chinese Americans adopted as they tried to survive with a modicum of
dignity in America. Some avoided physical confrontations, not because
they were cowardly or stoic, but because common sense compelled
them to do so: They fought back only when they were certain that they
would not be outnumbered. Such occasions were rare because Chinese
were a minuscule minority in most places. As Chin Cheung of Seattle
remembered: "When I in San Francisco they treat me very bad. . . .
Young fellows throw stones, cans, bricks; make lots trouble all the
time, but I always run away. I have no trouble that way because I never
stay a fight. Too many white people; same number Chinamen, lots of
fight; not many Chinamen[,] no can fight."[94]

As a survival tactic, avoidance is not as passive as it may appear.
Rather, it can be seen as one form of what the political scientist James
C. Scott called "weapons of the weak."[95] In the face of overwhelming
odds, people who are relatively powerless have a limited range of options. By deciding *when* to fight back, such individuals or groups make
a strategic choice. Historically, not only did Chinese Americans often
choose the occasions when they would resist, but some of them also
chose what *form* such resistance would take. Those who tried to maintain their equanimity were trying consciously not to let disturbing situations "get to" them. Lew Kay of Seattle said: "I was born and raised
here, . . . [so I] know what to expect and what others get. . . . I generally
know the places where discrimination is shown and I make no attempt
to go. That has been my policy after high school and University."[96]
Chin Cheung stated that after he moved from San Francisco to Seattle,
"I never have trouble in get[sic] my hair cut in barber shop or have
trouble to go in restaurant and not have them serve me. I know where
they treat Chinese all right, then I go. I stay away from other places."[97]

One Chinese American young woman admitted, "Of course I resented it, but not enough to fight back or to be embittered."[97] It was important for Chinese Americans not to become embittered lest chronic anger would deprive them of any semblance of a normal life.[99] In time, conditions did improve. According to David Young of Seattle, "In my young days, when they see any Chinese walking around, they would throw bricks and stones, but not now. Everything is better."[100]

Others took a more active approach by trying to combat negative images of the Chinese. According to Chingwah Lee, "In order to avoid being mistaken for . . . prostitutes . . . Chinese housewives would wear nothing but black [as Chinese prostitutes wore brightly colored clothes]."[101] A few Chinese Americans became tour guides "to combat these sightseeing companies" that spread erroneous and biased information about Chinatown to tourists.[102] (See Chapter 6 of this book, for further discussion on this topic.)

A handful of individuals went even further and refused to accept assignments that were stereotypically Chinese. Luke Chess, who was born in San Francisco in 1890 and claimed to be the first Chinese American to be accepted for enlistment in the U.S. Navy, recounted the following incident, speaking of himself (like Jade Snow Wong) in the third-person singular:

> The commander officer of the U.S.S. Charleston wanted to command him to be a COOK to the Captain, but he enlisted rated as 2nd class fireman U.S. Navy. Chess have had the most patriotic courage to replie his commander officer, and said to him, "I came to serve and to die might I need for my Country. And I shall not serve as servant to be a cook for the Captain." . . . Stopped! all the nonsense, the Commander officer said. . . . You know that I have the power to put in the Brack (lock-up) and lock you in there, if you do refused me to go to the Galley for cook to the Captain. . . . Fool! you understand that? Yes sir I do. . . . I rather take the Brack, . . . I am here and ready to serve for the U.S.A. and not for cook and servant to the Captain.[103]

His pride in himself for being courageous enough to refuse to be relegated to the role of a domestic servant shines through even his garbled English. His motto was "Give me Equal or give me death," while his goal in life was to "fight the battle of the prejudice and narrow minded . . . Unamericanism."[104]

Unlike Luke Chess, who managed to have a most unconventional career as a technician first in the U.S. Navy and later in a number of manufacturing companies on the East Coast, Chinese Americans on the West Coast found it virtually impossible to secure jobs in the fields in which they had been trained in college. C. C. Wing, who graduated magna cum laude from St. Ignatious School of Law (now part of the University of San Francisco), recalled: "They told me I could not make a living practicing law on account of my race."[105] By taking in every kind of case, however, Wing managed to eke out a living as Chinatown's one and only lawyer. Alice Fong Yu, the first Chinese American ever hired as a public-school teacher, had difficulty persuading the president of San Francisco Teachers College to allow her to enroll. "Nobody is going to hire you when you graduate," he said, "so why study to be a teacher?" He finally accepted her application only when she told him, "I'm not going to stay here; I'm going to China to help my people."[106] Elizabeth Ling-So Hall, who became the first Chinese American principal in the San Francisco public school system, could not land a job after receiving her teaching certificate. So she began her career by teaching English in Chinatown and later working at a private nursery school.[107] Daisy Wong Chinn recalled that the only American corporations that hired any Chinese Americans were those with a branch in China or Chinatown.[108]

When Jade Snow Wong was a senior at Mills College, she received the following advice from the placement office: "If you are smart, you will look for a job only among your Chinese firms. You cannot expect to get anywhere in American business houses. After all, I am sure you are conscious that racial prejudice on the Pacific Coast will be a great handicap to you."[109] The vocational counselor who made this statement thought that she was being kind. She wanted Jade Snow to have a realistic idea of what the world after college would be like.

At such a point in their lives, college-educated Chinese Americans stopped perceiving China as that strange land from which their parents had come and considered it, instead, as a place where they might find an outlet for their talents. Sun Peter Lee of Los Angeles told an interviewer, "I am directing my studies toward a course in electrical engineering, after which I plan to go to China, where I will find greater opportunities than in America, where they will not employ me because I am Chinese."[110] Louise Leung, also of Los Angeles, likewise noted, "The Chinese who are trained in the schools here do not expect to remain in the United States, but they are looking toward China for the future. . . . I myself am planning to go to China to teach."[111] Jade Snow Wong's father urged her to think about going to China as she was about to graduate from high school, because, as he told her, "a Chinese could realize his optimum achievement only in China."[112] After experiencing multiple rejections—by Euro-Americans, mainland Chinese Americans, and students from China alike—the young woman from Hawaii came to the dejected conclusion that

> Verily, I am a "man without a country." I love America and would be her citizen but she would not have me; . . . I am . . . feeling more sympathetic for China—a great deal more sympathetic than I have ever been before. I am acquiring a love for her as I never had before. I am beginning to feel a sense of nationalism. . . . While I love America, I love China also now. I see no place in American life for me; and I see very little place for me in China but there is more hope there than there is here.[113]

As David Young of Seattle said more succinctly, "The prejudice against the Orientals, you get sick of it and feel you would like to go back."[114]

The tragic irony, of course, is that to "go back" is a misnomer: Most of the Chinese Americans had never been to China! Nonetheless, whether their future lay in China or in America was the main topic of discussion among Chinese Americans in the 1930s. The *Chinese Digest,* founded by Thomas Chinn and Chingwah Lee as the first English-language journal for Chinese Americans, published essays submitted for a nationwide debate on this topic. The debaters on each side offered many reasons for choosing one country or the other.[115] (See Chapter 6 of this book for more details on this debate.) The true significance of the question that they addressed, however, was not cognitive but psychological. By finally allowing China to occupy a place in their consciousness, by reconciling themselves to the Chinese part of their ethnic identity, Chinese Americans learned to accept themselves as whole persons. Victor Wong of San Francisco described the process in the following way: "The funny thing is that after I consented to return to the culture I felt much better as a person. And much easier to live with. . . . Much more quiet inside myself since I returned."[116]

Conclusion

In an earlier work, I argued that "the history of Asians in America can be fully understood only if we regard them as both immigrants and members of nonwhite minority groups. As immigrants, many of their struggles resemble those that European immigrants have faced, but as people of nonwhite origins bearing distinct physical differences, they have been perceived as 'perpetual foreigners' who can never be completely absorbed into American society. . . . [T]he acculturation process experienced by Asians in America has run along two tracks: even as they acquired the values and behavior of Euro-Americans, they simultaneously had to learn to accept their standing as racial minorities."[117]

The European-immigrant analogy does not apply fully to Asian immigrants because although some of them—like the parents of Pardee Lowe, Thomas Chinn, and Jade Snow Wong—did acculturate (that is, they learned to think and behave like Euro-Americans), structural barriers prevented them from fully assimilating (that is, they were not allowed to become members of mainstream organizations and social group). Whereas acculturation depends mainly on the immigrants' efforts, assimilation is contingent upon the immigrants' efforts *as well as* on the receptivity shown by members of the majority society. Thus, if Asian immigrants did not assimilate as speedily as their European counterparts did, the reason was not entirely their proclivity to "cling" to Asian culture, as commonly alleged.

The racial minority analogy is not fully applicable to Asian Americans, either. Much of our theoretical understanding of racial minorities is based on studies of African Americans. However, unlike African Americans whose connections to Africa were ruptured in many ways during slavery, Asian Americans retained strong ties to their ancestral homelands. When Chinese in America encountered discrimination and became discouraged, some of them found a psychological refuge that was not available to African Americans: The immigrant parents dreamed of returning to China to retire, while their American-born offspring looked to China as a place where they might find employment commensurate with their education.

The historical experience of second-generation Chinese Americans was even more complex than that of their immigrant parents. Their sense of self changed as they grew up and interacted with different groups of "significant others." Wanting desperately to be accepted as Americans during their childhood, they resisted their parents' attempts to teach them the Chinese language, in which was encoded the values and norms of Chinese culture. Because many of their Euro-American teachers and schoolmates had accepted them when they were children, their self-identification as "Americans" seemed justified. As they became adolescents, however, they increasingly experienced rejection from their former Euro-American friends. They were stunned to discover that the identity imposed on them as "Chinese" (or worse, as "Chinks" and "Chinamen") was far more powerful, in terms of determining their "place" in American society, than whatever labels they might have fashioned for themselves. Nevertheless, fervently believing in the American dream, they insisted on going to college and worked to pay their way when their parents declined to give them financial support. Only after they had received their college degrees and entered the adult world of work did American racism hit them full force. Job discrimination was something that their parents had always warned them about, but they never realized its impregnable power until they sought employment outside their own ethnic communities. Under such circumstances, they paradoxically began to look to *China* as a place where their *American* ambitions might best be fulfilled. However, when some of them did "return" to China, they had difficulty fitting into the land of their parents. Suspended uneasily between two cultures, they had no choice but to try with quiet determination to create a new world of their own—a Chinese American world.

Notes

1. The total Chinese-ancestry population had declined from a peak of more than 107,000 in the early 1880s to a low of 61,639 in 1920 as a result of the Chinese exclusion laws. From this nadir, the number began to climb slowly as more children were born on American soil and, in the late 1940s, as Chinese war brides entered the country. Only in 1950 did the Chinese-ancestry population finally outstrip the figure shown in the 1890 census.

2. According to U.S. law, children born in China to fathers (but not mothers) who were U.S. citizens were considered derivative citizens who could enter the United States even during the years when the Chinese exclusion laws were in effect. Between 1878, when the *In re Ah Yup* decision explicitly denied Chinese the right of naturalization—a decision affirmed in the 1882 Chinese Exclusion Act—and 1906, when the San Francisco earthquake and fire destroyed all official records in the city, one can assume, with rare exceptions, that persons of Chinese ancestry with U.S. citizenship had been born in the United States. However, after the earthquake, some foreign-born Chinese claimed to be American born because no records were available to prove or disprove their claim. Individuals who managed to acquire American citizenship in this manner could then bring their China-born children into the country as derivative citizens. After 1906, therefore, the number of Chinese with U.S. citizenship and the number of American-born Chinese cannot be assumed to be the same. Chinese finally regained the right to become naturalized citizens in December 1943, when Congress repealed all the existing Chinese exclusion laws.

3. For details on how the California legislature, the U.S. Congress, and the various federal courts tried to minimize the number of Chinese women who

could enter, see Sucheng Chan, "The Exclusion of Chinese Women, 1870–1943," in *Entry Denied: Exclusion and the Chinese Community in America, 1882–1943,* ed. Sucheng Chan (Philadelphia: Temple University Press, 1991), 94–146.

4. The Survey of Race Relations archives housed at the Hoover Institution of War, Revolution, and Peace at Stanford University contain many more life histories, most written in the third-person singular by the project's field researchers. I chose to use only the documents written in the first-person singular because I am analyzing autobiographies, not biographies.

5. Philip Gleason, "American Identity and Americanization," in *Harvard Encyclopedia of American Ethnic Groups,* ed. Stephan Thernstrom (Cambridge, Mass.: Belknap Press, 1980), 31–58.

6. It is outside the scope of this study to cite the voluminous amount of literature on European immigration and its relationship to American identity, but a review essay by Rudolph J. Vecoli, "European Americans: From Immigrants to Ethnics," in *The Reinterpretation of American History and Culture,* ed. William H. Cartwright and Richard L. Watson, Jr. (Washington, D.C.: National Council for the Social Studies, 1973), 81–112, offers a useful overview of the writings published up to 1972. Only selected works that set the pace for American immigration and ethnic history (each pointed the field in a new direction either conceptually or methodologically) can be listed here. In chronological order by date of publication, they include Horace M. Kallen, *Culture and Democracy in the United States: Studies in the Group Psychology of the American Peoples* (New York: Boni and Liveright, 1924, reprint., New York: Arno Press, 1970), which contains a reprint of his famous essay, "Democracy and the Melting Pot: A Study of American Nationality," first published in 1915 in *The Nation;* William I. Thomas and Florian Znaniecki, *The Polish Peasant in Europe and America: Monograph of an Immigrant Group* (Boston: Richard G. Badger, 1918–1920; 2d ed., New York: Dover, 1927, reprint, 1958; abr. ed., Urbana: University of Illinois Press, 1984); Ray Allen Billington, *The Protestant Crusade, 1800–1869* (New York: Macmillan, 1938); Carl F. Wittke, *We Who Built America: The Saga of the Immigrant* (New York: Prentice-Hall, 1939); Marcus Hansen, *The Atlantic Migration, 1607–1860: A History of the Continuing Settlement of the United States* (Cambridge, Mass.: Harvard University Press, 1940); Marcus Hansen, *The Immigrant in American History* (Cambridge, Mass.: Harvard University Press, 1940); Edward G. Hartmann, *The Movement to Americanize the Immigrant,* Columbia University Studies in the Social Sciences, no. 545 (New York: Columbia University Press, 1948); Oscar Handlin, *Boston's Immigrants, 1790–1865: A Study in Acculturation* (London: Oxford University Press, 1941; rev. enl. ed., Cambridge, Mass.: Belknap Press, 1959); Oscar Handlin, *The Uprooted: The Epic Story of the Great Migrations That Made the American People* (Boston: Little, Brown, 1951, 2d enl. ed., 1973); Brinley Thomas, *Migration and Economic Growth: A Study of Great Britain and the Atlantic Economy* (Cambridge, England: University Press, 1954); John Higham, *Strangers in the Land: Patterns of American Nativism, 1860–1925* (New Brunswick, N.J.: Rutgers University Press, 1955, 2d ed., 1988); Charlotte Erickson, *American Industry and the European Immigrant, 1860–1885* (Cambridge, Mass.: Harvard University Press, 1957); Stephan Thernstrom, *Poverty and Progress: Social Mobility in a Nineteenth-Century City* (Cambridge, Mass.: Harvard University Press, 1964); Rudolph J. Vecoli, "*Contadini* in Chicago: A Critique of *The Uprooted,*" *Journal of American*

History 51, no. 3 (1964): 407–417; Frank Thistlewaite, "Migration from Europe Overseas in the Nineteenth and Twentieth Centuries," in *Population Movements in Modern European History*, ed. Herbert Mollor (New York: Macmillan, 1964); 73–92; Louis Hartz, *The Founding of New Societies: Studies in the History of the United States, Latin America, South Africa, Canada, and Australia* (New York: Harcourt, Brace and World, 1964); Timothy L. Smith, "New Approaches to the History of Immigration in Twentieth-Century America," *American Historical Review* 71, no. 4 (1966): *1265–1279;* John Higham, "Immigration," in *The Comparative Approach to American History*, ed. C. Vann Woodward (New York: Basic Books, *1968), 91–105;* Rudolph J. Vecoli, "Ethnicity: A Neglected Dimension of American History," in *The State of American History*, ed. Herbert J. Bass (Chicago: Quadrangle Books, *1970), 70–88;* Rowland Berthoff, *An Unsettled People: Social Order and Disorder in American History* (New York:: Harper and Row, *1971);* Stephan Thernstrom, *The Other Bostonians: Poverty and Progress in an American Metropolis* (Cambridge, Mass.: Harvard University Press, *1973);* Josef J. Barton, *Peasants and Strangers: Italians, Rumanians, and Slovaks in an American City 1890–1950* (Cambridge, Mass.: Harvard University Press, *1975);* Dino Cinel, *From Italy to San Francisco: The Immigrant Experience* (Stanford: Stanford University Press, *1982);* Jon Gjerde, *From Peasants to Farmers: The Migration from Balestrand, Norway to the Upper Middle West* (New York: Cambridge University Press, *1985);* Kerby A. Miller, *Emigrants and Exiles: Ireland and the Irish Exodus to North America* (New York: Oxford University Press, *1985);* and Bernard Bailyn, *Voyagers to the West: A Passage in the Peopling of America on the Eve of the Revolution* (New York: Alfred A. Knopf, *1986).*

7. C. Wright Mills, *The Sociological Imagination* (New York: Oxford University Press, 1959).

8. Among Erikson's writings, the most pertinent to my study here are Erik H. Erikson, "Ego Development and Historical Change—Clinical Notes," in Erik H. Erikson, *The Psychoanalytical Study of the Child*, vol.2 (New York: International Universities Press, 1946), 359–396, reprinted in *Psychological Issues* 1, no. 1 (1959): 18–49; "Growth and Crisis in the 'Healthy Personality,'" in *Symposium on the Healthy Personality*, ed. M.J.E. Senn (New York: Josiah Macy, Jr., Foundation, 1950), reprinted in *Personality in Nature, Society and Culture*, ed. Clyde Kluckhohn and Henry A. Murray, 2d enl. ed. (New York: Alfred A. Knopf, 1953), 185–225, and reprinted in *Psychological Issues* 1, no. 1 (1959): 50–100; *Childhood and Society* (New York: W. W. Norton, 1950, 2d rev. and enl. ed., 1963), especially chapters 7 and 8; "Ego Identity and the Psychosocial Moratorium," in *New Perspectives for Research in Juvenile Delinquency*, ed. H. L. Witmer and R. Kosinsky (Washington, D.C.: U.S. Children's Bureau, 1956), 1–23; *Young Man Luther: A Study in Psychoanalysis and History* (New York: W. W. Norton, 1958, repr., 1962); "Human Strength and the Cycle of Generations," in Erik H. Erikson, *Insight and Responsibility: Lectures on the Ethical Implications of Psychoanalytic Insight*, (New York: W.W. Norton, 1964), 111–157; *Identity: Youth and Crisis* (New York: W. W. Norton,a 1969; reprint, 1968), especially chapter 3; *Gandhi's Truth: On the Origins of Militant Nonviolence* (New York: W.W. Norton, 1993); and *Life History and the Historical Moment* (New York: W. W. Norton, 1975). Erikson discussed the "eight ages of man" in several of his writings; the most succinct exposition is found in chapter 7 of *Childhood and Society.*

9. Erikson, *Identity: Youth and Crisis*, 309.

10. For useful overviews on the psychology of adolescents, see Glen H. Elder, Jr., "Adolescence in the Life Cycle: An Introduction," in *Adolescence in the Life Cycle: Psychological Change and Social Context*, ed. Sigmund E. Dragastin and Glen H. Elder, Jr. (New York: John Wiley and Sons, 1975), 1–22; James E. Marcia, "Identity in Adolescence," in *Handbook of Adolescent Psychology*, ed. Joseph Adelson (New York: John Wiley and Sons, 1980), 159–187; Ruthellen Josselson, "Ego Development in Adolescence," in *Handbook*, ed. Adelson, 188–210; Sigrun-Helde Filipp and Erhard Olbrich, "Human Development across the Life Span: Overview and Highlights of the Psychological Perspective," in *Human Development and the Life Course: Multidisciplinary Perspectives*, ed. Aage B. Sorensen, Franz E. Weinert, and Lonnie R. Sherrod (Hillsdale, N.J.: Lawrence Erlbaum, 1986), 343–375; Jean S. Phinney, Bruce T. Lochner, and Rodolfo Murphy, "Ethnic Identity Development and Psychological Adjustment in Adolescents," in *Ethnic Issues in Adolescent Mental Health*, ed. Arlene Rubin Stiffman and Larry E. Davis (Newbury Park, Calif.: Sage, 1990), 53–72; and Jean S. Phinney, "Ethnic Identity in Adolescents and Adults: Review of Research," *Psychological Bulletin* 108, no. 3 (1990): 499–514.

11. The social scientific writings on ethnicity, acculturation, and cultural conflict are even more voluminous than historical studies of the same topics, so no comprehensive listing is possible here. The journal articles and books that began to appear in the late 1920s were authored mostly by sociologists trained at the University of Chicago by Robert E. Park, Meredith Burgess, Louis Wirth, William I. Thomas, Florian Znaniecki, and their colleagues. Interest in ethnicity reached a new crescendo in the 1960s and early 1970s, when racial and ethnic minority groups struggled for their civil rights partly on the basis of their newfound ethnic consciousness. Among the books that helped define the field in that tumultuous period, see Milton M. Gordon, *Assimilation in American Life: The Role of Race, Religion, and National Origins* (New York: Oxford University Press, 1964); Nathan Glazer and Daniel Patrick Moynihan, *Beyond the Melting Pot: The Negroes, Puerto Ricans, Jews, Italians, and Irish of New York City* (Cambridge, Mass.: MIT Press, 1963, 2d ed., 1970); Fredrik Barth, *Ethnic Groups and Boundaries: The Social Organization of Culture Difference* (Boston: Little, Brown, 1969); Michael Novak, *The Rise of the Unmeltable Ethnics: Politics and Culture in the Seventies* (New York: Macmillan, 1972); William M. Newman, *American Pluralism: A Study of Minority Groups and Social Theory* (New York: Harper and Row, 1973); Andrew M. Greeley, *Ethnicity in the United States: A Preliminary Reconnaissance* (New York: John Wiley and Sons, 1974); and Harold R. Isaacs, *Idols of the Tribe: Group Identity and Political Change* (New York: Harper and Row, 1975). Pierre L. Van den Berghe, *The Ethnic Phenomenon* (New York: Elsevier, 1981; paperback ed., New York: Praeger, 1987), and John Rex and David Mason, eds., *Theories of Race and Ethnic Relations* (New York: Cambridge University Press, 1986) are useful introductions to issues related to race and ethnicity.

12. William L. Yancey, Eugene P. Ericksen, and Richard N. Juliani, "Emergent Ethnicity: A Review and Reformulation," *American Sociological Review* 41, no. 3 (1976): 391–402.

13. The pervasiveness and strength of this conviction may be an artifice of the research design of the Survey of Race Relations. Because Robert E. Park, the director of research for this project, and his colleagues were so concerned about the assimilation—or lack thereof—of "Oriental" Americans, they tried dili

gently to gauge the extent to which their subjects had become Americanized. Furthermore, because none of the researchers could speak any Asian languages, they had to rely almost entirely on college–educated Asian American informants who were fluent in English, articulate, and at ease with social scientific research to supply them with the life histories that they desired. For a lengthier discussion of Park and the Survey of Race Relations, see Chapter 7 of this book.

14. "Life History and Social Document of Ying Foy," Survey of Race Relations, major document no. 184, 2.
15. "Life History as a Social Document of Mr. Chin Yen," Survey of Race Relations, major document no. 186, 2, 4, 6, 7.
16. "Life History as a Social Document of Bong Chin," Survey of Race Relations, major document no. 172, 6.
17. "Life History as a Social Document of Mr. Chin Cheung," Survey of Race Relations, major document no. 187, 3.
18. "Life History and Social Document of David Young," Survey of Race Relations, major document no. 272–A, 2.
19. "Life History as a Social Document of Bong Chin," 2.
20. "Life History and Social Document of David Young," 8.
21. Thomas W. Chinn, Bridging the Pacific: San Francisco Chinatown and Its People (San Francisco: Chinese Historical Society of America, 1989), 164.
22. "Life History of Chinese Student," Survey of Race Relations, major document no. 233, 7.
23. Pardee Lowe, Father and Glorious Descendant (Boston: Little, Brown, 1943), 106.
24. Ibid., 146–147.
25. Ibid., 190–191.
26. Ibid., 190.
27. "Life History and Social Document of David Young," 10–11.
28. "Life History as a Social Document of Bong Chin," 3.
29. "Life History and Social Document of Lew Kay," Survey of Race Relations, major document no. 194, 7.
30. "Interview with Lillie Leung," Survey of Race Relations, major document no. 76, 1.
31. "Interview with Flora Belle Jan, Daughter of Proprietor of the Yet Far Low Chop Suey Restaurant," Survey of Race Relations, major document no. 225, 1.
32. "Life History of Chinese Student," 8.
33. "Story of a Chinese Girl Student," Survey of Race Relations, major document no. 56, 4–6.
34. Ibid., 6.
35. Ibid., 9.
36. Jade Snow Wong, Fifth Chinese Daughter (New York: Harper and Row, 1945), p. 93.
37. Jade Snow Wong, No Chinese Stranger (New York: Harper and Row, 1975), 6.
38. Ibid.
39. "Interview with Lillie Leung," 3.
40. "The Life History of a Hawaiian-Born Chinese Girl, F.L.," Survey of Race Relations, major document no. 310, 8.
41. Ibid., 8.
42. "Story of a Chinese College Girl," Survey of Race Relations, major document no. 54, 4.

43. "Life History of Chinese Student," 2.

44. "Interview with Lillie Leung," 2.

45. "Life History of Chinese Student," 3.

46. Erikson, *Childhood and Society*, 262–263.

47. J. S. Wong, *Fifth Chinese Daughter*, 83–84.

48. Ibid., 88.

49. "Interview with Louise Leung," Survey of Race Relations, minor document no. 63, 1.

50. J. S. Wong, *Fifth Chinese Daughter*, 27.

51. Ibid., 109.

52. Ibid., 109–110.

53. J. S. Wong, *No Chinese Stranger*, 54.

54. "Story of a Chinese College Girl," 1–3, 9.

55. "Interview: Esther Wong, Native Born Chinese," Survey of Race Relations, major document no. 239, 5.

56. Lisa Lowe, "Heterogeneity, Hybridity, Multiplicity: Marking Asian American Differences," *Diaspora* 1, no. 1 (1991): 24–44.

57. Pardee Lowe, *Father and Glorious Descendant*, 91, 131–132.

58. Ibid., 131.

59. Ibid., 129.

60. Ibid., 139.

61. J. S. Wong, *Fifth Chinese Daughter*, 20.

62. On the historical relationship between Chinese immigrants and various Prostestant denominations, see Wesley Woo, "Chinese Protestants in the San Francisco Bay Area," in *Entry Denied*, ed. Chan, 213–245.

63. Pardee Lowe, *Father and Glorious Descendant*, 168.

64. "Life History and Social Document of Lew Kay," 8.

65. Pardee Lowe, *Father and Glorious Descendant*, 192.

66. J. S. Wong, *Fifth Chinese Daughter*, 113–114.

67. Pardee Lowe, *Father and Glorious Descendant*, 142–143.

68. "The Life History of a Hawaiian-Born Chinese Girl, F.L.," 8–9.

69. Chinn, *Bridging the Pacific*, 157, 192.

70. "Interview with Lillie Leung," 2.

71. "Life History of Chinese Student," 7.

72. J. S. Wong, *Fifth Chinese Daughter*, 72.

73. J. S. Wong, *No Chinese Stranger*, 15.

74. J. S. Wong, *Fifth Chinese Daughter*, 14–15.

75. Ibid., 230.

76. Ibid., 5.

77. Pardee Lowe, *Father and Glorious Descendant*, 13.

78. Ibid., 18.

79. Ibid., 68.

80. Ibid., 176–178.

81. Victor G. and Brett de Bary Nee, *Longtime Californ': A Documentary Study of an American Chinatown* (New York: Pantheon, 1972), 162, 164–166.

82. J. S. Wong, *Fifth Chinese Daughter*, 3, 67.

83. Victor Wong, "Childhood II," in *Ting: Chinese Art and Identity in San Francisco*, ed. Nick Harvey (San Francisco: Glide Urban Center, 1970), 69.

84. Chinn, *Bridging the Pacific*, 157–158.

85. Pardee Lowe, *Father and Glorious Descendant*, 112, 110.

86. "Life History as a Social Document of Mr. Chin Cheung," 4.

87. Ibid.
88. "Life History as a Social Document of Bong Chin," 3, 5.
89. "Life History and Social Document of Ying Foy," 3–4.
90. Pardee Lowe, *Father and Glorious Descendant,* 186.
91. J. S. Wong, *Fifth Chinese Daughter,* 128.
92 Pardee Lowe, *Father and Glorious Descendant,* 184.
93. Nee and Nee, *Longtime Californ',* 169.
94. "Life History as a Social Document of Mr. Chin Cheung," 2.
95. James C. Scott, *Weapons of the Weak: Everyday Forms of Peasant Resistance* (New Haven: Yale University Press, 1985). Although Scott studied peasants in Southeast Asia, I think the concept that he proposed is applicable to the behavior of Chinese Americans during the Chinese exclusion era.
96. "Life History and Social Document of Lew Kay," 3–4.
97. "Life History as a Social Document of Mr. Chin Cheung," 2.
98. "Life History of Chinese Student," 3.
99. This is a point that some Asian Americans who became political activists during the 1960s and 1970s seem to have difficulty understanding. Since the 1960s, because overt resistance has been possible, has enabled various minority groups to fight for their civil rights, and has consequently been greatly valorized, there has been a tendency to disparage the subservient behavior of individuals who lived in earlier years—under conditions far more oppressive than today's Asian Americans can even begin to imagine.
100. "Life History and Social Document of David Young," 7.
101. Chinn, *Bridging the Pacific,* 222.
102. Ibid., 223.
103. "Autobiography of Mr. Luke Chess," Survey of Race Relations, major document no. 193, 3.
104. Ibid., 3–4.
105. Chinn, *Bridging the Pacific,* 195.
106. Ibid., 236.
107. Ibid., 242.
108. Ibid., 251.
109. J. S. Wong, *Fifth Chinese Daughter,* 188.
110. "Interview with Sun (Peter) Lee," Survey of Race Relations, minor document no. 62, 1.
111. "Interview with Louise Leung," 1.
112. J. S. Wong, *Fifth Chinese Daughter,* 95.
113. "The Life History of a Hawaiian-Born Chinese Girl, F.L.," 10–11.
114. "Life History and Social Document of David Young," 9.
115. For a reprint of the essays, see either Chinn, *Bridging the Pacific,* 138–144, or Chinese Historical Society of America, ed., *Chinese America: History and Perspectives, 1992* (San Francisco: Chinese Historical Society of America, 1992), 150–175.
116. Victor Wong, "Childhood II," 72.
117. Sucheng Chan, *Asian Americans: An Interpretive History* (Boston: Twayne,Publishers, 1991), 187.

CHAPTER 6

"Go West . . . to China": Chinese American Identity in the 1930s

GLORIA H. CHUN

"WE WERE 'GHETTOIZED' WITHIN JUST THESE FEW SQUARE blocks," stated Thomas Chinn, who grew up in San Francisco's Chinatown during the 1930s. To enable members of the second generation like himself to "break out of the shell of Chinatown," he helped to found the San Francisco-based, English-language newspaper/magazine the *Chinese Digest,* which ran from 1935 to 1940.[1] This publication served as a crucial conduit through which young second-generation Chinese Americans could voice their thoughts and feelings. The articles mirrored these young people's responses to and reflections on various issues and concerns, such as the Japanese invasion of China, the economic depression, their exclusion from the mainstream job market, the preservation of Chinatown against foreign entrepreneurial and cultural encroachments, and their involvement in the Chinese section of the 1939 World's Fair. The *Chinese Digest,* along with recorded interviews, memoirs, and autobiographical writings, provides a window into the lives and thoughts of American-born generations of Chinese in the pre-World War II years.[2]

How these American-born youths came to negotiate their identity is the focus of this chapter.[3] I found little evidence to support the widely held assimilationist thesis, which states that second-generation members of ethnic groups generally identify with mainstream American culture and eagerly adopt and emulate its norms and values in the hope of being accepted. This perspective, predicated on the Euro-American immigrant model, cannot explain the experiences of those who have been marginalized as second-class citizens and rendered as the racialized Other. Unlike their European counterparts, who could change their last names and blend in, the American-born Chinese, by virtue of their physical appearance, had to contend with their already constituted identity firmly etched onto the minds of many Euro-Americans by both the print and visual media. The question of Chinese American identity was made all the more poignant by the fact that they were, as a rule, barred from the mainstream job market, rendered politically invisible, and socially segregated into Chinatowns. By examining and analyzing the "Great Debate of 1936" and Chinese American participation in the 1939 World's Fair, I show the complex processes involved in the formulation of Chinese American consciousness and identities in the 1930s.

Social Isolation and Exclusion

Before World War II, the Chinese in America were a largely ignored and forgotten people. Isolated from the larger society and racially segregated, most Chinese were concentrated in urban ghettos. "We were not allowed to come out and mingle with other people outside of our community. We were too strange and were even discriminated against physically," recalled Thomas Chinn.[4] The emerging second- and third-generation Chinese Americans, who constituted more than half the Chinese American population by the 1940s, had a status imposed upon them by laws and various social institutions similar to that of blacks in the South. Outside Chinatown, Chinese Americans were customarily refused service in restaurants and cafés. A Chinese American could not lawfully marry a white person. "Oriental" schools were designated for Chinese pupils; the few who attended "white" schools were prevented by racial prejudice from participating in extracurricular activities and student organizations as well as from using public swimming pools, other recreational facilities, and social clubs. Those who desired to play sports, to dance, or to debate had to form their own clubs.[5]

Exclusion from jobs was even more pronounced, particularly during the Great Depression. American-born Chinese with college degrees and special training were largely excluded from mainstream jobs. As a result of such discrimination, along with the decline in tourism during the Depression, many were either unemployed or underemployed. The graduating class of 1936 at the University of California, Berkeley, included twenty-eight American-born Chinese, many of whom had earned degrees in engineering, economics, architecture, optometry, pharmacology, and commerce.[6] Few found jobs in the fields in which they had been trained because most firms refused to hire second-generation Chinese Americans, even if they were well educated and equipped with special talents. Nate R. White of the *Christian Science Monitor* reported a similar situation in San Francisco. He found that for some five thousand young San Franciscan Chinese there seemed to be "no future worthy of their skills."[7] According to the Oriental division of the U. S. Employment Service in San Francisco, more than 90 percent of its placements were for those in the service industries, mainly in the culinary trades.[8] Instead of being employed in the areas for which they had been trained, many were carrying trays, washing dishes, cutting meat, ironing clothes, drying fish, and selling herbs.[9]

Working at these jobs was demoralizing. Educated in American public schools, the American-born generation understood what constituted respectable occupations. Having grown up in Chinatown, they also knew all too well that to work as a cook, a restaurateur, a laundryman, or a waiter involved long, laborious hours. A survey of Chinese high school students showed that engineering and teaching were the most popular professional aspirations. Less than 1 percent expressed a desire to walk in the vocational footsteps of their fathers.[10] In fact, however, many were forced to enter their parents' businesses, whereas others ventured to open their own small businesses in Chinatown.

The Depression heightened the economic and social isolation of the Chinese within Chinatown. The American-born Chinese likened their situation to that of individuals "trapped" in one of the crowded, dilapidated tenements in Chinatown "without windows and two-feet wide hallways."[11] By 1935, contrary to the common belief that the Chinese would "take care of their own" or that they had a special talent for silently enduring hardship, more than 350 families in San Francisco's Chinatown were receiving assistance from the San Francisco Relief Administration. A survey of 119 of the families receiving relief aid showed that on average 2.2 persons were consigned to a room, only 40 families had private kitchens, and 25 had private bathing facilities.[12] Memories of living in Apartment #301 remained vivid for David Gan:

> It had two rooms and a closet-sized kitchen with a window facing other apartments. George and I slept on a sofa bed. Ma and Pa slept in the bedroom with Virginia, Norman and Hank, I think. The dimly lit and narrow hallway had brown linoleum and I rode my tricycle at times. There

was no bathroom. Each floor had a communal bathroom, consisted of a tub and a toilet, shared by four or five apartments' tenants.[13]

Stereotypes of the Chinese

Fu Manchu versus Charlie Chan
and Other Negative Images

In addition to social isolation and economic deprivation, Chinese Americans had to endure demeaning popular images of themselves. What American-born generations asked of America was that they not be ridiculed. They protested the representation of the Chinese as Fu Manchu, "the sleepy celestial enveloped in mists of opium fumes," and as "long-fingered Mandarins chasing sing-song girls at chop suey joints." The editor of the *Chinese Digest* stated, "We are tired of comedies."[14]

A creation of the British author Sax Rohmer, Fu Manchu was the embodiment of the "Yellow Peril." A popular theme present in almost all of Rohmer's forty-one novels, as well as a significant collection of his short stories, was that yellow hordes were on the verge of sweeping through the world. Fu Manchu's bizarre assassination tactics and his other unusual cruelties helped to epitomize the image of the Asian threat to the West.[15] His horrid actions were matched only by his physical appearance, as described by Rohmer:

> Imagine a person, tall, lean and feline, high-shouldered with a brow like Shakespeare and a face like Satan, a close-shaven skull, and long magnetic eyes of true cat-green. Invest him with all the cruel cunning of an entire Eastern race, accumulated in one giant intellect, with all the resources, if you will, of a wealthy government, which, however, already has denied all knowledge of his existence. Imagine that awful being, and you have a mental picture of Dr. Fu-Manchu, the yellow peril incarnate in one man.[16]

If Fu Manchu was the paragon of Chinese evil, Charlie Chan was the model of the friendly Chinese. The film scholar Dorothy Jones confirmed that John Stone, the producer of the original Charlie Chan films at Fox Studios, saw the characterization of Charlie Chan "as a refutation of the unfortunate Fu Manchu characterization of the Chinese."[17] Devoid of any assertiveness and sexuality, Charlie Chan was self-effacing to a fault. Typically, he said things such as, "I am so sorry. I have made stupid error. Captain—is it possible you will ever forgive me?"[18]

Charlie Chan, a creation of Earl Derr Biggers, who wrote six Charlie Chan novels between 1925 and 1932, was a benign, overweight detective speaking in pidgin with pseudo-Confucian aphorisms: "The Emperor Shi Hwang-ti, who built the Great Wall of China, once said: He who squanders today talking of yesterday's triumph, will have nothing to boast of tomorrow."[19] Unlike Fu Manchu, however, Chan was on the side of the law, solving murder mysteries with his uncanny wit. The stories were serialized in the *Saturday Evening Post*, were published as books, and appeared in forty-eight feature films.[20]

Scientific and academic institutions also created an image of the Chinese as decidedly strange and peculiar. A Works' Project Administration (WPA) task force project purportedly aimed at examining health-related issues of Chinese Americans in San Francisco's Chinatown turned into a study of physical anthropology. Photographs marked with measurements of Chinese American children's heads, faces, and body stature, along with samples of their hair, were sent to museums across the country. Professor Alfred Louis Kroeber of the University of California at Berkeley and Professor Allen Danforth of Stanford University were key scientists behind the study. From such a study, an effort was made to "classify" the "physical racial type" of the Chinese.[21]

A Chinese American young woman related a "humiliating" incident that she experienced as a result of such studies. She was made to stand in front of the class as the teacher used her as a "specimen" when her class was studying about China. According to her, "She [the teacher] pointed out all the characteristics of the Chinese. 'There were the slant, almond eyes, the black hair—coarse and straight, you notice, don't you, class? The nose that was practically no nose, the cheek bones, and the general blank look.'[22] Actually, her "blank look," the author explained, "concealed a wealth of emotions underneath."[23]

Chinese as the Humble and Gentle People

Another prevailing stereotype was that of a humble, gentle people. The wide popularity of a novel by Pearl S. Buck, *The Good Earth* (1931), was largely responsible for the more humane characterization of the Chinese. The novel follows the story of a Chinese peasant and his wife who struggle against natural disasters, political turmoil, and human cruelty. The couple persevere, however, and do not forsake their lives rooted in the soil. At a time when Americans were struggling

during the Depression, many people easily identified with the protago-
nists in *The Good Earth*. And, at a time when China was receiving
much news coverage because of the Sino-Japanese War, the American
public, largely moved by the portrayal of the Chinese in the novel,
came to view the Chinese as a brave and noble people unjustly attacked by the cruel Japanese. Harold Isaacs has argued that the book
was the single most powerful force in garnering national sympathy for
the Chinese during the Sino-Japanese War.[24] According to the John Day
Company, its many editions and renditions sold more than two million
copies. In 1937, the novel appeared as an enormously popular film that
was seen by some twenty-three million Americans.[25]

The Great Debate of the 1930s

Given the plethora of stereotypical depictions of the Chinese,
the American-born generations became all the more eager to define for
themselves who they were and what being a Chinese American meant.
A national debate on the future of the Chinese born in America set the
grounds for doing just that.

The Ging Hawk Club—a women's social club based in New York—
sponsored a national essay competition in 1936 entitled "Does My Future Lie in China or America?" This competition unwittingly sparked
a verbal battle involving Chinese American communities across the
nation. "In America lies my future," answered Robert Dunn at the beginning of his first-prize winning essay. Kaye Hong, the second-place
winner, expressed the opposite view; he thought his future lay in
China: "The old adage, 'Go West, young man,' no longer becomes applicable to this American youth. . . . It is for me, 'Go further west,
young man.' Yes, further west, across the Pacific to China.[26]

With the publication of these essays in the *Chinese Digest*, letters
flowed in from across the country. Dunn's position defending a future
in America seemed less appealing to his American-born peers. The
Chinese Students' Club at Stanford University became Dunn's main
opponents. The Stanford students wrote in the section of the paper ap-
propriately labeled "Firecrackers" that Mr. Dunn was "unwise" if not
outright "unpatriotic" to China. For months, the ideological war between Dunn and his opponents raged.[27]

This debate revealed much more than the writers' political consciousness. It also provided a forum for cultural creation. Behind the authors'
political or ideological consciousness lay certain basic assumptions about

how one could perceive one's ethnic or national identity. From the ensuing debate emerged two "generation units," to borrow Karl Mannheim's term, within the American-born second-generation Chinese. One generation unit, represented by Dunn, advocated allegiance to America and emphasized its members' Americanism.[28] Kaye Hong and the Stanford students, in contrast, favored a future in China and felt culturally closer to things Chinese. By taking their clashing political views into the public arena through their writing, both groups made positive assertions about their identity.

Robert Dunn, who was raised in Roxbury, Massachusetts, was an undergraduate at Harvard University. Although he did not grow up in a large Chinese community, he claimed that his upbringing was very Chinese. By his own description, Dunn was "radical" and "unconventional." His thinking was radical because to choose America over China was to break away from the views of the parental generation, whose members encouraged loyalty and service to China. "Ever since I can remember, I have been taught," wrote Dunn, "by my parents, by my Chinese friends, and by my teacher in Chinese school, that I must be patriotic to China." He was made to feel "obliged to render service to China." Breaking away from this expectation constituted a "radical" move, an "unconventionality" with regard to Chinese norms.[29] Moreover, his parents questioned how their son could be loyal to America, a country where "the Chinese are mocked at, trodden upon, disrespected, and even spit upon." For any Chinese to desire a future in such a country would amount only to "losing face."[30]

Dunn, like many others, however, defied parental advice and decided to make his future in America. The crucial factor for Dunn was his love for what he called "American" values and principles, which he preferred to "Chinese" ways and thought. After all, he had learned "to live by Christian ideals, by liberal attitudes, and by an optimistic outlook on life." Dunn saw these principles as the fabric of America. "I owe much pride and gratitude to America," he said, "for the principles of liberty and equality which it upholds for the protection of its government . . . , and for its schools and institutions in which I have participated. Without them, I certainly could not be what I am now."[31]

Dunn could not imagine how he could survive in China. He did not think that he could make many friends there who would share his values. "I shall be able to make few close relationships with the young men and women of China," Dunn decided, "for their background is of utilitarian ideals, conservative attitudes, and of a fatalistic outlook upon life." For Dunn, Chinese ways and American ways were irreconcilable.[32]

Although racism was prevalent in the United States, Dunn believed that Chinese Americans could still make a successful living there. "The color line," he wrote, "does not entirely prevent the American-born Chinese from getting jobs. . . . It cannot be said, therefore, that it is impossible for Chinese American youths to obtain remunerative positions in either China or America." In fact, he found that being Chinese worked in his favor at times. His experience at Harvard University was one example: "They [the white students] give me more respect because I am Chinese. Whatever I do in school and college in the way of extra-curricular activities or of attaining high grades, I am given much more credit and popularity than an American would receive, if he did the same things. Being a Chinese among American friends, then, is a sort of advantage."[33]

The Stanford students' main argument against Dunn was that he did not see the pervasiveness of racism and its damaging effects on the Chinese. They wrote, "Can racial prejudice disappear in America in a few years? When you [Dunn] fail to take cognizance of these facts in your essay, you cannot blame us for accusing you of lack of information."[34] Kaye Hong, the second-place winner, who had grown up in San Francisco and attended the University of Washington in Seattle, agreed that his patriotism toward China was shaped by his awareness of racism in America against the Chinese. Hong found the ideals propounded by American Christian democracy hypocritical. For instance, he discovered that the principle of equal opportunity did not apply to the Chinese. Hong wrote, "I have learned to acknowledge that the better jobs are not available to me and that the advancement of my career is consequently limited in this fair land." Hong bluntly stated that the cry to "make the world safe for democracy" left him "coldly unresponsive." Hong's patriotism was of a "different hue and texture," one "built on the mound of shame." "The ridicule heaped upon the Chinese race has long fermented within my soul," Hong explained.[35]

Hong's patriotism toward China was a product of his upbringing. Growing up in San Francisco's Chinatown, a place shaped by a long history of racism, Hong, along with many young American-born Chinese, was constantly reminded of racial injustice in America.

James Low, another Chinese American, grew up with the constant reminder from his elders that America held little security for his future: "Father used to tell me, 'Look at your boss, he was going to be an engineer, look what happened to him! What are you studying engineering for?'"[36] His father was referring to the fact that although James's boss had been trained as a mining engineer, he was working in a sewing factory. James's parents thus urged him to go to China.[37]

Thomas Chinn, a San Franciscan, was trained from an early age to think about a future in China. In preparation for such an outcome, he studied the Chinese language and received a Chinese education. Being the eldest son, he was sent to China in 1924 to get a "genuine" Chinese education, a practice common at the time. Such preparation grew out of his parents' fear that "if things became worse they might be forced to return to China." Particularly after China became a republic in 1912, Chinese parents hoped that their children would have a future in rebuilding China. Such a life seemed more promising than taking jobs as waiters, dishwashers, or janitors in America.[38]

Indeed the insurmountable barrier of the color line made hoping for an equal-opportunity future in America nearly impossible for the American-born generations. As mentioned previously, because of their race, many were barred from entering the mainstream labor market. Some states, such as California, had legislation against the employment of Chinese Americans in certain fields such as law, medicine, financial administration, dentistry, veterinary science, liquor store ownership, architecture, engineering, and realty, among others. More subtle forms of discrimination also existed. For instance, some jobs required union membership, a stipulation that automatically precluded the Chinese because they were barred from joining unions. Furthermore, the seniority system sanctioned the practice of hiring Chinese last and firing them first.[39]

Census records indicate that during much of the 1920s and 1930s, most gainfully employed Chinese in the United States were classified under domestic and personal service occupations. More Chinese were listed as servants and laundry workers than in any other job category. According to the 1930 census, of the 19,470 Chinese American males in California older than age ten who were gainfully employed, 7,773 (40 percent) were in domestic and personal service. Among these nearly 1,000 were in laundry work, and 4,774 did domestic work. Others worked as barbers, room cleaners, janitors, elevator operators, and bellhops. Opportunities for women were even slimmer: Fewer than 1,000 were gainfully employed.[40]

The chances of finding employment in their field of study were slight for the American-born Chinese who remained in America. Sam Lee, who headed the Asian branch of the California State Employment Service, stated, "The only Chinese ever to obtain a doctor's degree in architecture at Berkeley is glad to work in a barbecue stand." Lee also told about an electrical engineer who resorted to shopkeeping in Chinatown, and a young man with a master's degree in journalism who was chauffeuring a rich woman.[41] In yet another case, a graduate of a recognized school of mechanical engineering had been working in a steel mill for nine years. His education far surpassed that of his American coworkers. Yet, one by one they had been promoted, while he had received only small increases in salary. A draftsman when he first entered, after nine long years, he remained a draftsman.[42]

Economic Opportunities in China

One alternative to tolerating the racism in the United States was to go to China. One young Chinese American man had been trained as an engineer at the Massachusetts Institute of Technology and secured a position in a U. S. radio company. After some months, however, he was laid off. He applied to firm after firm, but on one pretext or another was refused interviews. He then signed up as a salesman with a Jewish meatpacking company, taking orders from Chinese restaurants and stores. He was paid strictly by commission, which did not amount to much. After a time, he became so disgusted that he resigned. He then became a waiter in a Chinese restaurant, saved some money, and went to China.[43] In another slightly different case, Mary Lam, the daughter of a well-to-do businessman, refused to marry the suitor chosen for her and decided instead to teach in China.[44]

While the exclusion of Chinese from American mainstream labor helped to push some American-born Chinese toward China, certain factors in China also worked to pull them there. War-torn China, eager to rebuild, advertised its need for American-trained workers. An advertisement in the *Chinese Digest* announced that the Shanghai Aviation Association was eager to get in touch with Chinese aviation students in America.[45] The Chinese embassy in Washington, D.C., relayed the message that the Ministry of Industry in China had requested engineers specializing in iron and steel smelting to apply for positions in Shanghai. The Department of Agriculture disseminated the news that the Chinese government would grant money, land, and machinery to Chinese farmers trained in the United States who were willing to work in China.[46]

This advertising campaign must have been effective, because it succeeded in luring an estimated 20 percent of the American-born Chinese to China in the 1930s. As late as 1936, Jane Kwong Lee confirmed, "Facts tell us that a minority is constantly going back to China." However, American-born Chinese going to China was actually an age-old phenomenon. Between 1920 and 1924, 2,510 more departed for China than entered the United States. In 1931, whereas only 1,365 entered the United States, 3,386 left for China. More than 10,000 more Chinese left the United States than entered between 1909 and 1932.[47]

For many, the decision to go to China was influenced by their cognizance of racial prejudice in America. As long as racism against the Chinese existed in America, many Chinese Americans felt as Kaye Hong did: They did not believe that they would be able to live and work in America. On the basis of this conviction, Mr. T. Z. Koo, an American-born Chinese, went to China and set up an organization to provide American-born Chinese with jobs. He explained, "It is an inescapable fact that an 'alien' [American-born Chinese in China] faces almost unsurmountable obstacles before any headway can be made," but Koo and many others knew that in America, little headway, if any, could be made. A Chinese American remained forever an alien in the United States.[48]

Many second-generation Chinese Americans understood that as long as China remained subjugated by the Japanese, prejudice would continue to depress their social and economic standing. A Berkeley student stated, "Henceforth we who are in America must lend all our efforts to the up-building of a strong united front, for the better development of the movement for national liberation in China."[49] Those who advocated a future in China tended to emphasize a collective purpose rather than personal satisfaction. Their rhetoric was nationalistic. One student wrote, "May we unite for teamwork and be proud of our country [China]."[50] Another echoed, "It is not so much a question of the individual as it is that of the country's welfare."[51] Kaye Hong wrote, "I merely intend to become a good citizen of the great Republic, I shall support the nationalist government which is now gaining strength with each succeeding day. I shall accept the national policies as being the best moves for China. As a whole, I shall place the welfare of the nation above my own."[52] Whereas those who advocated a future in America spoke much more about individual concerns, placing personal happiness above any national or group interest, the China advocates placed greater emphasis on the moral imperative to rebuild China.

The China advocates' identification with China was total, as evidenced in the language that they used to speak of China. They used the phrase "return to China" even though they had never been there. Denying America, their birthplace, they adopted China as their surrogate homeland: "In our own country, filling our niche of service, whatever it may be is the only place where our real future lies. So let us . . . set our faces toward our homeland."[53]

Those foreseeing a future in China saw themselves as "pioneers of a new frontier"—a frontier in China. Kaye Hong best expressed their conception of this frontier: "It will take hundreds of thousands, millions of young men with vision to build for the future. To start the wheels of industries, to weave a cobweb of railroads and highways across the expanse of all Cathay, to advocate, to send out a fleet of trading vessels, to develop the internal resources to build a richer life for one and all."[54] Another student had a similar vision: "Great highway systems will appear all over the country, linked with an efficient railroad net. Mines will be opened and rivers harnessed for power development and flood control, streaming lines of trucks will move rapidly from city to city."[55] Given their conscious efforts to identify with China rather than America, it is ironic that they expressed a vision similar to the miracle of industrialization found in late-nineteenth-century America. This similarity reveals that despite their nationalist penchant, their thoroughly Eurocentric education made their notions of economic progress and modernization a vision predicated on the grand, historical narratives of Euro-America.

These young people's enthusiasm for a future in China was fueled by reports from Dr. Charles R. Shepherd, who reported that Lai Sun of California had found a position with Texaco Company in Hong Kong and that Agnes Mark, a Canadian, worked as a secretary at the Shanghai Hospital. The full report contained an extensive list of names and occupations; most jobs fell into the categories of engineering, medicine, teaching, and research.[56]

Japan Symbolizes Racial Oppression

China came to symbolize a haven for a racism-free life. Only Japan threatened to spoil this plan. In the eyes of the American-born Chinese, the injustice of Japan's imperialist aggression against China paralleled that of America's discrimination against Chinese Americans. During a march protesting Japanese actions in China, one student waved a placard emblazoned with the slogan, "Racial Freedom and Liberty Forever!"[57] For this individual, as for many others, the struggle against Japanese imperialism in China went hand in hand with the fight against racism in America. Thus, increasingly, Japan, as the identifiable, common enemy, came to represent more than just an aggressor nation against China: It became the incarnation of racial oppression itself.

Young second-generation Chinese Americans grew up with the idea that Japan, Great Britain, and America were the imperialist enemies of China. In the Chinese-language schools, James Low recalled how he acquired his political consciousness: "Ever since I was small, the Japanese had been committing aggression in China." The Chinese school principal "was always attacking Chiang Kai-shek for not fighting the Japanese." Many of his Chinese teachers were always talking about "imperialism and prejudice, and how imperialism was the cause of China's downfall, how the British forced opium on the Chinese, et cetera, et cetera, and that the Chinese don't have a chance here." Although he did not always understand what was taking place, by the "demonstrations and parades" and "speeches on the playground" he "kind of got the feeling" that he did not have a "Chinaman's chance" to make it in America.[58]

Outcome of the "Go West . . . to China" Movement

At the Chinese Young People's summer conference, which was held at Lake Tahoe in 1935, when the question of where one's future lay was raised, balloting showed that 75 percent of the participants favored a future in China. Many insisted that second-generation Chinese *must* go back to China.[59] The prevailing desire among the American born to establish their future in China took on a symbolic significance and laid the foundation for a nationalist/separatist ideology. Much like the mid-nineteenth-century pan-Africanism led by Martin Delany, Paul Cuffe, and others, and that of the earlier half of the twentieth century led by Marcus Garvey, young Chinese American radicals in the 1930s advocated going back to China as a protest against American racism.

A discrepancy between theory and practice, though, was perhaps an indication that life in China had its difficulties too. Given the favorable relations between China and the United States just prior to and during the war, immigration records show that many Chinese Americans returned to the United States from China. Between 1940 and the start of the war, many American-born Chinese came back to the United States with hopes for a better life. The sudden swelling in the number of Chinese being admitted into the United States from China indicates that a substantial percentage of those entering were Chinese American returnees. The number being admitted into the United States from China rose sharply beginning in 1940, with 920 entering. In 1941, 1,003 entered, compared with 231 in 1934 and 297 in 1936. This shift suggests a reversal of the trend in the preceding two decades, which showed far larger numbers departing for China than vice versa.[60] "I was disillusioned after a few months," said a young engineer. "First of all, I found that I did not master the Chinese language and the upside down Cantonese that I had learned in those afternoon classes on Stockton Street only evoked hilarity over there." Besides, he discovered that he could not learn anything new in his field because his training made him far superior to his Chinese colleagues.[61] Others complained about the "filth and poverty of the Chinese villages," which appeared to be "worse off than Chinatown."[62] Furthermore, to do well in China, one had to be fully fluent in Chinese, to have a marketable skill, and to have some connections to influential persons. Many Chinese Americans were unable to meet all three criteria. Others, like Thomas Chinn, who went to China in 1933 with hopes of opening a sporting goods shop, returned when their business ventures failed.[63]

In the end, Kaye Hong and Robert Dunn each encountered a fate opposite the one that they had envisioned. Hong remained in the United States rather than going to China. He is now a retired businessman living in San Francisco. When asked why he decided to stay, he answered, "It was actually harder to find a good position in China, unless you had connections. Although in my heart, I wanted to serve China, practical circumstances—such as meeting my wife, getting married, and starting a family—led me to stay in America working at whatever odd jobs I could find to support my family."[64] Ironically, Robert Dunn went to China for a while after working with the Chinese UN delegation to help frame the UN Constitution. Fortunately for Mr. Dunn, he had connections to high officials in China who offered him a position that he found "hard to pass up." Much to his surprise, his stay in China was pleasant. There, he married a woman born and raised in China. He also made friends with Chinese individuals whose values and ways of thinking were similar to those in the West. After the Communists occupied the Chinese mainland, however, he returned to the United States with his spouse and resided in Maryland.[65] When asked why he went to China, he answered that although he is bicultural, he has always considered himself "first and foremost a Chinese."[66]

Actually, Dunn and Hong shared some deep-rooted similarities. Whether they felt greater loyalty to China or to America, they could not escape the fact that they felt more Chinese. Identifying with Chinese culture had more to do with feelings that emerged from their marginalized status in American society and less to do with any familiarity and learning in classical Chinese art, history, or literature. Neither

Dunn nor Hong wanted to live in the shadow of the "ancient glories" of the Chinese cultural past, however. Despite what his parents had told him, Hong stated, "We, the younger generation, have nothing to be proud of except the time-worn accomplishments of our ancient ancestors."[67] Similarly for Dunn, his parents' constant harping that he "should be proud of China's four thousand years of glorious and continuous history" left him "unmoved."[68] These exemplars of the two generation units knew that no matter how glorious China's past had been, China in the present was seen by the United States as a weakling nation, economically destitute, socially backward, and politically impotent. They were convinced that they, the Chinese living in America, would be more respected if modern-day China were stronger.

Two options were available for achieving this end. Dunn's ideological solution was to stay in America and become a good "ambassador" in America, to "serve China by building up a good impression of the Chinese among Americans, by spreading good-will and clearing up misunderstandings, by interesting the Americans in the Chinese through personal contacts."[69] In contrast, Hong thought that a better method would be to build up China physically with hammer and nail. "Then and only then," avowed Hong, "can the present generation of Chinese really save their faces."[70] "While China's industries are unborn, her resources yet underground, and her people jobless and starving, the present generation of American-born Chinese cannot save their faces."[71] As long as China remained "subjugated" by the Japanese, many young Chinese Americans believed that their "economic as well as social status" would suffer "among the Americans."[72]

Ultimately, the American-born Chinese hoped for an "America in the heart," free of racism.[73] "As long as the 'bok gwais' [literally, 'white devils'] ruled over America," a young man explained, "the possibility of a happy life in America was just a dream."[74] An "America in the heart" would be a place that the Chinese could claim as their own. What better way would there be to claim America than if it had been discovered by a Chinese? One can imagine the surprised delight of American-born Chinese when they heard about *Steel of Empire,* a book written by a Canadian, John Murray Gibbon, who asserted that there was "sufficient data to prove that a Chinese Buddhist monk [Hui Sien] was really the very first discoverer of America" a thousand years before Columbus and about five hundred years before Leif Eriksson. A favorable review of this book by William Hoy received four full columns in the book section of the *Chinese Digest.* However remote the possibility, still a smile—the kind that smooths angry brows—must have come over the faces of some American-born Chinese who, upon reading this, began to entertain extravagant thoughts about claiming America as their own—even if doing so seemed dream years away.[75]

The 1939 World's Fair

Although their hope of equality seemed a difficult accomplishment, Chinese Americans seized what opportunities there were for improved well-being. Some believed that reforming the general image of Chinatown would help to improve the way that they were viewed. When the 1939 World's Fair came to San Francisco, Chinese Americans had their chance to implement these reforms. Eager to shed the "sordid aspects of the old Chinatown," according to the *Chinese Digest*, they set out to "modernize" the place in preparation for the World's Fair. The event offered them no less than an opportunity to recreate Chinatown. They were tired of the age-old tales found in popular literature from the late nineteenth century through the 1940s that depicted Chinatown as the abode of mysterious Chinese, where horrible crimes were perpetrated, where so-called hatchet men killed one another at the slightest provocation, where vices were indulged in by both Chinese and unfortunate Caucasians who were lured into its "dens of iniquity," and where "every almond-eyed girl who peeps out from a tenement house window at the passing throng was a sing-song girl."[76] The editors of the *Chinese Digest* lamented that "no people in America were more misunderstood than the Chinese." They blamed "the pulp magazines and Hollywood" for keeping "this illusion alive."[77]

The tourist trade had also been built up on these exotic fantasies. Sightseers by the tens of thousands thronged the streets of Chinatown to see the "Oriental" iniquities and mysteries. In fact, the tourist industry encouraged the perpetuation of these racist images of the Chinese by disseminating sensational tales that the tourists then spread. Compared with these disparaging stereotypes, Pearl S. Buck's image of the Chinese as humble and gentle people was preferred. Chinese Americans eagerly promoted Buck's image over the negative, sensationalized images, in the hopes of being better received by the larger society.[78]

"We look forward to the time when our own generation will sponsor some projects for the coming San Francisco Exposition which will be remunerative to us and educational to the public," said an editor of the *Chinese Digest*.[79] This hopeful prediction became a reality. The World's Fair allowed the Chinese Americans to refurbish Chinatown and to build a model Chinatown on the fairgrounds proper. The Fair directors offered to spend $1 million to build a Chinese village on Treasure Island to occupy more than a city block of space. Many American-born Chinese marveled at this opportunity to build an ideal Chinatown, a Chinatown of their dreams to serve as a model and an inspiration for the real Chinatown on Grant Avenue. The leadership of the planning committee was composed largely of American-born Chinese and Chinese-born merchants. Ching Wah Lee, who served as an editor for the *Chinese Digest*, and George Jue, another American-born community activist, were the main leaders of Chinese Factors, Inc., the planning committee. Representing the interests of the American born, they were careful to emphasize "genuine" Chinese expressions instead of re-creating the falsified, tourist-trap inventions that inundated parts of Chinatown. When certain members of the merchant class, whose primary interest had always been financial profit, suggested that they add nude girls jumping out of cakes as a tourist attraction, the leadership of Chinese Factors, Inc., protested, reasoning that doing so would be both "tasteless" and "not Chinese." The Reverend Edward Lee, who was tangentially involved with the Fair, recalled that many such arguments arose between the merchant class and the American-born Chinese. "The merchants were primarily interested in profits," stated the Reverend Lee, "whereas the American-born Chinese wanted to do things with more integrity."[80]

In their efforts to reform Chinatown, these young Chinese Americans sought to change the premise of tourism as it had come to be known in Chinatown. Tourism was no longer to be a thrill show, but an educational experience. The tourist was to learn about China and Chinese culture by being exposed to genuine expressions of things Chinese. The underlying principle behind the effort to reform Chinatown architecturally was the following motto: "If we must modernize Chinatown, do it. But do it by using Chinese forms and color as a basis for this development."[81] Apparently, China, not Chinese America, was to be the source of the cultural and aesthetic adornment of Chinatown.

When the World's Fair Chinese village was finished, Chinese Factors, Inc., and the others who were involved were sure that they had been relatively successful in their aim. Approximately a million Fair visitors entered the Chinese village through the towering gateway that mimicked the Peking Palace entrance. Once inside, they encountered a Mandarin theater, a Home of Fortune, a temple, a cocktail lounge, and many shops displaying Cathay's arts and handicrafts made by native Chinese artisans. In addition, the crowds were delighted by a beautiful willow teahouse and a Chinese garden. In the background stood a 130-foot-tall pagoda that held a formidable collection of Chinese art such as jade carvings, tapestries, and paintings from ancient China.[82] David Gan remembered the pride that he felt upon visiting the fairgrounds and seeing the Chinese village decorated in black, crimson, and gold, which made it the most colorful section at the Fair.[83]

To cap it all, the Fair opened with a Chinese New Year's parade because the New Year fell on February 19, a day after the Fair's opening. Two monstrous dragons four hundred feet long, one gold, the other silver, led the procession. Like everything else, these dragons were designed and assembled by skilled artists and craftspeople in China. Adding to the fanfare, the Chinese YMCA Bugle and Drum Corps led the parade for the Exposition.[84]

Less spectacular, but genuinely Chinese, was a Chinese farming village, which represented village life from interior China. Within the village, one found a typical farmer using an old wooden plow drawn by a water buffalo, a village temple, and a small shop where craftspeople sold their goods. Even the topsoil was imported from China. Chinese Factors, Inc., called this farming village "The Good Earth Settlement," after Pearl S. Buck's famous novel. Although the village settlement bore little resemblance to the farming village described in the novel, the connection was obvious insofar as both the novel and the settlement served to humanize the Chinese, and to show them as industrious peasants who worked the earth.[85]

Back in Chinatown on Grant Avenue, Chinese businesspeople refurbished their stores in Chinese colors and constructed modern bars and coffee shops, which began to attract more visitors. Chinatown acquired a new image. It was no longer an alien world teeming with vice and intrigue, fit for only the wild or the criminal at heart, but a safe, educational, and colorful place fit for all. David Gan and his brother, George, benefited from the resurgence of tourism:

> We went into a family business selling Chinese candy to the tourists who visited Chinatown. We started by sitting at the concrete flower bed curb in front of Old St. Mary's Church on Grant Avenue and California Street. . . . Then George and I traversed our side of Grant Avenue and asked tourists to buy the candy. Sales were much improved by this direct contact approach. On a good day, we both sold ten dollars gross and it was good money those days.[86]

By the late 1930s, many once-failing businesses had rebounded from the economic depression. As the tourist trade began to improve, the Chinese import business, which had declined precipitously since 1931, began to recover, and by 1935 it was about a fourth of the 1929 level. George Jue, the managing director of Chinese Factors, Inc., reported in 1939, "Chinatown is enjoying the biggest business boom in a decade."[87] In 1938, tourism in Chinatown had increased to an annual value of five million dollars.[88] In addition, two hundred new jobs were created at the fairgrounds as well as fifty in Chinatown, particularly for young women who served as hostesses, secretaries, cigarette girls, and waitresses.[89] Even after the Exposition, tourism did not decline and the American-born generations continued in their efforts to improve Chinatown's new image.

The American-born Chinese saw the Fair, however, as more than simply an opportunity for employment or increasing their incomes. By examining the process through which the American-born generations shaped a public image of themselves for the wider public, we get a rare glimpse into the cultural politics of Chinese American identity and representation in prewar America. Motivated by the hope of winning greater acceptance, and perhaps more crucially, respect from the dominant society, they carefully crafted a self-image that was antithetical to the negative portrayal of the Chinese as a morally decadent and barbarous people. To counteract the prejudice that they encountered, the American-born generations invented themselves in the image of the "genuine" Chinese, as if they had acquired a pipeline transference of culture from ancient China. Above all else, the American-born Chinese, motivated by the desire to present themselves in a more favorable light, so as to curb the racial prejudice against them, designed the Chinese segment of the World's Fair to achieve this end.

This somewhat Luddite insistence on displaying "genuine" expressions of things "Chinese"—even to the point of importing the topsoil of the Chinese village from China—is evidence of their need to authenticate the "truthful" version of Chinese America and counteract the "false" Hollywood representations of them. By making a positivistic assertion about what constitutes "Chineseness," they were complicit in objectifying the Chinese. Also noteworthy is the sheer absense of any discussion about claiming a Chinese American heritage and identity in either the planning of the Fair or the actual building of the Chinese sector. Their failure to assert any linkage to Chinese America certainly was not due to any historical blindness. Rather, I contend that their move "to go back to China" in hopes of retrieving an identity and a culture hitherto buried, was for the American-born generation, a viable and enabling act of self-assertion, given that they lived in a society that simply could not see the Chinese—even those born in America—as "American." Although the

American-born generations could not wholly escape internalizing their "otherness," they remade themselves in ways that challenged and subverted the stereotypical rendition of the Chinese made by Americans.

The Guardians of Chinatown

The Fair further revealed that the American-born Chinese saw themselves as not only makers but also guardians of Chinatown. Ostracized by the dominant society, Chinatown was their only home. Only a few wealthy Chinese could afford to buy houses outside Chinatown in such places as the Nob Hill district by paying higher than market value. Otherwise, economic constraints and prejudice confined the Chinese to Chinatown. "Keep Chinatown Chinese!" against the vendors of "fake" culture, cried the American-born Chinese.[90] "Chinatown makes its last stand not only against general decay," wrote Pardee Lowe, "but also against the aggressive competition of China's ancient kin and modern invaders, the Japanese." He described the increasing number of Japanese as a threat. Lowe explained that whereas U.S. census takers in 1880 counted only 148 Japanese, compared with 105,465 Chinese, the scales had turned by 1930: The Japanese numbered 138,834, compared with 74,954 Chinese. This increase in the number of Japanese would have been less threatening had not Japanese merchants been taking over Chinatown shops. Pardee Lowe explained how the Japanese presence had changed the face of Chinatown: "Waiting to greet the tourists in this new background of dwarfed trees, tori gates, and countless paper lanterns are the bobbed hair, American-born, college-educated Japanese sales girls dressed in their colorful native Kimono, obi and sandals."[91] Virginia Lee in her book, *The House That Tai Ming Built*, also recalled that stores along Grant Avenue called "Nippon Trading Company, Nara Art Store, and Yamamoto Curios" sold not only cheap souvenirs but also expensive woodcuts.[92] In fact some thirty of fifty bazaars in the Chinatown enclave came to be owned by Japanese immigrants. Many Chinese Americans feared that just as "the Japanese took Manchuria" so would they take Chinatown if they were not stopped.[93]

Co-opted not only out of their businesses, but also out of history books, some of which depicted China as a mere appendage of Japan, the American-born Chinese demanded that the books be corrected. According to a *Chinese Digest* editorial, the assertion that "during the war and afterwards Japan played a part in China utterly different than anything previously known by entering into the affairs of that great and disorganized country, imposing the Twenty-One Demands of 1915 and beginning an economic penetration in it by lending money and opening factories" was nothing but "propaganda favoring Japan."[94]

Pride in things Chinese also meant protecting the forms of livelihood traditionally held by the Chinese. When the laundry business was threatened, many youths came to its rescue not only because a considerable number of people depended on it for a living, but also because it was a trade that had been in the hands of the Chinese for as long as they had been in America. In 1936, San Francisco passed a series of laundry laws that mandated closing on Sundays and holidays. Laundries also were not allowed to remain open later than 7 P.M. on weekdays. Regular health checkups for employees who delivered the laundry were also proposed. Such laws, Chinese Americans argued, existed for no other purpose than to harass and eventually drive the Chinese laundrymen out of business. At least half the existing Chinese laundries faced the possibility of closing down under the new stipulations. Many young Chinese community leaders, wise to the ways of survival in America, did not need fancy theories to tell them that this policy was an effort by the bigger laundries to use the state to crush the smaller laundries. One young leader expressed the view that the Chinese were "being cheated out by the Anglo, financial pigs" who are the "late-comers" to a business that had been in the hands of the Chinese dating to the mid-nineteenth century.[95]

Providing for the welfare of Chinatown was yet another expression of Chinese Americans' ethnic pride. Some young women studied to become teachers, fueled in part by the realization that nursery schools, adequately equipped and staffed to care for the community's preschool children while their mothers worked, were in high demand. Still others studied education administration to help organize and erect new educational centers and evening schools for adult English classes. Yet others trained to become health technicians or welfare and sanitation managers to curb the spreading tuberculosis epidemic. Among the graduating class of 1936 at the University of California, Berkeley, were many who chose as their field of study education, education administration, pharmacology, dental hygiene, social welfare, and architecture.[96]

Conclusion

In the period before World War II, Chinatowns such as the one in San Francisco were self-contained neighborhoods equipped with not only Chinese restaurants, "Oriental" schools, and herb shops, but opera houses as well. The residents had little day-to-day contact with members of the dominant society, other than with tourists. Many young American-born Chinese, far from being filled with assimilationist desire, saw themselves primarily as "Chinese" and kept to themselves. Their ethnic identification and solidarity were less the result of making choices based on a knowledge of things Chinese than the consequence of a lack of choices, given the social and economic isolation imposed on them by the larger society. Robert Dunn's assimilationist stance was certainly unpopular and perhaps even premature: Not until World War II, when the American public began to view the Chinese as a friendly race, did Chinese Americans in larger numbers adopt the assimilationist stance. That is, in the 1930s, even as some protested their parents' imposition on them of traditional Chinese ways, they felt "un-American" because of institutional and societal racism. They had little choice except to identify themselves as "Chinese." In short, one's self-identification as an "ethnic" in the 1930s was predicated on one's awareness of his or her social, economic, and political marginalization vis-à-vis the broader society. Although most of the American-born generation had arguably acculturated to the norms of mainstream America, only a few believed that assimilation into its sociocultural matrix was truly possible. A spectrum of identities could be said to exist in the prewar years. The debate on the future of Chinese Americans and the Chinese input in the World's Fair, among other factors, point to an emergent nationalist consciousness in the American-born generations in the 1930s.

Notes

1. Thomas W. Chinn, "A Historian's Reflections on Chinese-American Life in San Francisco, 1919–1991," interview conducted by Ruth Teiser, Oral History Office, The Bancroft Library (Berkeley, California: Regents of the University of California, 1993), 54.
2. The *Chinese Digest* is an invaluable resource for researching this time period. Established in 1935, it was the first truly Chinese American newspaper in the English language. Its contents included happenings in China, articles on Chinese art and tradition, news about San Francsico's Chinatown and other Chinese American communities, and, occasionally, cultural and social essays on Chinese American life. The newspaper folded in 1940. For a further discussion on the subject, see Julie Shuk-yee Lam, "The *Chinese Digest*, 1935–1940," in *Chinese America: History and Perspectives, 1987*, ed. Chinese Historical Society of America (San Francisco: Chinese Historical Society of America, 1987), 119–137.

3. This chapter is based on a portion of my doctoral dissertation, entitled "Of Orphans and Warriors: The Construction of Chinese-American Identity, 1930s to the 1990s" (University of California, Berkeley, 1993). Although it covers happenings mainly in California, the discussion lends itself more broadly to issues of Asian American culture and identity. The phrase "Go West . . . to China" comes from Kaye Hong's essay in *Chinese Digest*, May 22, 1936, 3.

4. Chinn, "A Historian's Reflections," 54.

5. For a more in-depth discussion of the social isolation of American-born Chinese, see the introductory chapter in Hsien-ju Shih, "The Social and Vocational Adjustments of the Second Generation Chinese High School Students in San Francisco" (Ph.D. dissertation, University of California, Berkeley, 1937).

6. *Student Registry*, 1935–36, University of California, Berkeley, The Bancroft Library.

7. Nate R. White, "Chinese in America," *Christian Science Monitor*, February 1, 1941, 4.

8. Shih, "The Social and Vocational Adjustments," 72.

9. White, "Chinese in America," 4.

10. Shih, "The Social and Vocational Adjustments," 59.

11. Ethyl Lum, "Chinese during the Depression," *Chinese Digest*, November 22, 1935, 10.

12. Ibid.

13. David Gan, "A Letter to the Gan Family," in an unpublished manuscript, "History of the Gan Family," ed. Helen Gan and John Aston, San Francisco, 1991.

14. William Hoy, "Exploit Chinatown," *Chinese Digest*, November 22 , 1935, 8.

15. William F. Wu, *The Yellow Peril: Chinese Americans in American Fiction, 1850–1940* (Hamden, Conn.: Archon Books, 1982), 165–175.

16. Sax Rohmer, *Fu-Manchu: Four Classic Novels* (1916; reprint, Secaucus, N.J.: Citadel Press, 1983), 94.

17. Harold R. Isaacs, *Scratches on Our Minds: American Views of China and India* (1958; reprint, Armonk, N.Y.: M. E. Sharpe, Inc., 1980), 119.

18. Wu, *The Yellow Peril*, 178.

19. Ibid., 179.

20. Ibid.

21. The State Emergency Relief Organization, *Survey of Social Work Needs of the Chinese population of San Francisco, Calfornia*, "State Emergency Relief Institute of Governmental Studies Administration, *1935–1944*," University of California, Berkeley, The Bancroft Library, *18*.

22. Louise Chin, "I'm an American," *The Record*, January 11, 1935, 20.

23. Ibid.

24. Isaacs, *Scratches on Our Minds*, 157.

25. Ibid., 156.

26. *Chinese Digest*, May 22, 1936, 3.

27. The Stanford University students wrote on two separate occasions. See *Chinese Digest*, May 15, 1936, 3, 13; May 22, 1936, 3, 14.

28. Karl Mannheim refers to the diverse interest groups within the same generation as "generation units." See Karl Mannheim, "The Problem of Generations," in Karl Mannheim, *Essays on the Sociology of Knowledge* (London: Oxford, 1959), 276–322.

29. *Chinese Digest*, May 15, 1936, 3, 13.
30. Ibid.
31. Ibid.
32. Ibid.
33. Ibid.
34. *Chinese Digest*, July 3, 1936, 5, 14.
35. *Chinese Digest*, May 22 ,1936, 3.
36. Victor G. and Brett de Bary Nee, *Longtime Californ': A Documentary Study of an American Chinatown* (New York: Pantheon, 1972; reprint, Stanford: Stanford University Press, 1986), 169.
37. Ibid.
38. Thomas W. Chinn, *Bridging the Pacific: San Francisco Chinatown and Its People* (San Francisco: Chinese Historical Society of America, 1989), 93, 162.
39. Bernard P. Wong, *Chinatown: Economic Adaptation and Ethnic Identity of the Chinese* (New York: Holt, Rinehart, and Winston, 1982), 37–38.
40. Ibid., 40; U.S. Bureau of the Census, *15th Census of the United States, 1930: Population*, vol. 5, *General Report on Occupations* (Washington, D.C.: Government Printing Office, 1941), 95–97; *Chinese Digest*, August 7, 1936, 6.
41. Ernest O. Hanser, "Chinaman's Chance," *Saturday Evening Post* 213, no. 23 (December 7, 1940); 85.
42. *Chinese Digest*, August 7, 1936, 6.
43. Ibid.
44. Survey of Race Relations Collection, Box 22, Folder 20, Hoover Institution archives, Stanford University.
45. *Chinese Digest*, January 10, 1936, 2.
46. Ibid.; *Chinese Digest*, August 21, 1936, 8.
47. See Bureau of the Census, "Immigration Statistics," *Statistical Abstract of the United States, 1909–1933* (Washington, D.C.: Government Printing Office; 1933) 1272–1273. In an interview conducted by the author in October 1989, Ben Tong estimated that as many as 20 percent went to China during this period, basing his observation on his interviews with San Franciscan Chinese. See also Chinn, *Bridging the Pacific*, 134. In addition, see Lim P. Lee, "An Interview with Dr. Charles R. Shepherd upon His Return from China," *Chinese Digest*, February 1937, 11+, for full details. Dr. Charles R. Shepherd, superintendent of the Chung Mai Home for Boys, made a trip to China in 1937 and gave the following report: "Dr. John Y. Lee, owner and manager of the China Scientific Instruments Co., Ltd., of Shanghai; his brother, Jose, who holds an important position with the government railways; his sister Sarah, who teaches in a governmental school in Canton. Then there is Bill Poy, of Portland, who, about to finish his first term with the Hackett Memorial Medical College in Canton, was offered and has accepted the concurrent posts of Chief Surgeon of the Government Military Hospital and Chief Anatomist at the new Sun Yat-sen Memorial Medical College, both in Canton."
48. *Chinese Digest*, August 28, 1936, 5.
49. Chinese Students Club at the University of California, Berkeley, *A Statement from the Far Eastern Relations Committee of the Chinese Students Club*, vol. 1.The Bancroft Library, September 14, 1936, 1.
50. *Chinese Digest*, June 19, 1936, 14.
51. *Chinese Digest*, May 22, 1936, 3, 14.
52. Ibid.
53. Ibid.

54. Ibid.
55. Ibid.
56. L. P. Lee, "An Interview with Dr. Charles R. Shepherd, 11+.
57. *Chinese Digest*, December 1937, 14.
58. Nee and Nee, *Longtime Californ'*, 170.
59. *Chinese Digest*, July 3, 1936, 5, 14.
60. *Statistical Abstracts of the United States* for the years 1938 to 1944, published by the U. S. Bureau of the Census, shows a steady increase in the numbers of immigrants from China. The gap between those immigrating and those departing began to close, an indication that those who repatriated were returning and/or that fewer American born were departing for China:

Year	Admitted from China	Departed for China
1934	231	2,225
1936	297	1,663
1940	920	968
1941	1,003	816

61. Hanser, "Chinaman's Chance," 87.
62. Ibid.
63. Chinn, *Bridging the Pacific*, 160; Chinn, "A Historian's Reflections," 105.
64. Kaye Hong, interview by author, San Francisco, California, February 1990.
65. Robert Dunn, interview by author, San Franciso, California, February 1990.
66. Ibid.
67. *Chinese Digest*, May 22, 1936, 3, 14.
68. *Chinese Digest*, May 15, 1936, 3, 13.
69. Ibid., 14.
70. *Chinese Digest*, May 22, 1936, 13.
71. Ibid.
72. "A Statement from the Far Eastern Relations Committee of the Chinese Students Club," 1.
73. The phrase "America in the heart" is borrowed from the title of a book by Carlos Bulosan, the Filipino American author of *America Is in the Heart* (Seattle: University of Washington Press, 1943).
74. *Chinese Digest*, MAY 22, 1936, 3.
75. *Chinese Digest*, December 20, 1935, 9.
76. *Chinese Digest*, November 13, 1936, 13.
77. Ibid.
78. Ibid.
79. Ibid.
80. *World Fair's Highlights* 1, no. 7 (December–January 1937–1938): 8; The Reverend Edward Lee, interview by author, Berkeley, California, September 1990.
81. *Chinese Digest*, April 10, 1936, 8.
82. *World Fair's Highlights*, 9.
83. David Gan, interview by author, January 1993.
84. *YMCA: Chinese Branch Historical Sketch*, 50th Anniversary, Chinese YMCA 1911–1961, University of California, Berkeley, The Bancroft Library; *World Fair's Highlights*, 46.
85. *World Fair's Highlights*, 19.
86. David Gan, interview by author, January 1993.

87. *World Fair's Highlights, Clip Sheet*, no. 9.
88. Judy Yung, *Unbound Feet: A Social History of Chinese Women in San Francisco* (Berkeley and Los Angeles: University of California Press, 1995), 204.
89. Ibid.
90. *Chinese Digest*, January 31, 1936, 11.
91. Pardee Lowe, "Chinatown's Last Stand," *Survey Graphic Magazine* 24, no. 2 (February 1936): 86–90.
92. Virginia Lee, *The House That Tai Ming Built* (New York: Macmillan, 1963), 139.
93. *Chinese Digest*, January 31, 1936, 11.
94. *Chinese Digest*, March 6, 1936, 7.
95. *Chinese Digest*, December 6, 1936, 8; December 13, 1936, 11.
96. *Chinese Digest*, May 29, 1936, 3.

CHAPTER 7

The "Oriental Problem" in America, 1920–1960: Linking the Identities of Chinese American and Japanese American Intellectuals

HENRY YU

DURING SEVERAL DECADES OF THE MID-TWENTIETH CENTURY, the consciousness of American intellectuals of Chinese descent was profoundly shaped by the theories and writings of a handful of social scientists from the University of Chicago. Ever since Charles Spurgeon Johnson made his pathbreaking report after the Chicago race riots in 1919, the Department of Sociology at Chicago had been the physical locus for race relations research in America. From the 1920s to the end of the 1950s, it was a training ground for intellectuals and academics interested in what were called the "Negro problem" and the "Oriental problem" in America.

The group of sociologists who initially defined the "Oriental problem" in the 1920s created a set of ideas that structured the way that Asians were understood and the way that they were given a meaningful place in American society. The "Oriental problem" became an intellectual construction—a set of questions, definitions, and theories about Asian immigrants and citizens of Asian ancestry in the United States—which provided the vocabulary and the concepts for scholarly discussions about Chinese Americans and Japanese Americans between 1920 and 1960. At the same time, the "Oriental problem" was an institutional construction: Academic discussions and writings about "Orientals" were tied to a certain network of sociologists spread across the United States, a network whose members were united by their connection to the University of Chicago's sociology department, and, most interesting, a network that involved many students and researchers of Chinese and Japanese heritage.

The ideas and theories associated with the "Oriental problem" had a profound effect upon the identities and self-understandings of some of the researchers involved. The concept of the "marginal man" caught between two worlds—one of the ideas that the Chicago sociologists used to explain the "Oriental problem"—came to have a formative influence on the identities of pioneer Chinese American and Japanese American sociologists, who often used the Chicago school's theories to understand themselves. The marginal man theory described their existential dilemmas as "Oriental" Americans and offered them an important role in modern America, a role that gave them a respected position and place, in contrast to the widespread occupational exclusion that Asians had faced to that point. Many of the intellectuals who became involved with Chicago sociology were women, and their identities as women and as Americans were profoundly shaped by the definitions of "traditional Oriental" culture versus "modern American" culture. For them, becoming American involved not only leaving behind an immigrant community, but also being freed from restricted gender roles.

The theories used to explain the "Oriental problem" had another important ramification. In providing an intellectual framework for understanding the place of Asians in America, they buttressed a dichotomy between "white" America and the "Oriental" immigrants who were not quite American, reinforcing a perception that the American Chinese and Japanese, as well as the American Filipinos and Koreans, were to be categorized together as "Orientals." Although this "Oriental" identity was not commonly assumed by either the Chinese American or the Japanese American intellectuals who studied the "Oriental problem" during the mid-twentieth century—they were much more likely to identify with their "national origins" in China or Japan—the theories of the "Oriental problem" did affect Chinese American and Japanese American thinkers in similar ways. It is important to recognize how the definitions and theories of the "Oriental problem" created a consciousness that the dilemmas and situations faced by the Chinese and Japanese in America could be understood together. In relating the experiences of Chinese immigrants and intellectuals in America to those of the Japanese Americans, the "Oriental problem" concept contributed to the definition of an "Oriental" identity in America, an identity that emphasized the similarities between the situations of the Chinese and the Japanese in America more than any differences arising from national origin.

During the 1970s, the Asian American consciousness movement retraced the boundaries of the "Oriental" category; while rejecting the theories of the "Oriental problem," the movement nonetheless turned the category on its head by encompassing the experiences of the groups previously labeled "Oriental" under the new banner of "Asian American." Ironically, the line distinguishing Asian Americans from other Americans was initially almost identical to the line separating "Orientals" from the rest of America. Thus, the theories of the "Oriental problem" not only affected the identities of Chinese American and Japanese American intellectuals in the mid-twentieth century, but also laid the groundwork for the rise of Asian American consciousness several decades later during the 1960s and the early 1970s.

Chicago Sociology and the Survey of Race Relations

Beginning in the 1920s, several American sociologists who had been trained at the University of Chicago became interested in Chinese and Japanese immigrants in the United States. At the time, sociology was still a young science, less than thirty years old, and still establishing itself as a legitimate academic discipline in American universities. The University of Chicago's sociology department, one of the few training professional sociologists, supplied most of the faculty for the large number of fledgling departments across the country. Chicago sociology and Chicago sociologists such as William I. Thomas, Robert E. Park, Ernest Burgess, and Louis Wirth were becoming famous and well respected.

Robert Ezra Park, the driving force of Chicago sociology in the 1920s and 1930s, was invited in 1924 to become the director of research of the Survey of Race Relations on the Pacific Coast, a huge research project funded by the Rockefeller Foundation and organized by a number of Protestant social reformers. Many of the organizers had been missionaries to China and Japan, and now wanted to gather as much information as they could about what was commonly called "Asiatic" or "Oriental" immigration to the West Coast.[1] Park quickly set out to use the Survey of Race Relations to answer a series of questions about what he and his fellow sociologists labeled the "Oriental problem" in America.

Park's questions about "Orientals" developed out of his earlier research. Having worked as a journalist and for many years as Booker T. Washington's press secretary at the Tuskegee Institute before becoming a social scientist, Park had a long-standing interest in what he called the "Negro problem" in America. In his view, the "Negro problem" had extensive parallels with the "Oriental problem." Park's intellectual construction of the "Oriental problem" was also indebted to his work with William I. Thomas on the Americanization of immigrants for the Carnegie Foundation. Thomas, his colleague and close friend from the University of Chicago, also coauthored one of the most important books ever published about American immigration, *The Polish Peasant in Europe and America* (1918–1920).

Park linked his particular understanding of race relations between "blacks" and "whites" in America with the set of theories derived from the study of Eastern European immigrants in America by means of the "interaction cycle." Also known as the "race relations cycle" or the "assimilation cycle," this foundational concept would structure the "Oriental problem" for the next forty years. Park, and Thomas before him, characterized the contact between any two well-formed social groups as following a series of progressive stages of interaction that was a universal, natural process. Whether it occurred between "American Negroes" and "American whites" or between Polish immigrants and earlier settlers, the nature of the interaction remained the same. Whether the interaction consisted of contact between races (the "race relations cycle") or the adjustments of immigrants to America (the "assimilation" or "Americanization cycle"), the two groups always underwent the same series of adjustments involving four stages: competition, conflict, accommodation, and assimilation.

Competition for economic resources or status inevitably developed into open conflict, which was then mitigated by some situation of accommodation—for example, the defeat of one group by the other, some negotiated compromise, or the creation of a hierarchical system such as caste or slavery. In the end, though, as the two groups began to communicate and share memories and a common life, the assimilation of the two groups into a single community was also inevitable. In many ways, Park had translated the vision of America as a melting pot into a universal objective process. As he proclaimed: "Every nation, upon examination, turns out to have been a more or less successful melting-pot."[2]

Where did Asian immigrants fit into the conceptual schema of Park and Thomas? "Orientals" linked the Chicago sociologists' study of "black/white" relations and their study of the assimilation of immigrants. Asians seemed to constitute a racial group separate from so-called native stock white Americans, simultaneously providing an example of both race relations and immigrant assimilation. The "Oriental" immigrant embodied the dynamic link between the problems of the "Negro" on the one hand, and the problems of the Polish peasant on the other. Even more important, the harsh anti-Asian agitation of "white" nativists in the American West provided the theoretical test for the interaction cycle. Robert Park was fascinated by the progress of Asian immigrants through the assimilation cycle. By all appearances, "Orientals" seemed to be stuck somewhere in the gears of the cycle, unable to get past an uncomfortable accommodation with nativist whites, surviving on such marginal economic activities as laundries and chop suey restaurants, and herded into ethnic enclaves like Chinatown and Japantown. The "Oriental" in America was still an exotic oddity, foreign and seemingly unassimilated.

Here, then, was the crux of the "Oriental problem" as Robert Ezra Park saw it: Were "Orientals" in America assimilating, and if not, why not? This issue was significant to Park and his colleagues because, according to their theory, the assimilation cycle existed everywhere and for everybody. It should have been inevitable in all instances. If "Orientals" were not following the script, Park and his colleagues might have to abandon their theories. What was stalling "Oriental" assimilation into American life? Their answers to this query predictably did not cause the sociologists to abandon their theories, and the question of assimilation continued to structure research on Asian immigrants for the next four decades.

During the Survey of Race Relations on the Pacific Coast, which was conducted between 1924 and 1926, Park and his fellow sociologists Emory Bogardus, William Carlson Smith, and Roderick McKenzie, all University of Chicago graduates, soon encountered a number of research problems. None of them spoke Chinese, Japanese, or any of the other languages that they had identified as "Oriental," so they had to rely on informants, either missionary translators or "native" bilingual interpreters.

The language barrier was compounded by what both the missionaries and the sociologists saw as the enormous cultural distance separating Western culture from "Oriental" culture. This cultural divide, symbolized by the imaginary wall that seemed to separate Chinatowns and Japantowns from the rest of the American West (Park titled one of his essays "The Great Wall of Chinatown"), appeared uncrossable to the "white" sociologists. They needed translators who could not only bridge the linguistic gap between them and "Orientals," but also reveal all the cultural secrets of these mysterious ethnic enclaves. The sociologists found that university students of Chinese or Japanese heritage were particularly good informants—people such as Flora Belle Jan, an eighteen-year-old American-born Chinese student and aspiring writer who had been educated in American schools, occasionally writing for newspapers in her hometown of Fresno.

Students like Flora Jan did more than help the sociologists gather research data: They became subjects for the survey. Flora Jan became an exemplar of an "assimilated" Chinese in the eyes of many of the researchers. Robert Park wrote to William Thomas that Jan was "the most emancipated girl I have ever met. Clever, sophisticated, Americanized." J. Merle Davis, the executive secretary of the survey, reported to Park that she was the "only Oriental in town . . . who has the charm, wit and nerve to enter good white society." Winifred Raushenbush, Park's personal research assistant, became particularly enamored with Flora Belle Jan, singling her out in a report in 1925 as proof that "assimilation is going on," as well as mentioning Jan in her book about Park written fifty years later.[3]

The sociologists decided that ultimately their best assistants would be Asian students who were training to become sociologists themselves and who could frame their findings in the same analytic terms as their mentors'. Ernest Burgess, coauthor with Park of the seminal textbook of the Chicago school, *Introduction to the Science of Sociology*, explained the sociological interest in the Chinese in America, as well as their use of Chinese students: "As one of the cultural groups most deviant from the typical native American culture it provided sharp contrasts which clarified theoretical issues which otherwise might be vague. Also, the attendance of Chinese graduate students provided an opportunity for insightful research."[4]

Between 1920 and 1960, several dozen students of Chinese and Japanese heritage enrolled in the sociology department at the University of Chicago. Each studied some aspect of the "Oriental problem" in America. Although they were not numerous, because they were the *only* scholars studying Asian communities in America at that time, their work has had an impact far beyond what their small numbers would suggest. The coherent language and definitions that these sociologists espoused dominated scholarly discourse about Asians in America for decades. Within an academia still dominated by whites, they became validated as the legitimate experts on the "Oriental problem."

The "Marginal Man"

One theory in particular had an enormous effect on all the American-born students of Asian ancestry—Robert Park's formulation of the marginal man. According to Park, human migration in the modern world had created constant interaction between different cultures and social groups. Beyond the stages of the race relations and assimilation cycles, such interaction produced a type of individual whom he labeled the "marginal man," a person formed not within a well-organized, coherent community, but one caught between two worlds or cultures. Existing in the margins between the two, he or she was not a member of either group. Often, this individual was confused and lost.[5]

The theoretical concept of the marginal man, borrowed from German social scientist Georg Simmel's conception of "the stranger" and retooled by Robert Park, held a special resonance for many University of Chicago scholars with immigrant backgrounds—Asian, Jewish, Eastern and Southern European—because it seemed to mirror the self-perception of many of these intellectuals who indeed felt caught between two worlds. The theory served as a language of discontent that named and reified internal conflicts between perceived "American" and "traditional" traits. But the marginal man theory not only provided the scholars with descriptive expressions of personal situations, it also helped to embed their dilemmas in a larger theoretical framework that suggested greater ramifications and possible solutions.

According to Park, the marginal man was not a figure of despair. In fact, within his theory, the marginal man was the hope of the future, the most important individual capable of easing the tensions between cultures and races by acting as a go-between. That the marginal man could be an interpreter or a bridge between vastly different social groups was the key to his or her major role in the modern world. Moreover, marginal men were important not only for the social functions that they would perform: They embodied modernity itself. Because marginal men were not the products of a single culture, they could understand other cultures without ethnocentrism. Cosmopolitan and without prejudice, the marginal man's ability to empathize with all sorts of people and with differing viewpoints was the most important feature of a new urbanity and modernity in the world. Interestingly, this ability also was the prerequisite for what Park called the "sociological perspective." It was no accident that the marginal man and the sociologist had the same outlook.[6] Robert Park's admiration for Flora Belle Jan, the Chinese American journalism student whom he had met through the survey, made sense within this framework. It was not her mere emancipation from "traditional" Chinese society, but the ability for self-conscious appreciation of both "American" and "Chinese" values afforded her by this emancipation, that made her an exemplar for

Park of the marginal "man." She could understand both worlds, and, more important, she could help each understand the other.

In his 1928 doctoral dissertation on Chinatowns, sociology student Ching Chao Wu applied Park's conception of the marginal man specifically to Chinese immigrants. When a Chinese immigrant is subjected to such American influences as Sunday schools, public schools, and missionary efforts, Wu said, "he is, sooner or later, transformed into a marginal man, a new personality which is the subjective aspect of the fusion of cultures. The conflict of cultures which is inevitable when incompatible ideas and practices are brought together goes on just in the mind of the marginal man. His mind is the real melting pot of cultures."[7]

In discussing how the marginal man was often thought to be a detriment to society, Wu tried to connect this perception to the negative reputation of Chinese immigrants for immoral behavior (opium smoking, gambling, and prostitution). The advantage of making this connection was to categorize Chinese immigrants as misunderstood marginal men who were in actuality the true hope for the future.

> A man who has been under the influence of two cultures is often described in an unfavorable light. . . . The marginal man is not only described by others as confused and lost, but he himself often feels the conflict of two cultures in himself. It cannot be denied that a man who is pulled by two forces, often has no clear idea just which is the right way to follow. Under such circumstances, a man's behavior may be highly individualized, and an individualized behavior, as contrasted with conventionalized behavior, may sometimes be immoral or antisocial. This unfavorable aspect of the marginal man does not need any further elaboration. Most people recognize that, but few people know the important role that he has played, or will play in the future. In the modern days of racial and cultural contact, we need some people to interpret the other group for us. An interpreter is one who is conversant with persons and things of two groups. No one is more qualified to be an interpreter than is the marginal man.[8]

Although Wu saw Chinese immigrants in America as marginal men, able to mediate between the two worlds of China and America, he only loosely fit the description. Born in China, Wu had come to the United States as a college student, and although an insightful and conscientious observer, Wu was non-Cantonese in a world dominated by Cantonese-speaking immigrants. The linguistic and cultural differences between Cantonese speakers from Guangdong province and Chinese from other parts of China proved to be a barrier for most Chinese college students who had not come from South China.[9] Few of these students had much connection to the Chinese communities in the United States, so most researched topics about China. Predictably, Ching Chao Wu's insights into the marginal man were gleaned mostly from the hundreds of life-history documents that had been gathered during the Survey of Race Relations three years earlier. Wu and most of the students from China viewed themselves as purely Chinese and treated their American training as an interlude. Almost all the China-born sociology students returned to China: Some, including Wu, became prominent intellectuals there.

Foreign-born students, both Chinese and Japanese, may not have identified themselves as marginal men, even while using the concept to extol the importance of their "Americanized" compatriots. In contrast, many American-born students explicitly saw themselves as marginal men and seized upon the concept's powerful description of the important role that they might play as cultural translators.

Almost every one of the Chinese American and Japanese American students who became involved with researching the "Oriental problem" had been born in the United States. Most had been raised outside "ethnic ghettos" like Chinatown or Japantown and were much more comfortable with white American friends than with their immigrant parents. The marginal man theory gave them not only a powerful language for describing their existential situations, but also a sense of purpose and self-worth. Many of the students had been caught in situations of self-loathing and had harbored feelings of worthlessness. Because of discrimination, their career options were few, and they were extremely self-conscious of being different. For them, the marginal man theory was like a release from bondage, naming them as the future and giving them the most important role in race and cultural relations. Accordingly, the concept had a profound impact on their self-identity. Embracing the concept also marked the point at which they devoted themselves to becoming social scientists.

Two "Oriental" Sociologists

Frank Miyamoto and Rose Hum Lee, two "Oriental" sociologists who obtained doctorates from the University of Chicago, illustrate the ways in which the theories of the "Oriental problem" affected Chinese American and Japanese American students. Like Flora Belle

Jan, they both identified with the marginal man, and as graduate students in sociology they each studied Asian immigrant communities.

Shotaru Frank Miyamoto

Shotaru Frank Miyamoto, born in Seattle in 1912, was the son of Japanese immigrants. His father, who operated a furniture business, moved his family outside the bounds of the tight-knit community of around six thousand Japanese Americans in Seattle. Although Frank Miyamoto knew many of the Japanese in town, he was raised outside the geographic and social territory of Japantown. In his master's thesis in sociology at the University of Washington, Miyamoto explored what was widely regarded as the extraordinary social solidarity of the Japanese community in Seattle, a phenomenon that sociologists had speculated might have retarded the "assimilation" of the Japanese in America and that Miyamoto and his family had tried in many ways to escape.

After completing his master's degree at the University of Washington, Miyamoto went to the University of Chicago in 1939 to obtain a doctoral degree in sociology. While telling Ernest Burgess his life history and discussing the reasons for his interest in sociology, Miyamoto explained how his becoming a sociologist had much to do with his cultural background:

> The strongest criticism of American society which I felt as a child was concerning the matter of race prejudice. Because of my father's early desire of finding a better home than those offered in the Japanese community, our family rode at the forefront of an ecological invasion, and we took the brunt of white-American disapproval. I felt deeply the injustice of the whole affair, and naturally began searching for means by which these injustices might be removed. Thus, the problems of Japanese-American relations came to take on personal meaning for me . . .[10]

Becoming a sociologist had allowed Miyamoto to understand the social forces that had affected his youth—racial prejudice resulting from the "ecological invasion" (a technical term used by Chicago sociologists to describe the movement of new populations into an urban area) of which his family was just a small part. The science of sociology gave Miyamoto a resonant vocabulary and conceptual framework for naming the "problems" of the Japanese in America, so much so that his life before becoming a sociologist now made sense in terms of the theories of sociology. In a statement that showed the deep effect of the concept of the marginal man on his self-identity and memory, Miyamoto re-marked how it was the

> . . . circumstance of the Japanese culture being superimposed upon the American culture, vividly contrasting the two, that further stimulated my interest in social problems. It led me, at certain points, to be criti-cal of the one or the other of the cultures, for from my particular per-spective, I felt a step removed from both and no strong subjective attachment to either. In this way I was developing the attitude of de-tachment fundamental to the sociologist—I was becoming, in a sense, a "marginal man."[11]

In his grammar school days, Miyamoto had dreamed of becoming a novelist, but like many Japanese American and Chinese American stu-dents of that time, the almost nonexistent career prospects due to racial discrimination against "Orientals" led him to choose a "safer" career option in college, in his case, engineering. He disliked, though, what he felt was the cold and inhuman nature of engineering; with his first exposure to sociology courses, his interest in that discipline began to grow. As the "science of human society," sociology appeared to be both analytic and humanistic. Better yet, a genuine interest in Asian immigrants seemed to exist within the discipline. Miyamoto's choice to become a sociology major seemed to him at the time to have been made on a whim, almost by chance, but with his "increased powers as a social analyst" gained through graduate training, he began to see that an array of factors in his background had determined his ultimate in-terest.[12] It was no accident that his understanding of how he decided to become a sociologist was couched in the language of sociology.

The theoretical descriptions of the marginal man resonated strongly with Miyamoto's understanding of himself and his role in the world. In short, the insights that many of the Chinese American and Japanese American students gained by studying sociology enabled them to ana-lyze and explain the larger contexts for events in their personal lives.

Rose Hum Lee

Perhaps the sociologist who spent the longest time studying the "Oriental problem," and who tried hardest to play the roles of "cul-tural translator" and "middle man," was the Chinese American Rose Hum Lee. Born in 1904 in Butte, Montana, Rose Hum was the second oldest of four girls and three boys. Her father, Wah Lung Hum, had come from Guangdong province in China in the 1870s and worked his way from California to Montana doing the manual labor typical of Chinese immigrant workers—ranching, laundry work, and mining. By 1900, he owned a Chinese merchandise store in the tiny but thriving Chinatown of Butte,[13] and he was so successful that he was able to return to China and bring a wife to the United States—a considerable achievement because Chinese women, with few exceptions, were excluded by federal law.[14]

Rose Hum and her siblings, composing one of the few "complete" Chinese families in town, were all honor students at Butte High School and all went on to professional careers. Rose Hum graduated from high school in 1921. After attending the local college for a short time, she fell in love with Ku Young Lee, a China-born engineering student from the University of Pennsylvania. They were married and she went with him to China after he graduated, living mostly in Canton for nearly a decade. Their marriage failed, and Rose and her older sister, who had also moved to China after marrying a Chinese student, pushed for a divorce. In 1939, at the age of thirty-five, Rose Hum Lee (she kept her married name) returned to the United States with an adopted daughter, determined to pursue a career as a writer, teacher, and social worker. Supporting herself by doing odd jobs, earning fees from the lecture circuit, and selling Chinese merchandise, Lee put herself through college and in 1942 graduated with a bachelor of science degree in social work from the Carnegie Institute of Technology in Pittsburgh. She then began graduate study at the University of Chicago's School of Social Work and Administration, eventually switching to the sociology department.[15]

In 1947, she finished her doctoral dissertation, "The Growth and Decline of Rocky Mountain Chinatowns," based mostly on her hometown of Butte. She spent 1949 in San Francisco studying the "adjustment" and "acculturation" of recent Chinese immigrants to the region. By 1956, she had achieved the zenith of a prolific career at Roosevelt University in Chicago by becoming the first woman, and first Chinese American, to head a sociology department at an American university.[16]

Rose Hum Lee took up the "Oriental problem" as if its questions and theories had been tailored just for her. Throughout her career, she explored the progress of Chinese immigrants along the path of the assimilation cycle, and in a manner like that of no other Chinese American theorist or sociologist, accepted the ultimate validity of Americanization with an ideological fervor. Robert Park had constructed the basic framework of theories and concepts through which the "Oriental problem" was to be researched in the mid-1920s; it is amazing that when Rose Hum Lee reexamined the marginal man concept in 1956, thirty years later, her discussion still used the language and terms of 1926. Describing the negative aspects of marginality, Lee suggested that only assimilation could erase the perceived problems of the marginal man:

> Culture conflict is responsible for his marginal feelings, composed of guilt, depression, instability, anxiety and frustration. These feelings are more pronounced in the second, or marginal, generation of settlement in a new society than in the one preceding it and in the ones to follow. When the "cultural gaps" are closed, so to speak, the cultural hybrid no longer poses a problem to himself and others. This is brought about by the processes of acculturation and assimilation.[17]

The major difference, however, between Lee's analysis and that of the earlier sociologists lay in their views about solving the assimilation problems of "Orientals." Park had not offered any specific solutions to the problem but emphasized that, on a theoretical level, assimilation was inevitable. Rose Hum Lee, after struggling her whole career with the inability of the Chinese in the United States to be accepted as completely "American," prescribed the universal intermingling of cultures and individuals. In the sentence following the passage just quoted, Lee added to the standard definition of "cultural assimilation" the eradication of all physical evidence of foreignness: "Ideally, the completion of the processes includes the mixing of cultures and genes so that there are truly no 'dissimilar people.'"[18]

This vision of the assimilation cycle reached far beyond what might be termed the "culturalist" theories of the sociologists who had carried out the Survey of Race Relations. Physical differences, Park had said, had nothing to do with differences between the races except for their effects on self-consciousness—culture was a purely mental and social phenomenon. For Park, then, the ultimate "melting pot" that lay at the end of the assimilation cycle was built purely out of shared memories and experiences: Actual physical amalgamation was extraneous and unnecessary.

In her early writings, Lee stayed well within the theoretical bounds of the "Oriental problem" as it had been defined and discussed in earlier texts. By 1960, though, after some fifteen years as a sociologist, Rose Hum Lee argued for an absolute commitment to "integration," a term that had never been important in the lexicon of the "Oriental problem." And her use of the term departed significantly from the usage current in the 1950s and 1960s. "Integration" at that time had become a political banner word, invoking debate and battle over racial segregation and civil rights; Lee's use of the term completely outside that context comes as a surprise. Lee used "integration" as a shorthand for the Chicago school's description of the assimilation cycle and the racial prejudice that blocked it: "The final objective of integration is a culturally homogeneous population. The barrier to complete integration is racial distinctiveness."[19] If "integration" was the assimilation cycle encapsulated, though, it was no longer the value-neutral, natural process that Park and Thomas had described. Lee's highly political use of the term "integration" and her commitment to it as a goal shows a personal advocacy that would have made Park cringe.

Lee's vision of a physically as well as a culturally homogeneous America without a trace of "foreignness" or distinctiveness, a place where no "dissimilar people" existed, may not have been a nightmare in the context of 1950s America, but it was certainly a utopian dream derived from difficult personal struggles against those whom she thought were hindering the assimilation of the Chinese. By the time she published her summary work in *The Chinese in the United States of America* in 1960, Lee saw the eradication of physical and cultural distinctiveness as the only way to eliminate ultimately both racial prejudice and the "clannish" tendencies of many Chinese in America.[20] At times, Lee abandoned the analytic prose style that had characterized her earlier sociological work for bitter invective: She railed against Chinatown social institutions and organizations that she blamed for hindering the unreserved integration of the Chinese in America.[21] Lee's desire for the elimination of all traces of Chinese identity even extended beyond the shores of America. In the preface to her book, she opened the discussion of the Chinese in America by placing them within the global diaspora of overseas Chinese, extending the goal of total integration to them as well:

> The Chinese in the United States of America are but a small segment of the Overseas Chinese. Chinese emigrants live scattered throughout the world. Many of them have become so integrated in the societies where they themselves or their ancestors settled that they are indistinguishable from the local population: that is the ultimate ideal to which all Overseas Chinese should aspire.[22]

Lee's exaltation of total integration toward the end of her career must be seen in the context of her struggle to define her own identity within America, while her commitment to "Americanization" should be understood within the context of her identity as a Chinese American woman. The opposition between "Chinese" and "American" took on the additional aspect of "traditional" versus "modern" gender roles, and for women like Flora Belle Jan and Rose Hum Lee, a struggle to escape what they believed were the restrictive roles of "childbearers" and "homemakers" was mapped onto the assimilation spectrum. The association of "Chinese" or "traditional" with "domestic" gender roles, and "American" with "modern," "equal opportunity," "educated" roles for women goes far to explain why Rose Hum Lee held such a particularly strong commitment to the desirability of "deethnicization." The great irony of Rose Hum Lee's commitment to "Americanization" as a means of overcoming domestic gender roles is that she espoused such a connection during the 1950s—a time when the ideology of domesticity was perhaps the most pervasive in twentieth-century America.[23]

For both Lee and Flora Belle Jan, the eradication of "traditional" notions of the family equaled the emancipation of women from oppressed roles. Lee often pointed to the progress from her mother, an uneducated and illiterate immigrant, to Lee herself, the first Chinese American woman to head a sociology department (an achievement of which Lee was deservedly proud) as a canonical example of the proper progress of immigrant women from "traditional" to "American."[24]

Lee had not only seen firsthand the difficulty that Chinese American women had to undergo to break out of "traditional" Chinese gender roles, she had lived the process. Her marriage and decade of life in China had been a torment: She was unable to conceive a child, and her husband's family constantly criticized her for her failure to fulfill a woman's duty. Her final break with her husband and return to America can be seen not only as a denial of her attempts to assume some of the "traditional" roles of Chinese womanhood, but also as a new journey to America. Lee's commitment to the assimilation cycle was reaffirmed as she left behind everything negative that she associated with the "old country." In a way, Lee rediscovered the importance of her American identity, and it was inextricably linked with her ambitions to be a modern, educated, professional woman. Lee remained proud of her Chinese heritage but was selective in choosing which traits defined her own "Chineseness," omitting those that she considered negative, such as "traditional" gender relations and "clannishness," and emphasizing those that she could be proud of in the context of America, such as Chinese art and philosophy or symbolic rituals such as Chinese New Year.

The way that gender identity interacted with theories of assimilation and "Americanization" shows how a commitment to and identification with the assimilation cycle could intersect with any number of aspects of the sociologists' self-identity. The role of marginal man was not restricted to men. As a woman trying to escape what she saw as the Chinese American community's strictures on what were proper roles for women, Rose Hum Lee was comfortable playing the role of a translator of Chinese culture to Americans, and indeed found in Park's modern marginal man an emancipatory self-identity.

When Lee wrote in her dissertation about "traditional" Chinese reactions to the education of women, she told of the gossip and criticism within Butte's Chinese community that news of her college ambitions had caused. The sociologists may have welcomed Lee as an interpreter of the Chinese American experience, but many of the subjects whom she was studying often did not accept her as such. Lee's position in relation to the Chinatown communities of the United States was always precarious, and in both her private and published writings she repeatedly noted the negative reactions to her work by those whom she termed Chinatown "traditionalists."

For a time in the mid-1950s, Lee's second husband, Glenn Ginn, an American-born Chinese lawyer from Phoenix, lived in hiding, afraid that powerful Chinatown tongs were pursuing him. Lee had only recently married Ginn in 1951 when his legal work, as well as a messy divorce from his first wife, engaged them both with Chinatown organizations. Rose Hum Lee Ginn, as she now referred to herself, became almost paranoid about a conspiracy fomented against her by Chinatown tongs, Communist spies, and her personal enemies; she was certain that her sociological work had somehow made her dangerous to these disparate groups.[25] Whether her academic work was the main cause of her troubles is unknown; much more likely, her new husband's divorce created the problem between them and the Chinatown associations.[26]

In personal letters to her daughter, Lee wrote extensively about what she saw as the connection between her difficulties and her ability to present the "true" picture of Chinatown to the rest of America. She saw herself as alienated from her own community, critical of its social and political life, yet she also saw herself as the true representative of the Chinese in America, bearing the qualities of Chinese culture that were respectable in America and forsaking those that hindered the assimilation of the Chinese.

The position of the marginal man as a respected interpreter and expert provided Lee with a forum and an audience of fellow sociologists, but it also gave her a stake in an America that respected her as a woman and a thinker. The possibilities that the opposition between traditional and modern gender roles and that between Chinese and American culture might not map onto each other perfectly, and that perhaps America was sometimes not the land of emancipated and modern women, were doubts that she avoided. Instead, she remained strongly committed to assimilation and her belief that Americanization was the process that not only had saved her personally, but also would do the same for all Chinese in America.

Beyond the "Marginal Man"

The rewards of playing a role in sociology's "Oriental problem" were institutional as well as existential. Overall, the entrance of more than a dozen Chinese American and Japanese American students into academic sociology had an important effect. Like many of the African American sociologists who were Park's protégés, most of the Asian American sociology students went on to successful professional careers, making contributions in all manner of fields and subjects.[27] Unlike the study of "black/white race relations," though, where many scholars from all disciplines and viewpoints were studying the "problem," the Chicago-trained "Oriental" sociologists were for many years virtually the only scholars studying Asians in America. Their institutional role as expert interpreters of Asian immigrants for academia made their impact as researchers and teachers much greater than their small numbers might indicate.

Most Chinese Americans and Japanese Americans who helped research the "Oriental problem" did not work on it exclusively. They went on to do other things as theorists, social workers, or teachers. The role of marginal man was just one of many aspects of self-identity in their lives, if perhaps one of the most powerful explanations for their place in American society. Frank Miyamoto went on to a long and distinguished career as a sociologist at the University of Washington, eventually serving as chairman of the department, and became a noted contributor to collective behavior theory, particularly the Chicago-school branch known as "symbolic interactionism." He remains a professor emeritus in the department and lives with his wife in Seattle.

Neither did Rose Hum Lee, the sociologist most deeply affected by the "Oriental problem," study Chinese immigrants exclusively. A respected researcher in the field of urban sociology, her 1955 work, *The City: Urbanism and Urbanization in Major World Regions*, was the

epitome of Chicago-school urban theory. She traveled the world, studying urban development and observing overseas Chinese communities.
Sadly, Lee's life and career ended prematurely when she had a stroke in
1964 at the age of sixty.

Perhaps the most poignant story among those of the students who
became involved with the "Oriental problem" was that of Flora Belle
Jan. As Robert Park did for many people whom he encountered in his
extensive research travels, he became a mentor to Jan, arranging for her
to attend the University of Chicago to study journalism and housing
her while she was in town. He had great hopes for her as a writer and
as the kind of sophisticated observer that resulted from her unique status as a marginal "man." She took his hopes to heart and tried to fulfill
the ideal. Unfortunately, a difficult marriage similar to Rose Hum
Lee's first marriage caused problems too great for her to overcome, and
she never lived up to Park's or her own expectations. She marked the
death of Robert Park in 1944 with the sad regret of a sense of failure:

> I was depressed by a letter from Mrs. Robert E. Park, who told me of Dr.
> Park's death. . . . The underlying reason for my depression was that I
> had not accomplished anything during his lifetime. He had expected so
> much of me and had hoped that I would write something worthwhile,
> but here I am beginning all over again, somebody's stand-on with secu-
> rity as far away as Mars.[28]

As much as the marginal man concept was a vision of hope for Chinese American intellectuals in the mid-twentieth century, it was a
promise difficult to fulfill, especially for an "Oriental" in an often hostile America. However, if nothing else, academic interest in the "Oriental problem" opened sociology to Chinese American and Japanese
American students who otherwise were unlikely to have had academic
careers.

By the time Rose Hum Lee was writing her most proassimilationist work, the "Oriental problem" as an intellectual and institutional
framework had faded in significance. Park had died in 1944, and the
Chicago sociologist who was next most influential in directing students on "Oriental problem" research, Ernest Burgess, had retired
from the faculty soon afterward. Institutionally, a strong and thriving
sociology department at the University of Hawaii would carry on
Chicago-style research on race relations for many years. However, the
demise of the "Oriental problem" was inevitable given the changing
nature of sociology.

By the 1950s, the theoretical bases of the "Oriental problem" had eroded, in particular the assimilation cycle concept. After the 1924 quota restrictions, immigration slowly but surely declined as a factor in American life, and the sociologists had failed to connect the assimilation cycle with race relations in America. Park's explanations and solutions for America's "race problems" were being eclipsed.

For Park and Thomas, the science of sociology had always been one deeply rooted in the highly descriptive style of journalism—eminently readable and largely untheoretical. Their emphasis on empathy and human understanding had earned their style of sociology the reputation of being "soft" science.

By the post-World War II period, a new type of sociology was informing the dissertations and theses of sociologists-in-training. More technical in prose style than the work of Park and Thomas, the writings of ascendant sociologists such as Talcott Parsons and Robert Merton became popular. With a marked bent toward the theoretical, the newer genres of sociology were often characterized by a prose that the uninitiated found difficult to read and understand. In Park's desire to convert as many scholars as possible to the science of sociology, he and his forebears at the University of Chicago had never demanded the intense and labyrinthine methodological rigor of the new practitioners; indeed, the sturdiness and structural coherence of the construction of the "Oriental problem" likely owed much to its reliance on just a few key theoretical concepts.

With the passing of the "Oriental problem" as an intellectual and institutional framework in the 1950s, sustained and coordinated interest in Asian immigrants and communities in America did not revive until a new wave of Asian immigrants followed the revision of immigration laws in 1965, ending more than half a century of Asian exclusion. The intellectual construction of the "Oriental problem," first defined in the 1920s, may have disintegrated as a coherent framework by then, but many of its ideas resulted in important legacies. The sociologists, by defining the "Oriental problem" as the shared experiences of Chinese and Japanese in being excluded from the "white" experience of "successful assimilation," had lumped Chinese and Japanese under the rubric of "Orientals." Ironically, this externally imposed aggregation of Chinese Americans and Japanese Americans laid one of the foundations for the emergence of an Asian American consciousness, as "Orientals" suffering from similar types of oppression were transformed from "problems" of sociology to empowered individuals aware of a shared social and political identity.

The creation of interdisciplinary Asian American Studies programs in the 1970s was a movement that in many ways tried to distance itself from the theories and texts of the early "Oriental problem" researchers. The Asian American activists saw the Chicago school's theories on race relations and immigration as backward and outdated, and deliberately maligned many of the earlier researchers. Park was labeled a conservative and a racist.[29] Many of the original Chinese Americans and Japanese Americans who had become sociologists were attacked as proassimilationist apologists, treated with derision and scorn, or, worse, viewed with pity for their attempts to enter "white" society.

If we were to take at face value the 1970s wholesale repudiation of the earlier sociologists, though, important legacies of the "Oriental problem" within American culture and intellectual thought would be too readily dismissed. The 1960s and 1970s generation of "Asian American" thinkers, in rejecting the theories of the "Oriental problem," overlooked their own use of Chicago immigration studies and theories. Even more important, the "Oriental problem" had paradoxically shaped nascent "Asian American" thought by being the target of its attacks and arguments.

Conclusion

The "Oriental problem" as an intellectual construction defined the place of Asians in American life, giving Chinese American and Japanese American intellectuals a language with which to understand themselves, as well as an opportunity to perform a valuable role in academia. They found in sociology the chance to express themselves and to write for an interested audience about subjects in which they were already interested. For many of the second-generation American-born Chinese and Japanese students who came into contact with Chicago-style sociology, Robert Park's marginal man theory stood out as a vision of hope, placing modernity and the social relations of the future in the hands of individuals, like themselves, who did not seem to belong to any one culture. In their minds, the marginal man theory was like a prophecy, leading them into a destiny as social scientists.

This chapter has provided a new look at the intellectual construction of the "Oriental problem" in the early twentieth century. Moreover, it has argued that without recovering the ways in which Chinese American and Japanese American identities were affected by these old theories and definitions, we cannot fully map the terrain on which

Asian American consciousness arose. The Asian American Studies movement, in the ways that it reacted against the theories of the "Oriental problem," was nonetheless shaped by those theories. Without delineating this process, we will never come to grips with that legacy. At the same time, we need to understand the struggles of the Chinese American and Japanese American intellectuals who tried so diligently to define themselves and Asian immigrants within a harsh and uninviting America.

Notes

Acknowledgments: Research funding for this chapter, and the dissertation of which it is a part, was provided by doctoral fellowships from the Social Sciences and Humanities Research Council of Canada, Princeton University's Department of History, and the Woodrow Wilson Society of Princeton University. The author thanks Frank Miyamoto, Tom Shibutani, Elaine Lee, and Ralph Hum for their kindness and generosity in candidly sharing their memories. Many thanks also to the colleagues and friends who helped on earlier drafts.

1. The reformers were all associated with the Institute of Social and Religious Research in New York, an organization that steered Rockefeller funds toward social research projects such as the race relations survey and Robert and Helen Lynd's famous "Middletown" research in Muncie, Indiana—*Middletown: A Study In American Culture* (New York: Harcourt Brace Jovanovich, 1929). The Institute was also closely connected with the YMCA International, and many of the missionaries had returned from overseas work to run YMCAs in the United States.
2. Robert E. Park, "Human Migration and the Marginal Man," from Volume One of Park's collected writings, *Race and Culture,* ed. Everett C. Hughes et al. (Glencoe, Ill.: Glencoe Free Press, 1950), 346. On the subject of Park's theories as the transformation of American ideals of exceptionalism into "natural process," see Dorothy Ross, *The Origins of American Social Science* (Cambridge, England: Cambridge University Press, 1991).
3. Park's and Davis's quotations are from Winifred Raushenbush, *Robert E. Park: Biography of a Sociologist* (Durham, N.C.: Duke University Press, 1979), 113. Raushenbush's quotation is from the papers of the Findings Conference of the Survey of Race Relations, held at Stanford University, March 1925, found in the Papers of the Survey of Race Relations, Hoover Institution archives, Stanford University. My thanks to Judy Yung for sharing her research on Flora Belle Jan's life. For an excellent discussion of the gender dynamics of growing up as a Chinese American woman in twentieth-century America, see Judy Yung, *Unbound Feet: A Social History of Chinese Women in San Francisco* (Berkeley and Los Angeles: University of California Press, 1995).
4. Ernest Burgess and Donald Bogue, *Contributions to Urban Sociology* (Chicago: University of Chicago Press, 1964), 326. *Introduction to the Science of Sociology* (Chicago: University of Chicago Press, 1969), called the "green bible" for its distinctive cover, was first published in 1921.

5. Park, "Human Migration," 340. It is interesting how Chicago theorists used "marginality" to examine what were perceived to be both "negative" and "positive" results of group interaction and contact. For instance, Park used Simmel's conception of the "stranger" to extol the cosmopolitan nature of a "marginal" perspective, but Paul Siu later used a variation, the "sojourner," to explain the lonely and demoralized existence of Chicago's Chinese laundrymen. The "sojourner" was the subject of his 1953 dissertation, which was published decades later as *The Chinese Laundryman: A Study in Social Isolation* (New York: New York University Press, 1987).

6. For a discussion of Park's use of "mobility," and one that I follow here, see Fred Matthews, *Quest for an American Sociology: Robert E. Park and the Chicago School* (Montreal: McGill University Press, 1977), 143–145. In 1938, Everett Stonequist, a student of Park's at the University of Chicago, completed his dissertation, "The Marginal Man: A Study in the Subjective Aspects of Cultural Conflict," but the original idea had been Park's. Perhaps the original American model and best example of the marginal man was taken by Park from his student E. B. Reuter's discussion of "The Mulatto in the United States: A Sociological and Psychological Study" (Ph.D. dissertation, University of Chicago, 1919). Robert E. Park Papers, Regenstein Special Collections, University of Chicago, Box 7, Folder 4.

7. Ching Chao Wu, "Chinatowns: A Study of Symbiosis and Assimilation" (Ph.D. dissertation, University of Chicago, 1928); see chapter 16, "The Marginal Man," 327–328.

8. Ibid. 329–330.

9. Many students like Wu had been trained initially in American missionary colleges such as Yenching University or Tsinghua University in Beijing prior to coming to the States for advanced degrees. Before the Communist revolution in 1949, all of them, like Wu, returned to China following their American training. See Siu-lun Wong, *Sociology and Socialism in Contemporary China* (London: Rutledge and Kegan Paul, 1979) for a description of what he calls "American missionary sociology." Tsinghua University was established in the 1930s from Boxer Indemnity Funds paid to the United States, with the specific goal of preparing Chinese students for study in the United States, whereas Yenching University had been established by American missionaries at the turn of the twentieth century. The Institute of Social and Religious Research of New York City (and through it the Rockefeller Foundation) was also crucial in promoting sociological research in China. In 1926, it donated enough funds to finance a new Institute of Social Research in Peking for ten years. Ching Chao Wu was one of many Chinese students who went to Chicago through the auspices of American missionary colleges in China. Those who studied topics relating to China included Ernest Ni, Ai-ti Huang, and Yung-teh Chow (none of whom practiced Park's style of sociology—they were all statistics-oriented demographers in the style of Park's methodological nemesis at Chicago, William Fielding Ogburn). Those who, like Wu, studied the Chinese in America included Ting-chiu Fan, Paul Chan Pang Siu, and Yuan Liang (all of whom wrote papers on the Chinese in Chicago for Ernest Burgess). Of the group, all returned to China except Yuan Liang, who remained in the United States because of China's civil war, and Paul Siu, who spent the rest of his life in the United States. Perhaps the most interesting of the China-born students, Paul Siu, was raised in China, but his father had long been a laundryman in Chicago. Of all the sociology students who studied the Chinese in America,

Siu was undoubtedly the best field researcher, empathizing with his subjects the most and probably understanding them best. He worked as a social worker for a decade and a half while completing his doctoral degree, and his understanding of the Chinese immigrant worker as a "sojourner" owed much to the Chicago school's conception of the marginal man, as well as to his own sympathy for his subjects. See John Kuo Wei Tchen's fine introduction to Siu's book (see Note 5).

10. From page 3 of "Background Paper" written by Shotaru Frank Miyamoto, Ernest W. Burgess Papers, Regenstein Special Collections, University of Chicago, Box 170, Folder 1. Burgess asked each of his students to write a paper describing his or her life history and how each had become interested in sociology.

11. Ibid.

12. Ibid., 1.

13. Butte was a frontier mining town with a relatively large population of around forty thousand at its height, 10 percent of whom were Chinese. "China Alley" was one city block in size. Rose Hum Lee, "The Growth and Decline of Rocky Mountain Chinatowns" (Ph.D. dissertation, University of Chicago, 1947).

14. Because of U.S. exclusion laws, the ratio between male and female Chinese immigrants for the period between 1882 and 1945 was highly skewed. Rose Hum's father, as a merchant, had an easier time bringing his wife over than most Chinese men in the United States did. Sucheng Chan, "The Exclusion of Chinese Women, 1870–1943," in *Entry Denied: Exclusion and the Chinese Community in America, 1882–1943*, ed. Sucheng Chan (Philadelphia: Temple University Press, 1991), 94–146.

15. Her master's thesis in 1943 was basically a social-work study based on her experiences in China: "Maternal and Child Health and Welfare Services in Canton, China."

16. Information on Rose Hum Lee is from her *Biographical File* at Roosevelt University archives; from interviews conducted in October 1992 with her younger brother Ralph Hum; from private letters and papers sent to her daughter, Elaine Lee (copies of which are in the author's possession); and from interviews with her roommate for a year at the University of Chicago, Beulah Ong Kwoh (who wrote her 1947 master's thesis in sociology on Chinese American undergraduate career prospects).

17. Rose Hum Lee, "The Marginal Man: Re-evaluation and Indices of Measurement," *Journal of Human Relations*, vol. no. 4 (Spring 1956): 27–28.

18. Ibid., 28.

19. Rose Hum Lee, *The Chinese in the United States of America* (Hong Kong: Hong Kong University Press, 1960), 406.

20. The two thousand copies of *The Chinese in the United States of America* published in February 1960 were paid for partly out of Rose Hum Lee's own funds.

21. Lee, *The Chinese in the United States of America*, 427–430.

22. Lee, *The Chinese in the United States of America*, vii.

23. See Elaine Tyler May, *Homeward Bound: American Families in the Cold War Era* (New York: Basic Books, 1988).

24. Lee often used her own family, especially her mother, as an example of the successful "assimilation" of a Chinese American family. Lee's dissertation contains an extended life history of her family in the appendix, as well as nu-

merous allusions to her own experiences. Of course, because of the genre of the detached sociological document, mention of her family and herself was usually cloaked in the anonymity of the third person.

25. Information on Lee's and her husband's fear of tong reprisals is from the author's interviews with Ralph Hum and from private correspondence between Rose Hum Lee and her daughter Elaine Lee, copies of which are in the author's possession.

26. Ginn's first wife had been born in China, and like many wives of Chinese Americans before World War II, had remained in China after their marriage. When she finally joined him in the United States, he could not get along with her and, in a manner that caused her to appeal to the Chinatown associations for help, he divorced her and married Lee. His first wife's grievance as a wronged wife was one of the types of disputes in which the associations commonly intervened. Interestingly, Lee was pilloried as a homewrecker, and her brazenly "untraditional" lifestyle was cited as evidence of the wronged wife's victimization.

27. Much has been written about Charles S. Johnson, E. Franklin Frazier, St. Claire Drake, Horace Cayton, and other African Americans who were Park's students. John H. Bracey, Jr. and August Meier, *The Black Sociologists in the First Half Century* (Belmont, Calif.: Elliot Rudwick, 1971); R. Fred Wacker, *Ethnicity, Pluralism, and Race: Race Relations Theory in America before Myrdal* (Westport, Conn.: Greenwood Press, 1983); and Stow Persons, *Ethnic Studies at Chicago, 1905–45* (Urbana: University of Illinois Press, 1987).

28. I thank Judy Yung for her permission to quote this passage from an unpublished paper on Flora Jan.

29. Paul Takagi, "The Myth of Assimilation in American Life," *Amerasia Journal* 2 (Fall 1973): 149–159.

About the Contributors

Sucheng Chan is Professor of Asian American Studies at the University of California, Santa Barbara. She has published many articles and a dozen books, including *This Bittersweet Soil: The Chinese in California Agriculture, 1860–1910* (Berkeley and Los Angeles: University of California Press, 1986) and *Asian Americans: An Interpretive History* (Boston: Twayne Publishers, 1991). Her newest book, *Major Problems in Asian American History* (Boston: Houghton Mifflin), will be available in 1998.

Gloria H. Chun is Assistant Professor of History and the Chair of Multiethnic Studies at Bard College. She received her doctoral degree in comparative ethnic studies from the University of California, Berkeley, in 1993. Her dissertation is entitled "Of Orphans and Warriors: The Construction of Chinese-American Identity, 1930s to the 1990s." She is the author of "The Good, the True, and the Marginal: Three Responses to Postmodern Literary Criticism," *Review* (1997), 207–217, and "The High Note of the Barbarian Reed Pipe: Maxine Hong Kingston," *Journal of Ethnic Studies* (Fall 1991), 19:3, 85–94.

Sue Fawn Chung is Associate Professor of History at the University of Nevada, Las Vegas. She received her bachelor's degree from the University of California, Los Angeles, where she worked with Roger Daniels on tracing the history of the Chinese American Citizens Alliance (CACA). She received her master's degree from Harvard University and her doctoral degree from the University of California, Berkeley, where she studied Chinese American newspapers published in San Francisco. In 1996, she received the Nevada Humanities Award for the numerous programs and exhibits that she has presented on Asian Americans in Nevada. She has written numerous articles and a book, *Beyond Gum San: A History of the Chinese in Nevada* (forthcoming from Reno: Nevada Humanities Committee and the University of Nevada Press, 1998), on the Chinese experience in Nevada.

K. Scott Wong is Associate Professor of History at Williams College. He received his doctoral degree in history from the University of Michigan in 1992. He is the author of " 'The Eagle Seeks a Helpless Quarry': Chinatown, the Police, and the Press. The 1903 Boston Chinatown Raid Revisited," *Amerasia Journal* 22:3 (1996); "Crossing the Borders of the Personal and the Public: Family History and the Teaching of Asian American History," *Magazine of History* 10:4 (Summer 1996); "The Transformation of Culture: Three Chinese Views of America," *American Quarterly* 48:2 (June 1996); "Chinatown: Conflicting Images, Contested Terrain," *MELUS (Multi-Ethnic Literature of the United States)* 20:1 (Spring 1995); "Liang Qichao and the Chinese of America: A Re-evaluation of his *Selected Memoir of Travels in the New World*," *Journal of American Ethnic History* 11:4 (Summer 1992) (winner of the Immigration History Society's Carlton Qualey Award, 1993); and "Our Lives, Our Histories," in *Multicultural Teaching in the University*, ed. David Schoem et al. (New York: Praeger, 1993). Along with Gary Okihiro, Marilyn Alquizola, and Dorothy Rony, he coedited *Privileging Positions: The Sites of Asian American Studies* (Pullman: Washington State University Press, 1995). He is currently writing a book on the impact of World War II on Chinese Americans.

Henry Yu is Assistant Professor of History at the University of California, Los Angeles, as well as a member of the Asian American Studies Center at UCLA. He received his bachelor of arts degree from the University of British Columbia and his master's and doctoral degrees in history from Princeton University. He is the author of "Constructing the 'Oriental Problem' in American Thought, 1920–1960," in *Multicultural Education, Transformative Knowledge and Action: Historical and Contemporary Perspectives*, ed. James A. Banks and Cherry McGee Banks (New York: Teachers College Press, 1996). His 1995 dissertation, "Thinking about Orientals: Race, Migration and Modernity in Twentieth-Century America," is due to be published by Oxford University

Press. Additionally, he has a forthcoming article, "Mixing Bodies and Cultures: The Meaning of America's Fascination with Sex between 'Orientals' and Whites," in *Sex and Love across the Color Line*, ed. Martha Hodes (New York: New York University Press).

Renqiu Yu is Associate Professor of History at Purchase College, State University of New York. He received his doctoral degree from New York University in 1990. He is the author of *To Save China, To Save Ourselves: The Chinese Hand Laundry Alliance of New York* (Philadelphia: Temple University Press, 1992; winner of the 1993 Outstanding Book in History Award, Association for Asian American Studies); "Imperial Banquets and the Emperor's Meals in Qing China," in *Culturefront* 5:1 (Summer 1996); "Chinese in New York City," in *Encyclopedia of New York City*, ed. Kenneth Jackson (New Haven, Conn. Yale University Press, 1993); "Little Heard Voices: The Chinese Hand Laundry Alliance and the China Daily News' Appeal for the Repeal of the Chinese Exclusion Act in 1943," in *Chinese America: History and Perspectives* (1990), 21–35; "Chop Suey: From Chinese Food to Chinese American Food," in *Chinese America: History and Perspectives* (1987), 187–195; "The Chinese American Contributions to the Educational Development in Toishan, 1910–1940," *Amerasia Journal* 10:1, (1983), 47–72; and other articles and short stories.

Qingsong (King) Zhang is President of the Asian American Association, an organization that serves 1.5 million Asian Americans and 200,000 Asian American businesses. He received his bachelor of arts degree from Nanjing University, China, in 1982, and came to the United States in 1984 as a Fulbright graduate student. He received his master's degree (1986) and doctoral degree (1994) in history from the University of Virginia. His dissertation is "Dragon in the Land of the Eagle: Exclusion of the Chinese from U.S. Citizenship, 1848–1943." During 1992–1993, he served as Executive Director of the Independent Federation of the Chinese Students and Scholars in the U.S.A. and coordinated a nationwide lobbying campaign for the 1992 Chinese Students Protection Act, which granted seventy thousand green cards to Chinese students and their families in the United States.

Also in the *Asian American History and Culture* series: